Indian Writing in English

Indian Writing in English

Edited by

Mohit K. Ray

ATLANTIC

PUBLISHERS & DISTRIBUTORS (P) LTD

Published by
ATLANTIC
PUBLISHERS & DISTRIBUTORS (P) LTD
7/22, Ansari Road, Darya Ganj, New Delhi-110002
Phones : +91-11-40775252, 40775214, 23273880, 23275880
Fax: +91-11-23285873
Web: www.atlanticbooks.com
E-mail: orders@atlanticbooks.com

Disclaimer

- The author and the publisher have taken every effort to the maximum of their skill, expertise and knowledge to provide correct material in the book. Even then if some mistakes persist in the content of the book, the publisher does not take responsibility for the same. The publisher shall have no liability to any person or entity with respect to any loss or damage caused, or alleged to have been caused directly or indirectly, by the information contained in this book.
- The author has fully tried to follow the copyright law. However, if any work is found to be similar, it is unintentional and the same should not be used as defamatory or to file legal suit against the author.
- If the readers find any mistakes, we shall be grateful to them for pointing out those to us so that these can be corrected in the next edition.
- All disputes are subject to the jurisdiction of Delhi courts only.

Printed & bound in India by Atlantic Print Services

Preface

It is a pleasure to place in the hands of our readers the Volume of *Indian Writing in English* in response to the growing demand for further volumes of the series. The nineteen essays that constitute this volume cover a wide range of authors and subjects. Starting with Nirad C. Chaudhuri, the man born in the nineteenth century and one of the greatest thinkers and most controversial writers, the essays shed new lights on different aspects of many eminent and not so eminent writers of Indian English literature: Mulk Raj Anand, R.K. Narayan, Manohar Malgonkar, Nayantara Sahgal, Bhabani Bhattacharya, Kasthuri Sreenivasan, Vikram Seth, Kamala Markandaya, Anita Desai, Arundhati Roy, A.K. Ramanujan and Kamala Das.

T.M.J. Indra Mohan tries to identify the nature of Nirad C. Chaudhuri's experience as an immigrant writer and argues that he has a dual identity that makes him equally at home in India and abroad.

U.S. Rukhaiyar analyses the narrative technique used by Anand in *Untouchable* and discovers that in his use of different registers and styles, recurring images and symbols he gives his narration a metaphorical structure that makes him easily comparable with novelists like Henry James, D.H. Lawrence and E.M. Forster.

Ramesh Kumar Gupta through a perceptive analysis of Mulk Raj Anand's *The Old Woman and the Cow* shows how Anand's humanism is inscribed in his treatment of Gauri *vis-à-vis* his criticism of contemporary society.

S. Rajalakshmi traces the stages through which Rosie passes to realize herself and become a completely liberated woman in R.K. Narayan's *The Guide*.

Anisha Ali examines R.K. Narayan's two novels, *Talkative Man* and *The World of Nagaraj* to show as to how chance encounters are used in the novel as catalysts in the restorative act in the life of the protagonists, and vindicate Narayan's pohilosophy of continuity of life aligning man and nature by creating a balance between order and disorder in the lives of the "insiders" and the "outsiders."

Anvar Sadhath, in his sharply critical essay tries to show as to how R.K. Narayan wrote within the confines of the cultural ideology of the dominant community so that in his works the characters from minority communities are always marginalized.

Shiv Kumar Yadav looks closely at Malgonkar's *A Bend in the Ganges* and finds it a fine critical assessment of the Gandhian ideal of *Ahimsa* or non-violence.

Abha Sharma brings out the contemporary relevance of Sahgal's perception of violence as reflected in her *Storm in Chandigarh* and contends that only a dedicated band of individuals like Vishal Dubey can be an answer to the deep-rooted problems of violence.

A.N. Prasad makes a critical survey of the novels of Bhabani Bhattacharya to underscore his social purpose and argues that in the description of the poor and the deserted he has no equal and hardly a peer in the western fiction.

Usha Rani examines in detail Kasthuri Sreenivasan's *The Light from Heaven* and shows as to how the protagonist's acute sense of alienation, dislocation and final salvation is presented in the novel through four facets of Balan's identity and four layers of his consciousness.

Kerstin W. Shands in his well-researched paper examines the roles of life style, gender and sexuality as primary factors in determining cultural identity in *A Suitable Boy* where shoes turn out to be politically salient signals of cultural identity and significant symbols linked to the seductions of rational love in both marriage and nation-building narratives.

U.S. Rukhaiyar focuses on the ironic vision in Kamala Markandaya's novel *Nectar in a Sieve,* identifies different kinds of irony used in the novel which enrich the form and content of the novel.

Usha Rani discusses Anita Desai's *Fasting, Feasting* to map out the different levels of realization and/or failure of the dreams of the main characters of the novel.

In her perceptive essay on Anita Desai, Devika argues that although the central theme of Desai's novels is the existential predicament embedded in the social milieu, Desai's existential concerns are largely frustrated on account of male interference in the lives of the females.

Ashwini Kumar Vishnu makes a fine anatomy of the sociological imagination of Arundhati Roy as reflected in her acute perception of social reality in presenting the world of *The God of Small Things* as a microcosm of the contemporary India.

Veena Singh tries to assess the achievements of the women novelists of the post-colonial India in transcending their middle class limitations and making valuable contributions to Indian English fiction in terms of themes, treatment and techniques.

Rajendra P. Lokhande offers a critical survey of post-Independence Indian English poetry marked by the spirit of nationalism which also eventually led to the realization of the identity of the nation.

In his fine analytical study, Saranga D. Baral tries to understand A.K. Ramanujan's conception of the self in the light of Bergson's notion of *élan vital.*

Bhabani S. Baral compares Kamala Das with the confessional poets like Sylvia Plath and Anne Saxton and the *sahajia* poets and Amaru, the author of *Amaruàataka* and, in the process, sharply defines her individuality.

I thank all the contributors for their insightful studies. I am grateful to my colleague, Professor Rama Kundu for her unstinting help in readying this volume.

I am particularly thankful to Dr K.R. Gupta, Chairman, M/s Atlantic Publishers and Distributors, New Delhi, for the confidence evinced in me and for seeing this Volume through the press.

MOHIT K. RAY
Editor

CONTENTS

1

Nirad C. Chaudhuri: Dual Identity

T.M.J. INDRA MOHAN

Around the world today when globalisation of economy, science and technology is taking place, literature cannot be the exclusive preserve of any nation and in that respect writers migrate from homeland to settle down in other countries for various reasons. When such a situation takes place, our immediate question is how well the writers would identify with the alien culture or they keep themselves isolated in order to maintain their national identity? It is a debatable question. In many countries such migrations of writers take place and there are instances where settled writers mingle with the native race and in a few cases identity crisis takes place, and in consequence, their writings are well anchored in their birthplaces. However, the problem any writer chooses to focus on in his work has been and by and large will be universal one. In that analogy, a writer's work focuses a problem confronted by any national: if treated partially at personal level, national race consciousness will find a place. The migrated writers sometimes find social and political compulsions pushing them towards certain views favourable or against the country to which they migrated. They also often become the factors for motivation and that force keeps the writer to go on writing.

Usually, for a migrated writer, the native moorings will give way and his main springs of the creative activity will get automatically transferred to the new-found land. James Joyce writes in *Dubliners* and *The Portrait of an Artist as a Young Man,* out of the depth of his Irish background. The self-conscious use of myth in *Ulysses* involves in many ways his religion and national experience. Chaudhuri is not an exception and from our readings of his works we understand that art emerges 'from the subtle and involuted tension between the remembered and the real, the potential and the actual, integration and dispossession.' This is rather a dictum for all migrated writers.

Affinities to the birthplace and loyalties to the settled nation more often than not become points of divergence; otherwise the universal concept of writers' sensibilities would continue to stay with them. They rather have a feeling that they do not belong to the migrated place; they are just living there. Among them one thing that stands out conspicuously is their commitment to the language which has been their chosen medium of expression and self-imposed affinity to the soil that provides them asylum. On the other hand, their status being peripheral to alien and native places, they are neither in nor out of it and that is the crux of the problem these migrated writers face or live with.

Nirad C. Chaudhuri belonged to this category, living in Britain with compromise though he can be rated as one of the migrated Indian writers. C.R. Mandy's remark on Chaudhuri is worth quoting here: "With such coruscating intelligence his brain dances like fireflies before the monsoon. I would always rate him—cerebrally and stylistically in the top class of Indo-Anglican writers."

Chaudhuri has deep faith in Indian's skill and ability in performing any feat devotedly. His arguments in *Defence of India* is an example to show Chaudhuri's faith in Indian army. He published it before his settlement in England. Indian army is a good fighting machine, he remarks. He is highly critical of the policies of the British; though he has very high admiration for the British, in this context his patriotism comes to the fore.

Chaudhuri's prominence came to limelight in 1951 when he published *The Autobiography of an Unknown Indian*. The book was an instantaneous success and deservedly he became famous. The admirer of Chaudhuri Khushwant Singh, wrote in the *New Statesman*, "Chaudhuri writes the English language better than any Indian has done before and is the most erudite writer in the country. His encyclopaedic knowledge has made him somewhat a legend; he is meticulously painstaking about what he writes and is particularly felicitous in expression. He is provocative and at times offensively anglophile at the expense of his countrymen."

Chaudhuri's second book after his visit to England, *A Passage to England* (1959) is much like a travelogue in which he praises the British. His controversial book *The Continent of Circe* is again an intellectual exercise. He is often more Indian than most Indians and also equally an avid Englishman. Despite his divided self he has a keen insight into human problems. *The Autobiography* is a kind of national history rather than personal. The places hold him a spell where he spent his boyhood days. Nationalist fervour and political climate make an impression in his mind; he himself says, "This book describes the condition in which an Indian grew to manhood in the early decades of this century. My intention is thus historical. The book may be regarded as a contribution to contemporary history."

Though a chequered career Chaudhuri has, his Indian sensibility looms large in his works. As regards Indo-English relationships, "My notion of what is proper and honest between Englishmen and Indians today is clear-cut and decisive. Either side in their political and public relations at the present moment is an honourable taciturnity. The rest must be left to the healing powers of Time." Here as well as on other occasions also Chaudhuri maintained a pliable position in his attitude towards Indo-English relations. In recording his impressions on Britain after his visit in 1955, he is comfortably at home in western literature, architecture and music. He is a serious writer and he looks at things in a childlike perspective.

In 1965, Chaudhuri published *The Continent of Circe*, which he called "an essay on the peoples of India," and here he wanted to analyze Indians' collective personality in the light of the historical evolution: his theory being that the Hindus are what they are because they are the victories of Circe. The "fair European-Aryan has become brown Hindu due to north Indian climatic conditions." He draws in this aspect a parallel between the plight of westerners in India and of the Europeans in Aryavarta. "Multiply the experiences of latter (the British) by fifteen and you get the Hindu...to put the matter briefly, the Hindu is a European distorted, corrupted and made degenerate by the cruel torrid environment and hostility." Though migrated, the moorings in India Chaudhuri has, undeterred and uncompromising. Often the Indianness unconsciously haunts him to write thus about husband and wife relationship: "For most Hindu husbands the wife is beautiful bath of gleaming porcelain, with both cold and hot water taps, with this difference, however, that the taps are not under control but flow as they list, and by turns the husband is bathed in a cool spray of love or scalded in a geyser of anger."

Humour apart, Chaudhuri's spirit of Indian attitude to social life impels him to such a commentary upon Hindu way of life; taken in lighter vein, this is not an exaggerated opinion; at the same time, idealism with which majority Hindus lead life as on today cannot be lost sight of, though settled in Britain.

Chaudhuri has a liking for Indian way of life compared to Britishers. The Britishers' reserve, he calls it, "nortorious English reserve" when he talks about their character in general. Drawing a distinction between silent reserve of the British and proximity of the Indians maintaining even with the total strangers make him feel that the Indianness has been a hallmark feature of our people which the Britishers lack. He has a soft corner though sometimes the behaviour of the Indians with the total strangers is excess. He cites an instance where a stranger whom he accosted on the way, within a few minutes becomes so affectionate and asks his address to send mangoes during the season.

There are many instances to show that the Indian faith is still persisting in Chaudhuri though he is trying to take root in an alien soil. Nonetheless, the migrated mind fails to severe its roots totally from the homeland. The migration is physically perfect but mentally not prepared for total alienation; that is why at the time of Chinese invasion of India, western countries wanted to lend a helping hand to India. In this context Chaudhuri compares the western powers with Mahabharata characters like Aswathama, Kripa, Kirthivaram. Chaudhuri is an intellectual colossus having one foot in India and one foot in Britain—a feature of the migrated writers.

WORKS CITED

Chaudhuri, Nirad C. *The Autobiography of an Unknown Indian.*

—–. *A Passage to England* (Bombay, 1951).

—–. *The Continent of Circe* (Bomaby, 1966).

—–. *The Intellectual in India* (New Delhi, 1967).

—–. *To Live or Not to Live.*

—–. "Indian Crowds."

Srinivasa, Iyengar, K.R. *Indian Writing in English.*

Narasimhaiah, C.D. *Commonwealth Literature: Problems of Response.*

Naik, M.K. *Studies in Indian English Literature,* New Delhi : Sterling Publishing, 1987.

2

Mulk Raj Anand's *Untouchable*: A Triumph of Narrative Skill

U.S. RUKHAIYAR

The narrative form of Mulk Raj Anand's novel *Untouchable* shows a skilful organization of the various tools of narration, *e.g.*, point of view, focus, atmosphere, characterization, etc. as also imagery. The novel shows how the untouchables at the time the novel was written lived in inhuman conditions and were subjected to worst kinds of humiliation, sometimes on trifles and sometimes without any cause whatsoever. Two of the keynotes of the novel are pathos and irony, or better say, irony upon pathos. But, though the novel begins on a note of despair, it ends on a note of hope, with echoes from Shelley's *Ode to the West Wind* and *Euganean Hills.*

Language is generally plain and simple. But, on occasions, there are images and symbols, some of them recurrent, charged with deep emotion. Sometimes words and phrases have subtle overtones. As we shall see, the book has been able to achieve an adequate narrative form.

We would do well to begin with what Mulk Raj Anand said about what he wanted to show in this novel.

"I wanted to bring to light the ghosts of the 'dead souls' murdered without a rite by the Dharamabugs. I wanted to beckon all the phantoms, so that they should haunt the dreams of the half dead, and awaken them, may be, to the lingering sparks of life [...] I wanted to burn and shine like

"Tiger, tiger, burning bright [...]."[1]

Another passage in the same article may shed more light:

> The chance of reading of Arthur Rimbaud's *Season in Hell* verified my own preoccupation with the sympathetic journey through hell which, I felt, the outcastes had been going through, with little or no hope of heaven. I do not believe in the theory of Karma. So I tried to take over the poetic truth of Blake, the pictorial truth of Picasso's blue period, and Theodore Powys' fabulous manner, to compensate myself for the disbelief of Rimbaud. And as these influences penetrated into my self-discovery, all the miscellaneous strains fused into Bakha. The real cry was not recorded in the book, and held back deliberately, but the echo might be feared if anyone wants to listen: 'A man is a man and he is born equal to all other men.'[2]

The narrator has used the third person point of view with all its three common devices, *viz.*, (1) omniscient point of view; (2) the intrusive narrator; and (3) the limited point of view.

At times there are internal monologues. Indianness is also there in both speech and atmosphere. Like *Ulysses,* this book deals with events of just one day.

The early pages show that the writer wants to draw our attention to two things—first, how the sweepers lived in an inhuman condition; and, second, how, even after being a sweeper, Bakha has some rare human virtues *e.g.*, sincerity and efficiency; and urge for life; an urge to rise above his station. "But Bakha was a child of modern India. The clear-cut styles of European dress had impressed his naive mind. This stark simplicity had furrowed his old Indian consciousness and cut deep, new lines where all considerations which made India evolve a skirty costume as best fitted for the human body, lay dormant. But Bakha looked at the Tommies, stared at with wonder and amazement. So he tried to copy them in every thing" (13). This note reappears with greater stress in another sequence:

> Bakha felt the keen urge of his sense of anticipation draw before his eyes the horrible prospects of all the

> future days of service in the town and the insults that would come with them [...]. And with this and other fashionable items of dress, he had built up a new world, which was his heaven, if for nothing else, because it represented a change from the old ossified order and the stagnant pools of the lane near which he was born. (87-88)

There is also a poet and singer in him. "And he slowly, slipped into a song" (20). "My work will soon be finished," he said poetically (21). He feels that during the dreary hours of his work, he heard sweet music, which must have been inspired by his conscious fondness for Ram Charan's sister, who is now going to be married. "During the day hours of his routine work at the latrines subsequently he had often heard the delicate strain of elfin music" (98). We know music is the natural ally of love.

That is not the end of it. In the same sequence, Bakha is hearing the strong call of biological adulthood, a Lawrencian impulse. He gets a vision of embracing, squeezing and ravishing Ram Charan's sister. But, soon he realizes how sinful it was on his part to think so of a friend's sister (98-99). This shows a conflict between the natural and the moral.

He has respect for his person as well as for his nation. When the English parson Col. Hutchinson wants to lure him to the Christian fold, he recoils, even though his own community has treated him so shabbily. Perhaps he knows the difference between the two kinds of servitude, and prefers the native to the alien.

The writer perhaps tries to underline the irony, the pity of situation—that is, how a noble soul, an honest and efficient worker, and a lovable boy like Bakha has to face all kinds of insult and humiliation only because he is an untouchable.

The narrative presents some four to five incidents, all of which look like variations upon the same theme, *i.e.*, how the untouchables at that time were subjected to all kinds of humiliation sometimes on trifles and sometimes without any cause, perhaps, just for sadistic delight. Anand first narrates the incident and then records Bakha's reflections thereon.

The first is the touching-in-the-bazar incident. It was a custom at that time that when sweepers entered the town, they had to beat a drum hung around their waist to announce their approach so that those who did not want to get touched by them would be on guard. One day Bakha is in a jolly mood. He walks into the town. He buys some *jalebis* to eat. But as soon as he wants to eat them, a *Lalaji,* that is, a man of upper caste, gets touched by him as Bakha had forgot to announce his approach. This creates an ugly scene. The Lalaji begins to hurl at him abuse and rebuke. He calls him swine, dog (53), dirty dog; son of bitch (53), offspring of a pig (53). Soon caste men gather there and begin to shower upon him abuse and humiliation. A shopkeeper, calls him 'rape sister' (57). A child says baselessly that one day Bakha beat him. Bakha was surrounded by a barrier, not a physical barrier but a moral one" (54).

The same image of barrier recurs in the Temple scene:

> And yet there was a futility written on his face. He could not overstep the barriers which the conventions of his superiors had built up to protect their weakness against him. (73)

And further:

> There was an inseparable barrier between himself and the crowd, the barrier of caste. He was part of consciousness which he could share and yet not understand. He had been lifted from the gutter, through the barriers of space, to partake of a life which was his and yet not his [...]. (153)

The recollection looks like an internal monologue. Bakha feels:

> The cruel crowd, all of them abused, abused, abused. Why are we always abused? The Sanitary inspector that always abused my father. They always abuse us. Because we are sweepers. Because we touch dung. They hate dung. I hate too. That's why I came here. I was tired of

> working in the latrines every day. That's why they don't touch us, the high castes. (58)

Another irony is that a Hindu humiliates a Hindu while a Muslim tangawallah is kind to him. He soothes Bakha and tells him to walk along.

> But he is a Muhammadan. They don't mind touching us, the Muhammadans and the Sahibs. It is only the Hindus, and the outcastes who are not sweepers. For him I am a sweeper, sweeper—untouchable! Untouchable! Untouchable! That's the word! Untouchable! Untouchable! I am an untouchable! (58-59)

It is to be noted that it may be one of the main grounds in the political equation in India today that the *dalits* feel closer to the Muslims than to the caste Hindus.

The repetition of the word untouchable about half a dozen times in quick spurts followed by the sign of exclamation, the jerking rhythm, very well delineates the agitation going on in the heart of Bakha at the moment.

Here, the author makes a fine use of irony upon pathos, "Like a ray of light shooting through the darkness, the recognition on his lot dawned upon him [...]." The use of light imagery in this context has a pungent irony. But Bakha is not a dead log like his father. He is very much alive. He does feel and react:

> But there was a smouldering rage in his soul. His feelings rise like spurts of smoke from a half smothered fire in fitful jerks when the recollection of abuse or rebuke he suffered kindled a spark in the ashes of remorse inside him. (57-58)

This image reminds us of the image of 'an unextinguished bearth/ashes and spark' in the last verse of Shelley's *West Wind.*

The same technique of action followed by Bakha's reaction to it is found in all the incidents.

Look at the Temple incident. The hypocritical priest Kali Nath calls Bakha's good-looking young sister Sohini to cleanse the temple toilets. But he molests her and makes evil suggestions.

Sohini screams. Pandit Kali Nath, for fear of being found guilty, starts shouting that he has been defiled by Sohini.

Now, this scene deepens the irony of the earlier incident. If a sweeper touches a Lalaji, he gets polluted. But a priest, a Brahmin, can touch an untouchable and that too for such a purpose. But there is much more to this irony.

(1) In the hierarchy of Hindu caste system, the Brahmins are supposed to be at the top, and they are revered by one and all. But here a Brahmin stoops so slow.

(2) What place has the Brahmin chosen to commit this unholy act? [...] A temple, the holiest place, the seat of God. What an irony!

(3) The caste men too take sides with him. They are not prepared even to listen to Sohini.

(4) Sohini gives a fair account of a modest Indian maid.

(5) Bakha fumes and gnashes to take revenge for the insult to his sister. But Sohini stops him from doing so because she feels that the caste men will jointly spring upon him and kill him.

The author's observation of Bakha's state of mind of the moment rings three notes: [...] (1) the oppression by caste men; (2) Bakha's urge to retaliate; and (3) his helplessness. The novelist observes:

> A superb specimen of humanity he seemed whenever he made the high resolve to say something, to go and do something, his fine form rising like a tiger at bay. And yet there was a futility written on his face. He could not overstep the barriers which the conventions of his superiors had built up to protect their weakness against him. He could not invade the magic circle which protects a priest from attack by anybody, especially by a low-caste man. So, in the highest moment of his strength, the slave in him asserted itself, and he lapsed back, wild with torture, biting his lips, ruminating his grievances. (73)

The real irony lies in Bakha's high resolve to take revenge being thwarted by *futility* written on his face. Why? Because the caste men have erected barriers of convention to protect their excesses from being questioned. The writer conceives of Bakha as a tiger, but a tiger at bay.

Such comments by the author make the reaction of Bakha clearer and stronger.

The Hockey Match incident sustains and develops the same note. When Bakha saves a small boy from being crushed in a stampede in a hockey match and takes him to his home, the child's mother, instead of thanking him for this admirable job, scolds him and says that it is he who must have been the root of the trouble.

That is to say, fault or no fault, the untouchables had to receive the abuse and rebuke of the caste men as daily food. The irony lies in this that Bakha gets rebuke where he should have got reward.

The Well incident shows how even for an essential thing like drinking water, the untouchables had to wait for long hours at some public well for some kind caste men who could show mercy and pull for them water from the well. And even when the hypocritical priest Kali Nath does so, it is inspired less by the service to the needy than by lust for the young women among them.

In the Sadhu incident, the housewife attends dotingly on a sadhu. But when Bakha asks for a piece of bread, she gives it to him after long entreaty, and that too after seasoning it with abuse and rebuke. Now, anybody can guess who needs bread more—the sadhu or the sweeper.

The same pattern is seen in the narration of minor events. But, with all this, the novel ends on a note of hope, and this suggestion comes three ways:

(1) Mahatma Gandhi himself appears in the novel and in course of his speech he observes:

> The fact that we address God as the purifier of the polluted souls makes it a sin to regard anyone born in Hinduism as polluted—it is satanic to do so. (164)

(2) When people in large numbers are going to attend the meeting of Gandhiji, they feel that evil may end:

> It was as if the crowd had determined to crush everything, however, ancient or beautiful, that lay in the way of their achievement of all that Gandhi stood for. It was as if they knew by an instinct surer than conscious knowledge, that things of the decadence may be destroyed in order to make room for those of the new. It seemed as if, in trampling on the blades of green grass, they were deliberately, brutally trampling on a part of themselves, which they had begun to abhor and from which they wanted to escape to Gandhi. (152-53)

Again we get echoes from the first verse of Shelley's *West Wind*:

> Pestilence-Stricken multitudes: O thou
> Who chariotest to their dark wintry bed
> The winged seeds, where they lie cold and low
> Each like a corpse within its grave. (1.5-8)

This passage seems to be logical corollary of the passages dealing with oppression to the downtrodden. It looks like the irruption of the congregated might of the 'smouldering rage' (58), tiger at bay (73) and a lion enmeshed in a net (105) and such other reactions taking the form of a volcano in the heart of Bakha and other *dalits*. This shows the narrative skill of the author. It sounds the destruction of the old order and the cherished construction of the new order. Perhaps that is why towards the end we find language becoming more metaphorical and symbolical anticipating an apocalypse.

(3) The last three pages (174-76) show a vision of dawn in a symbolic language:

> The fires of sunset were blazing on the distant horizon. As Bakha looked at the magnificent orb of terrible brightness glowing on the margin of the sky, he felt a burning sensation within him. (174)

* * *

> The sun descended. The pale, the purple, the mauve of the horizon blended into darkest blue. A handful of stars throbbed in the heart of the sky." (175)

These lines recall the following lines of Shelley's *Euganean Hills*:

> Noon descends around me now:
> This the noon of autumn's glow,
> When a soft and purple mist
> Like a vapour amethyst
> Or an air-dissolved star
> Mingling light and fragrance, far
> From the curved horizon's bound
> To the point of Haven's profound.
> Fills the overflowing sky. (lines 255-63)

We may also mark the last two paragraphs of the book and the verbal overtones of some of their words and phrases:

> He (Bakha) emerged from the green of the garden into the slight haze of dust that rose from the road and the paths. As the brief Indian twilight came and went, a sudden impulse shot through the *transformation of the space and time,* and gathered all the elements that were dispersed in the stream of his soul into a tentative decision: I shall go and tell father all that Gandhi said about us, he whispered to himself, and what that clever poet said. Perhaps I can find the poet on the way and ask him about his machine. And he proceeded homewards. (175-76) (Emphasis added)

Anand has used some images and symbols recurrently, perhaps to stress the main notes. The most important image is one of fire, with its variants. Fire stands for, among other things, revolution and purification:

> Then he picked up a long poker and prodded the fire. Quickly it flared up, suddenly illuminating the furnace with its leaping red, gold and black flames, *an angry consuming power.* (23) (Emphasis added)

* * *

> The burning flame seemed to ally itself with him. It seemed to give him a *sense of power,* the power to

> destroy. It seemed to infuse into him a manterful instinct somewhat akin to sacrifice. It seemed as if *burning and destruction were for him acts of purification.* (24) (Emphasis added. The verbal overtones are too clear to be explained.)

When Bakha receives abuse and rebuke in the touching-in-the-bazaar incident:

> There was a smouldering rage in his soul. His feelings would rise like spurts of smoke from a half-smothered fire in fitful jerks. (57-58)

After the Temple incident:

> As he sauntered along a spark of some intuition suddenly set him ablaze. He was tired with a desire to burst out from the shadow of silence and obscurity in which he lay enshrouded. (106)

The last pages of the novel (174-76) show a different use of fire image. In the previous images, fire suggests indignation, agitation and desire for revenge. But towards the end, fire suggests the effulgent glow of a new dawn. It shows the post-resolutive phase, the light that comes out of a long process of struggle and suffering. It is the light that comes towards the end in *Macbeth.* It is the light of hope that comes after the darkness of suffering.

> The fires of sunset were blazing on the distant horizon. As Bakha looked at the magnificent orb of *terrible brightness* glowing on the margin of the sky, he felt a burning sensation within him. (174)

The following suggestions come out:

(1) The fire of sunset may suggest the burning of the decadent order.

(2) The phrase "terrible brightness" recalls Blake's Tiger, of which Anand felt enamoured in the passage quoted on page 6. On two occasions in the novel Bakha has been likened to a tiger once "a tiger at bay: (73)," "a lion enmeshed in a net" (105). Just possible, Anand finds in him the Christ image. "In the juvenescence of the year/ Came Christ the tiger." (Eliot: *Gerontion*)

(3) That Bakha feels a burning sentation within him very well recalls the fire passages quoted above which suggest that he wished to burn the system but that he was helpless.

Now the hope is about to be fulfilled. And the subsequent passages give a vision of fulfilment "The sun descended" (175).

Similarly, the images of barrier, furrow, etc. also occur. Some of them appear in some of the passages quoted above.

On two occasions in the novel Anand has made a vitalist/organicist use of language. When Havildar Charat Singh gives Bakha a brand new hockey stick, he is astonished:

> He was overcome by the man's kindness. He was grateful, grateful haltingly, grateful falteringly, grateful, stumbling, grateful [...]. (122)

Similarly, the passage which describes Col. Hutchinson, uses so many polysyllabic and high-sounding words that we get an idea of the character of a hypocritical parson so well satirized by Chaucer and Langland.

> And he had swamped the overbearing strain of the upper middle class Englishman in him, by his hackneyed effusion of Christian sentiment camouflaged the narrow, insular patriotism of his character in the lingo of the white-livered humanitarian. (138)

This brief survey shows that in *Untouchable* Mulk Raj Anand has used not only a common, plain narrator's voice. When he describes a simple thing, he uses plain language. But when he describes an emotional sequence, he uses figurative language. He takes help of some powerful symbols and images. This device adds a poetic dimension to the novel. It seems he anticipated R.P. Blackmur's observation that if novel has to attain the stature of poetry or drama, it will have to cease to be mere chronicle and try to conform to the metaphoric structures. The narration is never dull, never flat. It is absorbing from the beginning to the end. The recurrence of the keynotes through plain narration as well as images and symbols reminds us of the methods used by Henry James, D.H. Lawrence and E.M. Forster. It is remarkable that Mulk Raj Anand made such a laudable attempt when Indian fiction in English was still in its infancy. It must have served as a model for many of the subsequent practitioners of this art.

NOTE

All the textual passages have been cited from the book *Untouchable*, Arnold Publishers, New Delhi (Revised Edition, 1970).

REFERENCES

1. Anand, Mulk Raj, "The Story of My Experience with a Write lie," *Indian Literature*, Vol. 10, No. 3, 1967. Reprinted in *Critical Essays on Indian Writing in English*, Macmillan, Silver Jubilee Students Edition, 1977, 18.
2. Anand 17.

3

HUMANISTIC NOTE: A STUDY IN MULK RAJ ANAND'S *THE OLD WOMAN AND THE COW*

RAMESH KUMAR GUPTA

> The creative artist of our age has to become a god, independent of his creation, revealing his omnipresence through a pervasive insinuation of his compassion or understanding of all his characters, through the varying tensions of their lives in search of personal relations.[1]

The most distinguished humanist of today is Dr Mulk Raj Anand, an internationally reputed Indo-Anglian novelist, short-story writer, essayist, art critic and poet. Mr Anand's emphasis on the dignity of man—irrespective of caste, creed and wealth, his plea for the exercise of compassion as a living value, his conception of the whole man, the deep significance he attaches to art and poetry as instruments for developing whole men, his crusade against superstition, feudalism, and imperialism—these are some of the chief characteristics of his humanism. The theme and subjects of Anand are chiefly aimed at portraying the contemporary social situation as seen and felt by the individual. More often than not, Anand's individual finds himself in an unenviable circumstance, being a prey of feeble traditions and savage customs, a defiled social order or a cruel administration. Delineating graphically the helpless individual in his pitiful and helpless state, Anand aims at touching the humanist chords of the reader's heart, with a message perhaps that only a concerted effort can examine the none-too-gay present social situation. Mr S. Lakshman Shastry, the editor of the *Contemporary Indian Literature*, rightly observes:

> Dr Mulk Raj Anand is a unique type of optimistic humanist who is capable to move the most pessimistic man to action. He is a very sensitive lover of all that is good and lovable on earth—good books, fine pieces of art, good manners. He stands for lasting peace and friendly relations between nations. At the same time he is also ruthless critic of all that is worn-out and decaying-dehumanising and degrading customs, manners, outdated social and political institutions, reactionary thoughts and ideologies. As a disciple of Tagore and Nehru, Dr Anand has made painstaking efforts to understand the soul of this land which has been expressing itself through Indian thought and Indian culture. It appears to us that it is the profound knowledge of Indian mind on the one hand, and critical assessment of the various outdated social systems and institutions on the other, that has made Anand an uncompromising agitator and organiser.[2]

Anand is thus a humanist to the core. It is his constant faith in humanism that has perhaps made him a lovable man with infinite charm and several interests. He is a true friend, a tireless worker, an excited organiser, a prolific writer, an unceasing champion of the cause of the poor and the submissive, a savage combatant against inequality and injustice, and above all, a trustworthy humanist with endless faith in man and creative arts on which his expectations are made evident by his letter of 3rd October, 1968 to G.S. Balrama Gupta:

> [...] if the 21st century is to be born, we must understand each other's humanness and cultivate the arts through which we may achieve the universal basis for no war, against stupidity, malice, aforethought and meanness of mind.

Anand exposes the contemporary situation through an analysis of the predicament of the men and women he knows. Anand saw India in terms of enslavement, caste, poverty, religious archaism, saluted the enduring heroism of the poor and oppression of the women. The women that reside in Anand's world are all preys of habit where man is ascribed the pride of place and thus allowed the socio-cultural confirmation of the female banishment. *The Old Woman and the Cow* presents the story of Gauri, a meek and gentle country-woman who suffers silently all the hardships and injustices imposed on her by her mother, mother-in-law, and even her husband till she meets the enlightened city doctor, Colonel Mahindra, under whose influence she grows glowingly conscious of her intrinsic worth as an independent individual. The leitmotif of this novel develops in Gauri's journey to emancipation. She is married to Panchi, "the holy bull." Gauri, "the gentle Cow" wanders from Piplan Kalan to Chota Piplan, symbolises a considerable fall in her destiny. Gauri's husband Panchi, also tries to free himself from the crushing and debasing influence of his uncle and aunt and the entire village bent on fault-finding and agitating him, but he fails. But his very combat, just as Gauri's, attracts our sympathy.

Anand's humanistic note in *The Old Woman and the Cow* (cited as *TOWC*) is obvious that presents the strong plea for the identification and approval of women's rights. The novelist's sense of disbelief in the Christian perspective of vice, his emphasis on the value of compassion in human affinities, his criticism of the cash-bond, and his usual reproof of uncritical faith in superstition, Karma, and God—these are the humanistic notes that form the plot of this novel.

In our conventional socio-cultural milieu, the woman remains unrealized, trapped, caged and oppressed. That women need equality with men is the chief principle of Anand's humanism which constructs the plot of this novel. The novelist presents the treatments of man's ideas and actions in respect of woman. Gauri's whole life is a tale of torture and trauma. The crowded and obstructed atmosphere of the joint family does not allot a room for making love between Gauri and her husband. She does nothing but groans and moans under the distress of male chauvinism. She is abidingly blamed of being an inauspicious creature, liable not only for the mishaps of the family but also for the drought in the village. Kesari, the traditional mother-in-law, does not want to loosen her hold on Panchi and continues to despise and distress Gauri. She is helpless. She finds a little love and tenderness in the corner of her husband's heart. Her husband, Panchi, is also a prey of the stratagems of the envious Kesari and artful Mola Ram. Despite his occasional love and compassion for Gauri, he is mostly seen savage peasant, a wild bull whose gruesome tendency comes in constant clash with Gauri's gentle nature. It is obvious in these lines:

> [...] there was the prospect of the prize of a girl—a girl whom he could fold in his arms at night and kick during the day [...]. (*TOWC* 5)

Panchi is a weak husband. He does not consider the veritable predicament of his wife, Gauri. He becomes a victim of Kesari's machination. Kesari makes him believe that Gauri is *de facto* inauspicious and immoral. But it is Gauri who probably succeeded in mollifying Panchi through her mere affection and endurance. Consequently she is conceived and becomes teemful. But it does not last for long. Gauri is bartered away by a malice and licentious uncle, Amru and a greedy mother, Lakshmi, for money and wiping out of mortgage on two houses and a cow, to the old and rude widower Seth Jai Ram Das in Hoshiarpur. She gets free from the Seth's house to Dr Mahendra's Hospital, with fever and malady and now she feels free from the clutches of the old Seth who entices her to live as his wife. Here she contends with Dr Batra, a beastly debauchee. Dr Mahindra's gentle behaviour and reformist ideas bring about a transformation in her. Her life takes a constant change in the company of Dr Mahindra. Now she has been changed from gentle cow to a self-willed woman with her own individuality. Once getting a chance she goes back to her husband but Panchi mistrusts her virginity in that she passed some days with the Seth Jai Ram Das and Dr Mahindra. Hence, he scolds and strikes her and gives order to desert his house. But Gauri is no longer a passive creature to avow this kind of behaviour. So she reacts and says:

> If I am a curse on you, I will go away [...]. And if you strike me again, I will hit you back. (*TOWC* 282-83)

Here Anand presents the symbolic aspect of modern women who are conscious of their rights and individualities. What she was now she is not. She is no longer a gentle cow. She takes compact decisions and raises the reasonable facts:

> He (Panchi) is not foolish. He is a weak, spoilt creature [...]. He pretended to be a lion among the men of the village. But really he is a coward. They are telling him that Ram turned out Sita because everyone doubted her chastity during her stay with Ravana. [...] I am not Sita that the earth will open up and swallow me. I shall just go and be forgotten of him [...]. (*TOWC* 283)

Gauri gets away from her husband's life and starts a new life of dedication to the dejected, poor and wretched.

Another aspect of Anand's humanistic note in this novel is the emphasis on the demand for deserting pain and barbarity and exercising mollification and softness. The novelist does this by depicting a true scene of the gloomy plot against which the tragedy of the novel takes place. At whatever place Gauri goes she meets with savage suffering but it is only Dr Mahindra who gives her solace. She tries to go to her every kith and kin for her shelter but she is hurt by each of them. They take rest after doing away with her from their house. Even her husband does it whom Gauri truly loves. Panchi thinks that she is his wife and he is her lord so he can hit and kick her. Kesari, aunt-in-law, tortures her upto the very end by using the envious conduct and by instigating Panchi against her. Lakshmi and Amru love their property more than their daughter so they sell her away to a sixty-year old Seth. Gauri does face all the severe tests in her life but thanks to Dr Mahindra who is sympathetic to her. As usual in India, rains fail and drought takes its place and it raises in the psychics of the villagers that unpropitious happening is due to Gauri. And thus the mishap instigates the villagers to their savagery. Even Gauri thinks that her husband, Panchi, would have probably sent her away due to his miseries and mishaps. Mr Anand explicates it through a minor character of the novel Rafique Chacha and indicates that poverty need not make people savage. Rafique Chacha is a poor man, but he is by nature gentle and keeps his goodness in spite of all miseries. He is kind enough to ask Panchi and his wife, Gauri, to come and live with him. He does not leave any attempt to make their lives lively and delightful. But Dr Mahindra's solace and generosity make Gauri a hopeful woman. Due to Lakshmi's and Amru's greed for money Gauri faces with hardships. Dr Mahindra tries to be up with the veritable evil of money and tells Lakshmi how people's greed for money, power, possession and property has dominated in their lives:

> [...] we pile up gold upon gold; silver upon silver [...] the Sethias, who buy and sell, have brought falsity into the life of the village. In the old days, there was often scarcity. But as no one owned the land, the five elders could give fertile land to whoever complained that his land was fallow [...]. And there was milk and butter and whey [...]. Now, every peasant owns his land and can sell it [...]. And cash has become more valuable than the earth. And thus there is wretchedness everywhere. Your Amru turns crook and you sell your daughter, even as folks in Gorakhpur district of Uttar Pradesh are selling their daughters. (*TOWC* 239-40)

Lakshmi's lure for money, "the new god" induces her to sell away her daughter. Even the hillmen do not flee from the enticement of money, and its consequences are calamitous. Lakshmi says to the city confectioner:

> [...]. Women always taught men to love [...]. But when you shopkeepers came with your money you taught us hill people to buy and sell girls [...]. I am not ashamed of having gone to bed with men, but I am ashamed that I had to sell my daughter [...]. (*TOWC* 226)

The novelist tries to combat against the man's faith in charms and omens, his power, possession, money, Karma, and God—all age-old notions which impede the development of the people. The denizens of the village are the victims of superstitions. Panchi sometimes feels it nugatory to believe in superstitions but he is not completely got rid of it only because he considers the destiny of Gauri who is a prey of mishaps. Kesari thinks that these mishaps are due to the wrong stars of

Gauri. Compelled by the circumstances Gauri herself thinks that she is probably an inauspicious woman as blamed by all. Like her husband, Gauri also believes in destiny and God, since she artlessly thinks that a day will come when she will be free from the reward of sufferings imposed by the kith and kin and the villagers. She contemplates that there is no means or no way for proving her virginity, for the Mother Earth would not open up and swallow her hence she decides to work out her own destiny herself. Here the novelist indicates that man must rely on himself for his livelihood rather than on luck or God. Anand does not believe in the dogma of rebirth which is the mythical aspect of our Indian 'religio-reliance.' That is why the novelist interprets it through Dr Mahindra:

> [...] the idea of deserving a higher birth, as a reward for good or bad deeds is, to my thinking, a myth promoted to keep men and women at work for the slave-drivers [...]. It is true that at the back of all wretchedness, there is the soul of man. And the soul remains when the wretchedness has passed [...] so the deepest good builds on the deepest human being, the whole man [...]. Any how, there is no question of rebirth. (*TWOC* 243)

Initially we find in the novel that Mr Anand presents a realistic picture of Gauri's sufferings. Gauri, a good and gentle woman, is aptly compared to a cow, for her endurance and immolation. The novelist again tries to evince the changes that come about in her. The credit goes to Dr Mahindra who has influenced her life, therefore she realises that her salvation does not remain in her endurance and obedience to an age-old corrupted society, but in an active opposition to it. Her company with Dr Mahindra opens out a new horizon of life. Gauri, on this very ground, defies her family, wrenches herself from it completely and starts to live a new life on a new ground. The whole plot is based on realism. The characters do not present only realistic ideas but they also depict the humanistic note of the novelist. Panchi, Lakshmi, Amru, Kesari, Mola Ram, Dr Batra all are meant to indicate the age-old victims of Indian family and society—savage, impassive and superstitious. Dr Mahindra tries to implant humanist ideas in Gauri by which she evinces how a person needs to depend on himself rather than on God for constructing his fate. The novelist tries to combat against falsity and hypocrisy, savagery and insensibility, and a defence of love and compassion, and all that goes to make man's life gaysome and lenient.

In this novel we find the whole process of the change of woman from a puppet in man's hands to the state of an independent woman who asserts her equal rights with man and demands recognition as such. The novelist adroitly makes use of the old myth of the *Ramayana* and suggests how it is no longer possible for man either to keep woman suppressed or to neglect her lawful liberty, equality, identity and individuality. The emphasis for the amelioration of woman is one of the significant aspects of Anand's humanism. Dr P.T. Raju, a reputed thinker, rightly says that "the present age is an age of humanism."[3] The works of Dr Anand are avowedly inspired by his compassion:

> And as my media as a writer were the memory and imagination, the substance of my work became the whole man, and the whole gamut of human relationships, rather than only one single part of it.[4]

We see that man is the chief exponent of humanism. The novelist says that it means what humanism has meant all along generally—"illumination or enlightenment in the interest of man, true to his highest nature and his noblest vision."[5] This way, "man is the measure of all things."[6]

NOTES AND REFERENCES

1. Anand, Mulk Raj. "Old Myths and New Myths: Recital *Versus* Novel," *Indian Literature of the Past Fifty Years* (ed. C.D. Narasimhaiah), Mysore, 1970, 119.
2. Shastry, S. Lakshman. "A Few words about This Issue" (Editorial), *Contemporary Indian Literature*, November-December, 1965, 10.
3. Raju, P.T. *The Concept of Man*, eds. S. Radhakrishnan and P.T. Raju (London, 1960), 15.
4. Anand, M.R. "Apology for Heroism" (Bombay, 1957), 18.
5. Anand, M.R. "Lines Written to an Indian Air" (Bombay, 1949), 7.
6. Stace, N.T. *A Critical History of Greek Philosophy* (London, 1962), 123.

4

Self-Discovery, Growth and Attainment: The Rising Graph of Rosie in R.K. Narayan's *The Guide*

S. RAJALAKSHMI

R.K. Narayan finds a pride of place among the illustrious Indian English creative triumvirate—the other two being, Mulk Raj Anand and Raja Rao. Unlike them, he never strays into the mazy intricacies of metaphysical fiction or the complexities of committed writing, but chooses to depict the foibles, follies, aberrations and absurdities found in the life of the common man. He is a conscious artist, writing being his only career, which he has mastered with superb skill, unflagging avidity and unswerving devotion. His reputation lies on his prolific fictional output—his captivating and enduring novels coupled with several short stories which have abiding interest for the common man.

With his demise on 13 May 2001, the brilliance of the Indian English firmament is truly diminished. A leading light is extinguished forever. What remains is the immortal Malgudi, the fictitious world of his rich creation, which has become a metaphor for India. The inhabitants of Malgudi have characteristic local flavour. With all their peculiar angularities, they are essentially human and share their kinship with all humanity. Human nature scarcely undergoes any considerable change, either with passing seasons and time or with varying geography. This quintessence of human life was comprehended by R.K. Narayan with firm conviction.

R.K. Narayan is richly endowed with the gift of seeing common characters from within and revealing them on their own plane. He has a keen eye for the common things that lie around us, choosing them to impart some random truths. Finding pleasure and happiness in simple things, is a recurring feature of existence, which is the hallmark of his writing. The core of his art lies in his singular gift, to present as valuable and beautiful anything that comes his way. This is his greatest asset as an artist. He makes no distinction between happenings small and events great. His art has the power to transmute the most ordinary, commonplace everyday experiences into everlasting expressions of artistic form and value. He portrays the various shades of human nature with deftness, ringing true to life, making his readers laud his works.

The Guide (1958) holds a place of eminence among his novels, bagging the much coveted Sahitya Akademi Award for the year 1960, for his "brilliant accomplishment." The rising fortunes of Rosie, the talented dancer with the able support of Railway Raju, form the motif of the novel. Rosie, the lovely girl passionately fond of dancing is suppressed by her husband Marco, an antiquarian, whose imagination is fired only by whatever is dead and decaying, "rather than things that lived and moved and swung their limbs."

In the initial stage, he aggressively defies the wishes of his wife who desires to see a king-cobra. He snubs her, "Don't expect me to go with you. I can't stand the sight of a snake—your interests are morbid." On the other hand, Rosie has a distaste for "Cold, old stone walls." She is perturbed by the fact that her husband, whom Raju calls 'Marco,' is more interested in books, papers, painting and old art, than in being a "real, live husband." He is too steeped in his zeal for archaeological studies, that he neglects his elegant and fascinating wife. Not realizing the invaluable treasure his wife is, he is "like a monkey picking up a rose garland!"

Rosie belongs to a family of professional dancing girls, devoted to the art, for whom dance is a part and parcel of life.

Seeing the cobra dance, she too unknowingly sways, imitating it, and for the shrewd Raju, "it was sufficient to tell me what she was, the greatest dancer of the century." She craves to dance and longs to express herself through dancing. But far from encouragement, Marco has compelled her to give up dancing, in return for a respectable life. His only enthusiasm is for collecting and annotating ancient art, and his icy temperament suggests an implacable malevolence towards love, warmth and life. She is pathetic, for she suffers from a bruised inward life. She becomes the victim of her husband's indifference and suffers psychologically as his discontented wife. Her mental anguish and incapacity to prove her prowess in dancing, torture her immensely. Marco is only interested in sculptured figures on walls and stones and not in his wife, "who as dancer was the living embodiment of those images."

She arrives in Malgudi with her husband, his interest in archaeology taking them there. Her association with the guide Raju, tends to open up the closed chapter of her life and gives a vent to her choice obsession of dancing. With Raju's assistance, her ecstasy for dancing is unbottled and she comes up gushing, frothing, effervescent and buoyant, excelling as a dancer. She is catapulted to dizzying heights of success, much applauded, living "in the glow of this radiant existence." She spends a great part of the day in her rehearsals and "one could hear the stamping of feet and the jingle of anklets." Her life becomes meaningful, "After all, she was living the life she had visualized." Her fascinating dance performances turn her into a celebrity and she basks in the glory of popularity.

Raju more or less creates 'Nalini,' the dancer, through his motivation. He performs the role of Rosie's business manager and publicity agent with relish and perfection, excelling as an impresario. He arranges her dance performances, bestowing great care up to the last detail. But she does not remain a mere toy in Raju's hands. For her, dance is not a means of making only money, but a cause, a devotion. She cherishes every garland that she gets, at the end of a performance. She feels that it is the best and worthwhile part of her entire activity. She emerges as a victorious new woman, breaking the shackles of serfdom under Marco. The social whirl makes her reach the pinnacle of glory.

Along with Rosie's rising graph towards fame, adultation and eminence, Raju too rises in stature. Wealth and success intoxicate him and he loses all sense of proportion. The company in which he moves, induces in him contempt for the law and he overreaches. With an almost childish irresponsibility, he forges Rosie's signature, and is subsequently jailed. Rosie works harder than before, giving dance performances to clear the debts incurred. Without Raju, she gains self-reliance, growing from "strength to strength." Neither Marco nor Raju had any place in her life, "which had its own sustaining vitality and which she herself had underestimated all along." Her dance performances take her to several places in South India, Bombay, Delhi and Ceylon. She deftly manages her life and her empire of dance expands. After repaying all her debts, she clears out of Malgudi "bag and baggage" and settles down at Madras "looking after herself quite well." So Rosie successfully wriggles out of her psychological trauma, attains her cherished ambition of becoming an accomplished dancer, ending up triumphant.

WORKS CITED

Balarama Gupta, G.S. "R.K. Narayan: In Memorial," *The Journal of Indian Writing in English,* Vol. 29, July 2001, No. 2.

Mukherjee, Meenakshi. *The Twice Born Fiction.* New Delhi: Arnold Heinemann Publishers (India) Private Ltd., 1974.

Narasimhaiah, C.D., *The Swan and the Eagle.* Shimla: IIAS, 1969.

Narayan, R.K. *The Guide.* Mysore: Indian Thought Publications, 2000.

Srinivasa Iyengar, K.R. *Indian Writing in English.* Bombay: Asia Publishing House, 1973.

Sundaram, P.S. *R.K. Narayan.* New Delhi: Arnold Heinemann India, 1973.

——, *R.K. Narayan as a Novelist.* Delhi: B.R. Publishing Corporation, 1988.

Walsh, William. *R.K. Narayan—A Critical Appreciation.* New Delhi: Allied Publishers Private Ltd., 1983.

5

THE CHANCE ENCOUNTER IN *TALKATIVE MAN* AND *THE WORLD OF NAGARAJ*

ANISHA ALI

By the time R.K. Narayan came to write *Talkative Man* (1986) and *The World of Nagaraj* (1990), his writing career almost reached its peak. Even in these two novels, he portrays the same pattern of order out of disorder. The usual motif of his writing brings in the tilt in the normal scheme of life, created by the encounter of an intruder who enthralls and excites the protagonist into an illusory state. Slowly the latter is enticed by certain activities which are quite alien to him. As a consequence, there is a rift between reality and illusion. This confusion dismantles the set order. Such a chance encounter usually does not conform to the usual social mores of life. The outsider is an embodiment of vitality and an individualist, alienated from the social values and yet accepted by the tame Malgudians who in spite of believing in order and continuity are vulnerable to the baser instincts at times. In *Talkative Man* (hence *TM),* Dr Rann arrives in Malgudi and invades the small world of the talkative man who as a young journalist struggles to establish his reputation in Malgudi as a talkative man who would "choke if [he] didn't talk" (*TM* 1).

In Narayan's writing, the outsider though bizarre to the Malgudian context always finds a response from the invaded. This is so because inside every ordered character lurks the principle of anarchy that needs to be mastered. Dr Rann, the outsider was completely "an oddity—dressed as he was in a blue suit, tie and shining shoes and holding a felt hat in hand."[1] Even his name was not Indian and he showed every sign of his foreign pedigree. Till the advent of Dr Rann into the world of the talkative man (alias Madhu as he was called in his boyhood days or the journalist who is rather called as the "universal correspondent") he enjoyed his "self-appointed role" (*TM* 3)—busy in his orbit of activities like despatch of the mail and always with unwarranted rush. The talkative man had dreams of becoming a journalist and so was busy in his own way with his usual tempo.

Dr Rann's sudden and presumptuous presence was almost a discomfiture to Madhu. The very entry of the former into the town of Malgudi created an annoying imposition on Madhu who was always on the lookout for a good story rather than encountering strangers. He was simply intrigued by the sudden presence of Dr Rann—"May I know what took you there and what has brought you here?"[2] Dr Rann arrived in Malgudi wearing a fancy blue suit and claimed to be researching on a project for the UN. He induced the talkative man into taking him home on Kabir Street where he started living as a house guest. Right from the beginning Dr Rann created distraught in Malgudi. His attire and manners seemed to have an overwhelming impact even on the puny station-master who was tantalized to find that the grand visitor had no intention of leaving the waiting room. In his thirty years of service, the station-master never came upon such an impossible situation that created so much confusion and disorder in the maintenance of rules in the railways. Narayan usually ascribes disorder in the form of greed, lust, destructiveness or adventurousness in the extraneous elements (the outsiders). In this novel too, the outsider Dr Rann with his adventurous research scheme comes and breaks the humdrum rhythm of life of the talkative man whose life turns topsy-turvy in meeting the demands of Dr Rann. The talkative man had a harrowing experience in finding a house for Dr Rann so that the latter leaves the waiting room to ease the grudging station-master.

Even after leaving the waiting room, Dr Rann with his impulsive air continued with his tantrums of 'outlandish habits'

(*TM* 27). With all his vanity, he quite eccentrically decided to stay with Madhu who offered his house out of sheer modesty. However, with his arrival at Madhu's door, things came to a sudden halt. This decision of Dr Rann makes "the whole of Kabir Street agog" (*TM* 27). People stood at their doors to see the new arrival. Soon Dr Rann assumes larger than life appearance with his grand research project. "He has come on a vital project on behalf of the UN and it's an honour for Malgudi that he chooses to work here." With Dr Rann's flamboyant project the talkative man as a journalist felt that he was at "the brink of some great event" (*TM* 29). Under Dr Rann's influence the Malgudian journalist becomes aspirant of a mighty career. Narayan as a novelist lays his craftsmanship in writing by creating an illusion "so pleasant that we are content to be lost in it."[3] It is this impression that makes the events or the actions flow and go to build up the structure of the novel in its form and content.

Narayan's heroes have the touch of creativity with their lively imagination, creating a new sense of life. The talkative man also has his chance to assert his creative self when he meets Dr Rann. Right after meeting him the talkative man gets enthused to work on the life and activities of the new scholar (Dr Rann) in Malgudi. It is always a meeting which precipitates the crisis of consciousness between reality and illusion. The talkative man soon dreams that Dr Rann, the man known to be from Timbuctoo would make an excellent news item. The whole idea gives him the feeling of doing service to the society, for he would then act as the eye for humanity. In order to be in the thick of the situation, the talkative man needed a photograph of "the Timbuctoo Man" (*TM* 24), to make his news item more effective. For the procurement of the photograph, the talkative man had to undergo a lot of trouble. It involved catching the service of a cameraman, borrowing the best Japanese camera from the councillor and above all catching hold of Rann to pose for the news item which would fetch the journalist all the pride in his society.

It is always the characteristic entry of the outsiders into the stable world of the protagonists that creates a tilt into the humdrum activities of life. Usually a sheer coincidence takes place in the set world of the heroes with a distinct touch of fantasy "Some miracle would happen, some chance or fortune be picked up on the doorstep."[4] Madhu or the talkative man realizes this when he meets Dr Rann that "one enters a new life at an appointed time and it is foolish to resist."[5]

All outsiders in Narayan's novels bear resemblance in being flamboyant and restless but they keep themselves busy with a practical ability. Dr Pal in *The Financial Expert* (*TFE*) remains equally busy in his creative activities as a journalist and writer. So is Dr Rann who in *Talkative Man* keeps himself busy in his assumed role of the research project for the United Nations. The impact of such individuals is extraordinary on the people they interact with. Dr Pal in *TFE* and Dr Rann in *TM* instill a new impulse but a short-sighted sense in the heroes like Nataraj and talkative man in the aforesaid novels.

It is noteworthy that the outsiders in the realm of order appear with their modern skills when the heroes are in a state of turmoil and confusion. The entry of the outsiders further aggravates the dilemma of the protagonists and makes their world chaotic. More so, these outsiders appear quite mysteriously with some avowed vocations always with a thrilling touch. Dr Rann like Dr Pal of *TFE* suddenly appears in the periphery of Malgudi giving the impression of obscurity and enthralment. Under the influence of the outsiders, the heroes get enticed with grand notions of life.

In *Talkative Man,* Madhu, the titular hero weaves his dreams of publishing and printing about Dr Rann and his alien world of Timbuctoo. Like Margayya in *The Financial Expert,* Madhu is also obsessed with the dream of being a journalist and perform a greater service to the society. His commitment is a kind of illusion in the sense used in the Hindu philosophy. His obsession is a form of attachment to things or *maya.* All his efforts to becoming a renowned journalist soon get threatened when he is rudely disturbed by the intrusion of Dr Rann's wife, Roja who comes on the lookout for her erratic husband. To Madhu, she almost looked "like a visitor from another planet" (*TM* 52). Both Dr Rann and his wife stand out typically as the creatures from the other world. Each of these extraneous elements gives a tilt to the sequence of events and creates a new momentum in the action of the novel.

It is after the advent of Roja that Madhu comes to know more of Rann's outlandish ways of living and the fact that he spends most of his time in flippant and scandalous acts, being "a regular lady killer" (*TM* 55). Roja divulges all her experiences with her husband and discloses to Madhu that Dr Rann has his own peculiar ways of seducing women as she herself was enticed by his ensnaring ways. She relates to the journalist how she became a victim to Rann's charming ways and ultimately eloped with him. Narayan depicts Dr Rann with "the same uncertainties, possibilities and potentialities."[6] At first Narayan projects him as a figure of overwhelming sense of a self-contained man given to scholarly pursuits as against Madhu who can hardly contain himself. Dr Rann has an assumed role of researching and so Madhu had "offered asylum" although for no reason. It had "just been an impulse to help him" (*TM* 42). Narayan's major heroes like Madhu or Nataraj in *The Man-eater of Malgudi* or Srinivas in *Mr Sampath* all have an impulsive nature for a temporary period in the alluring world. Except for this illusory period they remain static all through.

Dr Rann is eked out as a man of enormous strength with his research work for the UN. However as things turn out, his passion for dubious adventures with women soon perturbs the good temper of Madhu especially after he came to know about the facts from Roja who sought help from him to find out her husband. Dr Rann soon becomes the disrupting force in Madhu's world of peace and order. The latter now begins to doubt and harbours suspicions about Dr Rann's recklessness in the research work. He becomes impatient to find out "as to what game [Dr Rann] was trying to play, to warn him to keep

off and not to add one more desperate correspondent to his files" (*TM* 92).

Soon Madhu comes to know about Dr Rann's most irresponsible and scandalous behaviour when the latter starts frequenting the old librarian's house and shows extra care for the librarian's young granddaughter, Girija in her studies. Matters reach its peak when Dr Rann schemes in his mind to elope with Girija. This is divulged to Madhu by Gaffur, the driver who used to take Rann to Girija's house. Gaffur acts as a tertiary character or becomes the 'causality' of the novel. Girija in fact was misled by Rann after he promised to provide her any degree she chose from any university on earth. The knowledge of this relationship threw Madhu into a complex situation. Such act of Girija would create a public shock and the outcome of the scandal would mean her eventual desertion to some far off place. He makes up his mind to protect the old librarian from this shock. He decides to call upon Dr Rann's estranged and jilted wife, Roja who had earlier come to Malgudi pursuing her husband when she saw a photograph of him in the newspaper, *Telegraph.* It was the illusion of Dr Rann's intellectual pursuits that made Madhu keep Roja away and protect Dr Rann from "wifely intrusions" (*TM* 52) when she first came to Malgudi. This time Madhu after knowing Rann's scandalous indulgence intimates her and asks her to come to Malgudi immediately. He then resolves to unmask the true picture of Rann to the citizens of Malgudi who had so long respected him as a scholar. With the liaison between Rann and Girija reaching its cataclysmic peak, Madhu feels secured because he thinks that in no time Dr Rann would be "hounded out of Malgudi by its worthy citizens for being fooled with all that trumpeting about the Town Hall Lecture" on futurology and a menacing weed that he was to deliver at Lotus Club. To Madhu, Rann now appears "a callous and indiscriminate lecher" (*TM* 112).

However, the silver jubilee function of Lotus Club, graced by Rann ends in fiasco for his lecture on science was so preposterous that really told on the nerves of the audience and put the whole assembly in complete disarray. Madhu too works out his plan to inform Roja who arrives at this juncture. In the midst of all confusion and disorder Rann gets caught by his own wife who arrives at the opportune moment to round him off. It is at this point that the crucial circumstances come to an anticlimax. Rann's scheme of alluring Girija and duping the people thus comes to an end. Narayan very aptly juxtaposes the unholy thought of Rann to elope with Girija to his holy act of research amidst the celebration of the silver jubilee of Lotus Club. The author is more interested in the unpredictable qualities rather than the expected ones. He pins his attention on the potentialities of life. In *Talkative Man* the disturbance of order is followed by a return, a renewal and a restoration of normalcy, for all the threads get eventually settled. After Rann's departure from Malgudi there is a new sense of order. Madhu derives a new peace at the extermination of the extraneous element which misled him and Girija. Luckily Girija too seemed "to come through her escapade unscathed" (*TM* 113). After Dr Rann's departure, she resumes her studies and goes to her college regularly with the same tempo as before.

Narayan believes in the ultimate inheritance of righteousness. Man's better self always prevails. In his novels, action develops the character and the theme of order—disorder is unfolded with the outsider leaving at the end or the hero getting reformed. Herein Narayan shows that "each person must also face life's mutability."[7]

A portion of Narayan's authorial commentary in the novels urges the reader not to concentrate on specific behaviour and regard it as idiosyncratic. Much of his imagery is directed to arousing our imaginative comprehension not merely of why a character exists and acts, but also of how his existence and actions are at par with existence and actions of other characters. Narayan often compares characters in the same novel to bring out contrasts like Nagaraj and Tim in *The World of Nagaraj* who interact with each other by their opposing natures. Tim is always found recklessly involved in his mad pursuits of vagrancy while Nagaraj only beholds the reckless activities of adventure in a docile manner from his corner sitting on the *pyol*.

The World of Nagaraj (*TWN*) has equally wrought out meaningfully the central theme of creating a balance between order and disorder in the lives of the 'insiders' and the 'outsiders' of Malgudi. The insiders in this novel are Nagaraj and his wife Sita. The two live in a spacious family house leading a quiet and comfortable life. The outsiders are Tim, the son of Nagaraj's ambitious landowning brother Gopu and wife, Saroja. Tim leaves his home to live with his uncle Nagaraj who in spite of his worldly life as a middle class business partner has his greatest knack of writing a book on the sage *Narada*. There is the pressure of the outsiders who are inclined to the fascinating world of illusion and fantasy and who convey an air of eccentricity, a degree of crankiness and adventurousness. In short, none of them have the Malgudian propensities. The Malgudian characters unlike the outsiders are usually passive and inert, static in their ways and lead a life of order and stability. It is their irresistibility to new ideas and allurements which disturb their setting of order and calm. In the interactions of these passive characters with the outsiders, there is a hectic striving, a continual uncertainty among the inexperienced Malgudians. So Narayan finds Malgudi a ground of ungovernable and unpredictable forces. The world of Nagaraj in the novel is a world of chances where everything may not be in good order. It is a world of folly and futility—a realm of Don Quixote in a quixotic world. It projects the self-deception and stupidity of the Malgudians and the means to bring them to some positive consequences. All reel back to the correct comprehension of the inevitability of law and order out of disorder. The sense of humanity pervades through life quite subtly almost as if balancing all matters, all wrapped up centripetally.

The World of Nagaraj has a tight and a well-organized plot with integrated characters and incidents. The action is counterpoised between Nagaraj and Tim. The action is also circular in the sense that it ends where it begins. The opening of the novel shows Nagaraj taking pain to be “a man with a mission” (*TWN* 1) and the closing of the novel also depicts him working out his way to his mission. The circular action has a climax-anticlimax structure. Nagaraj’s world of quietness and comfort is suddenly invaded by Tim, his nephew whose life is based on reckless endeavours of sensuous life, secret late night activities entailed by the strong smell of spirits lingering behind him. However, Tim has his abrupt anticlimax. Nagaraj therefore has his shocking experience in his usual tranquil life but he soon regains normalcy like any other Narayan hero for “there is generally a flight, an uprooting, a disturbance of order—followed by a return, a renewal, a restoration of normalcy.”[8] The story, in a way, delineates the opposing forces in conflict.

In Narayan’s novels, action determines the character, Professor W. Walsh says, “Character is action, and action is plot and it is by means of the action of his character that Narayan summons up the world in which he lives.”[9] It is through his characters that Narayan portrays his insight into human nature. This makes his portraiture more charming. The novelist presents both his major and minor characters in an equally fascinating and amusing manner. There is the realistic and authentic delineation of their capacities to surprise the reader. This makes the characters unpredictable yet potentially capable of being ‘round’[10] as is observed in Tim and Saroja. The two are minor characters although they do not play a minor role. They are confident, practical and definite and have an integral part in the development of the novel. They have peculiar independent roles to enact. We see them in constant strife to achieve the fulfilment of their dreams. On the other hand, the major characters like Nagaraj appears to be fragile and prone to fantasies. More particularly, they have their free flight into the past and future particularly in times of tense situations. Likewise, Nagaraj likes to retrospect his bygone days with his land-owning brother Gopu living as a coherent family in their old village house (signifying order and tradition). This stands quite in contrast to the appalling conditions created by Tim (the impulsive force) who comes to occupy his house. "The life and the movement of Kabir Street"[11] (where Nagaraj is a well-known business partner of Coomar) are always in a state of flux.

Right from the beginning of the novel we find Nagaraj trying to affirm a life of austerity and devoutness. In a way Narayan believes that the best way of life lies in respecting one's own individuality, by maintaining a firm faith in the divine order wherein the play of evil is always temporary. It is the good angel that takes over ultimately to ensure the triumph of faith and reason over the impulsive forces. Narayan sharply concerns himself with the moral issues of life. It is the mind which gets involved in the intricacies of human relationships. He has actually translated his own experiences in life and in his later novels he clarifies a "Triple Vision of Man in relation to himself, his environment and his gods [...] all give new dimensions to his art as a novelist."[12] Nagaraj's grand plan to do research for his magnum opus on *Narada* and the human predicament in general gives him a philosophical outlook wherein the essential need is equanimity with human existence. Throughout the novel, the principle of anarchy in the form of evil ways of the outsider, Tim dismantles Nagaraj's world and makes the latter desperate. Nagaraj, however, with his level-headedness keeps himself away (quite scrupulously) from both Tim and Saroja. Tim's formidable strength, his gregarious behaviour and flippancy together with Saroja's ill-got sense of music and fun all create a dismantling picture in the tranquil atmosphere of Nagaraj and Sita's house. By keeping a distance from Tim's suspicious activities, Nagaraj paves his way to stability.

At the beginning of his research on *Narada,* Nagaraj had carved a niche of his own to create an environment in spite of the disturbances caused by the constant movement of his old mother over the whole place. Nagaraj's refuge to "seek asylum on the pyol" (*TWN* 52) gives him a peculiar sense of peace. His mind seems to philosophize on the life *of Narada* who according to ancient epics becomes catalytic in propelling the activities of life in the proper order "beneficial in the long run in an eternal perspective" (*TWN* 44). Nagaraj assumes that his research work on *Narada* would give him a way to harmony in the clash of order and disorder. Ruminating in the context of his stable life at home, he quite naturally melts into the great human forces in life. Before the intrusion of Tim "he could watch tranquility of the scenes in the street" (*TWN* 61). But now "Nagaraj's heart bled" (*TWN* 63) at the hostile notions that started troubling his head about the young fellow whose frisky and dubious ways make him look "full of charm but never meant what he said, and proved slippery" (*TWN* 58). Nagaraj soon learns to go alone in his business of living uninterrupted and absolve himself for, he could see the probability of "exaggeration and misapprehending" (*TWN* 63) as if bloated in the theme of disorder out of too much brooding. In Hindu philosophy, attachment to things entails fear and insecurity in life. The best way to pull one's mind back from the theme of disorder is to make an effort. The resoluteness of will alone can harmonize the discordant forces of life. Thus Nagaraj learns to accept the situation and that "each [is] moving in a fixed orbit as if nothing else mattered or existed."[13] For Nagaraj and also for Narayan, the research work on *Narada* was a symbol of a bridge between the past and the present for he continues his work with the same tempo and spirit throughout the novel. Nagaraj never started working without praying. He always wore the ochre robe and sat on the pyol with an introspective state of mind and watched the stars. So the engulfing spirit in the form of swarming activities of the buzzing town of Malgudi impresses upon him with calm thoughts much more like a conscientious man who grapples his "dignity and development."[14] The crisis of consciousness in Nagaraj's mind is closely linked with the expanse of life in the teeming population (that he always views from his pyol) which symbolizes the movement of life in Malgudi. This leaves an indelible impression on the theme of the novel.

Nagaraj pins his only hope on the outcome of the book on *Narada*. But Tim's erratic ways made his world confusing and vague. He became perplexed and did not know—whether he was helping Tim as his uncle or Tim was indirectly dictating him. The whole position was vague and obscure.

However, while in the throes of being a writer, Nagaraj cannot escape from his responsibility of looking after his nephew Tim's whereabouts. Soon Nagaraj's mind "conjures up visions of Tim's affluence" (*TWN* 82). Things get aggravated when both his brother Gopu and his wife arrive suddenly to fetch Tim. The crisis concludes when Gopu relates a marriage proposal from Delhi for Tim with rupees ten thousand as dowry. In a mysterious way, Tim happily accepts the proposition. So it is settled that Tim would be taken up by marriage and soon all the hassles and the speculations about the young man will get over.

Nagaraj has ample faith on the book on *Narada* which became almost a symbol of stability and revival of order. He wants to assert himself with his creative powers. He, therefore recounts the book as if it would pave a way to a predetermined force. This would help him in the search for an unknown stabilizing factor in his life. Tim leaves for marriage and that brings a deep sense of serenity in Nagaraj's house. Nagaraj soon gets "used to the silence of his home, where even street noises were muffled by the heavy door and the occasional monologues uttered by Sita in the kitchen which fell in tune with the surroundings" (*TWN* 93). His peace is however short-lived as Tim again returns, this time with his newly wed wife, Saroja. Nagaraj now faces a new phase of disturbances from the team of Tim and Saroja who occupy the middle room of the house. The couple turns out to be rowdy and their room seems to be emanated with the incessant chatter and giggling, with sudden outbursts of songs with the accompaniment of her harmonium. The turmoil and confusion especially with the torment of harmonium butting mercilessly makes him even more restless and doubtful. Surrendering himself totally to the chaos he missed the sheer peace of watching the street life with total surrender. In complete disgust he murmurs to himself, "What evil genius impelled me to undertake this task? What conceit? Waste of time. Ages since I sat on the pyol with a free mind" (*TWN* 141).

In the novel, we look upon Nagaraj as a man striving forth not in accordance to his wishes but complying with the dictates of a mysterious element. Whatsoever, he has to ultimately revert back to his own endeavour to complete the book. In pursuit of this, he needed to go to a Sanskrit *pundit* who only makes him "more desolate" for he "stood transfixed, staring after the retreating scholar" (*TWN* 99). Nagaraj again slowly starts wondering whether he would even be able to complete his work. He gets intrigued with the doubtful nature of the *pundit's* help and his mind becomes split between illusion and reality. At this juncture he comes upon the Talkative Man (*TWN* 161) who helps him to get lessons from the Sanskrit scholar at an auspicious day and hour. But then to his dismay, Nagaraj finds that the *pundit* hardly had any interest in doling out his knowledge *of Narada*. "It seemed to Nagaraj an endless quest" (*TWN* 115). Nagaraj felt that his life became more muddled. In his literary struggle, hunting for resources from library hardly gave him any books on the sage, *Narada*. Soon Nagaraj found that he had to even tolerate the card playing habit of the *pundit* in order to procure materials for his work. Bearing all these Nagaraj however derived an inspirational boost from the *pundit* who professed that writing is "Something that is churned out of a lot of mental struggle" (*TWN* 128). This gives Nagaraj the much-needed happiness that helped him to continue with his mission and also gave some stability in his life.

Nagaraj's literary preoccupations have had its stifling and harrowing part that constantly dissuaded and interrupted him. Yet again a calm and poise come when Tim becomes unpredictable and mysterious in his ways leaving behind Nagaraj and Sita with no reason to work in Kismet, an affluent hotel.

For once, "Life's pendulum, which had swung erratically was coming back to normal which meant that in the background *Narada* would once again appear and lend a meaning to daily existence" (*TWN* 177). The house would revert to quietness and normal order. Above all, Nagaraj felt free from responsibilities and custody of Tim. "He had a fresh lease of life" (*TWN* 177). However, this was for a short period only. Tim returned back with his wife as he had a quibble with the secretary of Kismet.

Tim's flippant and mysterious behaviour always gives a shaky picture to the mind of Nagaraj momentarily but the latter soon realizes that all these are passing phases and that it is existence which is pertinently felt and is inevitable. It is through his continuous struggle, "the war that is going on between man's inside and outside"[15] to his literary pursuits that ultimately gives a sense of order.

Narayan makes it a point to evolve the same cycle of events with the theme of survival and strife in the thick of changing circumstances. He tries to justify the value of existence only to reassert the stabilizing factor in knowing oneself, of deriving joy and peace with a sense of one's true identity. There is the ongoing principle of acknowledging the oneness of man and universe. It is Nagaraj's inner strength, resilient to the odds that come his way. His persistent involvement in trying to write about *Narada* (who is solely devoted to the cause of mankind) allows Nagaraj "to learn from nature how to control and create both the outer and inner life, that is to recreate his environment."[16]

Narayan's mission has invariably been to vindicate the philosophy of continuity of life and aligning man with Nature. Struggles are inevitable and persistently felt. In Narayan's scheme of writing, the advent of the outsiders is almost imperative. These extraneous elements have biphasic roles. They not only initiate the struggles but also act as catalysts in the restorative act in the life of the heroes. In *Talkative Man* and *The World of Nagaraj*, the outsiders, Dr Rann and Tim respectively have proved just that. The outsiders also play a crucial role in providing the comic relief in the novels. Most of Narayan's comedy is derived through the interactions between the heroes and the outsiders. With the expulsion of the latter, order is restored with an amusing sense of life's frailties and small dreams. In Narayan's character there is a continual self-analysis which entails brooding of personal destiny. This only gives a contemplative stance to his writing. There is an inert commitment to life in these characters which comes to light only through the external agencies albeit disaster that pushes them to the very brink of total defeat. This has been amply shown in the two novels discussed above.

REFERENCES

1. Narayan, R.K. *Talkative Man* (Mysore: Indian Thought Publications, 1986) 6.
2. *Talkative Man* 9.
3. Peery, Lubbock. *The Craft of Fiction*. J. Cape Paperback (1952) 6.
4. Narayan, R.K. *The Financial Expert* (Mysore: Indian Thought Publications) 79.
5. Narayan, R.K. *The Vendor of Sweets* (Mysore: Indian Thought Publications) 129.
6. Narayan, R.K. *The Man-eater of Malgudi* (Mysore: Indian Thought Publications, 1962) 30.
7. House, B. Elizabeth. "Artist and the Art of Living: Order and Disorder in Toni Morrison's Fiction," in *Modern Fiction Studies*, Vol. 34, No. 1 (1988) 28.
8. Iyenger, K.R.S. *Indian Writing in English* (New Delhi: Sterling Publishers, 1983) 385.
9. Walsh, Williams. *R.K.N.: A Critical Appreciation* (Great Britain: Heinemann, 1982) 135.
10. Forster, E.M. *Aspects of the Novel* (Australia: Penguin Books, 1971) 81.
11. Narayan, R.K. *The World of Nagaraj* (Mysore: Indian Thought Publications, 1990) 7.
12. Iyenger, K.R.S. *Indian Writing in English* (New York: Asia Publishing House, 1993) 300, 301.
13. *The Man-eater of Malgudi* 186.
14. Narayan, R.K. *Mr Sampath* (Mysore: Indian Thought Publications, 1949) 93.
15. *Mr Sampath* 6.
16. Sinha, Nandan Krishna and Ghai, Sisukumar. "Psychology of Social Development: A Modern View," in *Indian Writing in English* (New Delhi: A Heritage Publication, 1982)186.

6

Spirituality Syndrome and Cultural Exclusiveness in R.K. Narayan

ANVAR SADHATH

The most noticeable aspect of R.K. Narayan's novels is, perhaps, his commitment to Hindu ideals. Religious identity in general and caste identity in particular, form an ideological matrix from which Narayan appears to operate his consciousness. His novels are set in an "ideological space," the imaginative South Indian town, Malgudi. Hinduism and Malgudi demarcate Narayan's scope, and therefore he speaks as though from within the four walls of a confining culture, which is opposed to the all-inclusiveness of Indian culture, where private (or communal) is treated as more essential than the public (or national). The confined kingdom of Narayan thus exemplifies an underlying ideology which affirms cultural superiority and hegemony over the subordinate groups, or overshadows them with its blinding presence. Here I would like to focus upon two major traits, cultural exclusiveness and spirituality syndrome, which descend from the above said cultural identity, with special reference to *The Guide* and *The Bachelor of Arts.*

I

There is something very strange in the way the inhabitants of Malgudi are attracted to sanyasam and sanyasis. The way Chandran becomes a sanyasi in *The Bachelor of Arts,* the way people, without knowing his whereabouts, offer him food and respect; Chandran's mother's attitude to the self-declared sanyasi who lifted flowers from their garden; Velan's reverence to Raju when he appears in the temple in *The Guide,* and many such instances, show indications of what can be called a spirituality syndrome. Gita Mehta offers a number of such cases in her *Karma Cola* where she finds that thousands of westerners travelled to India in search of spiritual gurus who are expected to free them from the boredoms and despair of the realities of an increasingly material world (IX). Mehta's findings bear a negative picture of the spiritual enlightenment that Indian sages do offer, although she makes us believe that India can justly be called a "Rishi Bhoomi," the land of sages and sanyasis. For every seeker, it is understood that, there is a sage to teach him/her "true" enlightenment (81). Gita Mehta gives us innumerable cases in point to authenticate the worldliness of these sages, whereas Narayan portrays the manner in which the people of Malgudi approve sanyasis and he delineates the process by which sanyasis are made. Sanyasam, as per Hindu scriptures, is one of the four asramas through which a Hindu believer passes in his life. The other three are Brahmacharya (bachelordom), Grihastha (householder) and Vanaprastha (retirement to forest). The formulation of these asramas is expected to be in accordance with the purusharthas or purpose and end of life, *i.e.* "Dharama-Artha-Karma-Moksha (righteousness, seeking wealth, satisfying desires and liberation)" (Balakrishan 52). In Narayan, sanyasa is not an achieved state of renunciation through karma, that leads to moksha, but is forced upon individuals by their circumstances which are purely of the material kind. Therefore their renunciation is to be addressed as symptomatic of a syndrome. In *The Bachelor of Arts,* Chandran's abstention was "an alternative to suicide [...]. He was a sanyasi because it pleased him to mortify his flesh. His renunciation was a revenge on society, circumstances and perhaps, too on destiny" (108). In *The Guide* Raju's transfiguration from a tourist guide to a sanyasi, which is outwardly similar to the transformation of a highway robber to Valmiki, is achieved through karma. "But it is impossible to conceive that this progress might end in the condition of moksha" or liberation. Viewed from an orthodox Hindu point of view, Raju's situation "combines a subjective experience and an objective condition, which that experience can never fully account for [...]" (Swinden 78-79). Spirituality syndrome makes the people of Malgudi take Raju's refuge in the temple as sanyasam: "He is a big man, he may have thousand things to do [...]. He has renounced the world; he does nothing but meditate" (29). Velan is not ready to believe Raju when he puts down Velan's request to perform fasting to please rain-god saying that "I am not a saint Velan, I am just an ordinary human being" (99).

Having said that spirituality is a syndrome, let me relate these mysterious aspects of Indian life depicted by Narayan, to Edward Said's concept of Orientalism. Orientalism, to Said, is a western style of dominating and having authority over the Orient, "By making statements about it, authorizing views of it, setting it, ruling over it" (3). The concept of the Orient created by the western intelligentsia all through centuries helped Europeans or the westerners to define themselves (Said 1). These concepts include certain preconceived notions, dogmas and stereotypes as the mysterious nature of the Orient, its intellectual backwardness, "the absolute and systematic difference between the West which is rational, developed, human, superior," and the Orient "which is aberrant, underdeveloped, inferior and incapable of defining itself" (Said 300-01). The creations of Narayan have most of the qualities with which the Orient is identified by the accident. The lethargic Indians who seek refuge in spirituality in an effort to escape from the harsh realities of the world like Raju and Chandran, and failed entrepreneurs like Srinivas (*Mr Sampath*) are examples, which match the Orientalist stereotypes of Indians.

II

Narayan, not unlike many other writers, appears to be writing from the cultural sphere of Hinduism, which I would argue, determined the hierarchies and concepts of his time. Louis Althusser who called man "an ideological animal by nature," argued that ideology functions in a way that it recruits subjects through a precise operation named "interpellations" or hailing. In his view religious ideology addresses the individuals or transforms the individuals into subjects who obey the commandments of God (Selden 462). Ruling or dominant classes, according to Antonio Gramsci, exercise hegemony over the other classes largely through an ideological domination which includes the mastery of people's common sense (quoted in Selden 452). The social reality that Narayan extends is a product of the internalisation of the dominant ideology, which is obvious in his works. The most discernible aspect of this is what I mentioned as cultural exclusiveness and spirituality syndrome. While spirituality syndrome originates from the legitimating and approbations of some religious rituals as pious and redeeming, cultural exclusiveness stems from the delimiting of a writer through an ideological scrutiny by the state or the ruling ideology. The former, I have discussed in the previous section. There are numerous instances in Narayan for cultural exclusiveness. Primarily almost all the major characters in his novels represent the dominant community. Raju and Velan in *The Guide;* Srinivas and Sampath in *Mr Sampath;* Chandran, Mohan and Raman in *Bachelor of Arts;* Swami, Rajam, and Mani in *Swami and Friends;* Margayya and Dr Lal in *Financial Expert*; Nataraj and Vasu in *Man-eater of Malgudi;* Sriram and Bharathi in *Waiting for the Mahatma*; Ramini and Savitri in *The Dark Room* are examples. People of other community are rare birds in Narayan's novels. Even if they appear (for instance Gaffur and Joseph in *The Guide),* they are always marginalised or sidelined. Fear of the authority of the dominant group being thwarted, is prevalent in his novels. Raju in *The Guide* is not sent to Albert Mission School by his father because "it seems they try to convert our boys to Christianity and are all the time insulting our gods" (29). On another occasion when Rosie asks how Joseph became a Christian, Raju replies in a scornful fashion: "There was a Mission somewhere here, missionaries go and settle in all the sorts of places, you know" (89).

Critics, mainly western critics, tended to conceive Malgudi and Hinduism as forming a microcosm of Indian culture as a whole. Most of their critical remarks in this sense are quite misleading. Both Malgudi and Hinduism are exclusive categories in Narayan and therefore are not disseminating the variety and diversity of India. Malgudi is only a polished version of India, deriving from his religious indifference. His is rather an account of the dominance of a particular community, its social superiority, its cultural hegemony over the other groups, its sense of belonging to one place and its love of being free from responsibilities and changes.

Cultural exclusiveness makes Narayan's characters take refuge in spirituality. Both Raju and Chandran become sanyasis to free themselves from the realities of the world. They have confined their lives to the cultural code of Hinduism and Malgudi, and they rarely go out of these spheres. Their localness and domesticities make them narrow in their approaches. They don't care what happens to their country. Chandran is cynical about his friends who became guerrillas to fight against the colonial powers. When showed politics and religion, country and locality, Chandran and Raju would prefer the latter. This confining nature is purely in contrast to the colonising nature of the West, and thus Narayan's views are in tune with the Eurocentric vision. It is perhaps this vision that made Narayan popular in the West. Richard Cronin describes Malgudi as "Narayan's India," with a number of deities, the thwarting of which leads Vasu the taxidermist, in *Man-Eater of Malgudi,* to self-destruction. He finds India a country where myths overrule nationhood. Indian history in his view is "a sequence of invasions, Mogal, British, Chinese. In the face of every invader India is seen helpless and yet it is India that, apparently so disorganized and so passive that survives" (26). These stereotyped pictures of India and Indians are authorised in many of Narayan's novels. From Narayan what the western critic gets is a picture of Indians who believe in myths, who are basically opposed to the rationalist Europeans, who are so passive as opposed to the active Occident. What leads Narayan is, however, an escapist notion that, "Whatever happens, India will go on" as he is reported to have told V.S. Naipaul once.

III

Many critics considered seeking history in fiction and finding fiction in history as fallacious. But earlier Marxist critics and recently cultural critics who promulgated what Andrew Milner described a "sociological turn" in literacy studies, opposed this and they took literature as a cultural product. Marxist critics, Balibar and Machery held that there is an intricate relationship between the historical conditions of existence and literature (Rice and Waugh 62). While traditional literary studies showed a tendency to define literature as a timeless "aesthetic" category, "cultural studies would tend to see cultural value as socially constructed" (Milner 11). The historical conditions have been the locus of Indian fiction right from the early twentieth century. The dividing line between political history and fictions in Indian literary scenario is very narrow. From Mulk Raj Anand to Salman Rushdie, Raja Rao to Rohinton Mistry, writers of fiction took political history of India as the thematic focus of their works. Narayan is no exception. But the history that Narayan recreates in his novels doesn't have much of the events and problems that form India's history. The amount of political history available in his novels is minimal when compared to the works of writers like Mulk Raj Anand, Raja Rao, Chaman Nahal, Kamala Markandaya and Salman Rushdie. Perhaps, *Waiting for the Mahatma* is the only novel in which historical figures occupy a considerable space. The tendency to retire to the world of fiction is to be considered as part of Narayan's clinical aloofness, which again is inextricably linked to his cultural exclusiveness. As Cronin observes, "The cool sympathy with which Narayan views his characters and their doings, his ironic acceptance of the oddity of men and women and the oddity of their way," and his indifference to human pain stem from and is sanctioned by his Hinduism. Viewed from this angle, spirituality syndrome, which derives from cultural exclusiveness, is part of an escapist disposition, which was prevalent in the dominant ideology. The pangs of growth that India suffers during the early years of Independence, the worries of Partition, the political instability of the free India and the pathetic condition of the working class in India do not reach the closed walls of Malgudi, or its heroes, as if they belong to the ivory tower. Raju's love in the time of political violence (1950s), his running away to the inner recesses of spirituality, Chandran's sympathy for his friends who joined Resurrection Brigade to fight for the country are examples of Narayan's cultivating a religious indifference in the face of hard realities. But Narayan used to dream of a peaceful India. "At moment of crisis he retreats as Srinivas retreats from the noise of Ravi (in *Mr Sampath*) being thwacked into a visionary India, eternal, free from pain, an India that can only be seen in a vision, for it is a country that never existed" (Cronin 60).

These findings are more relevant if we associate them with the controversies arising from the revivalist trends in Indian history, which modern historians like K.N. Panikkar pursued in their works. The term revivalism is widely used in India to refer to a tendency to reconstruct the past so as to shape it in tune to the ideological intentions of a dominant culture. Panikkar, in his article, "Outsider as Enemy" published in *Frontline* (6 January 2001) argues that a section of the majority community which were not interested in the politics of the country, didn't participate in the freedom struggle and such path-breaking historical events. "They were rather collaborators of colonialism." Now these powers try to rewrite history to reconstruct their roles in the freedom struggle. "The main objective of rewriting history is to import certain historical legitimacy to communal politics" (Panikkar 78-79). What I would suggest here is that, the ambivalent attitude that Narayan and his characters have towards Indian political history is similar to the ambivalent attitude that some sections of the dominant group had for the freedom struggle and such historical and political events. Narayan's novels, thus, offer avenues of political and religious reading.

WORKS CITED

Althusser, Louis. "Ideology and Ideological State Apparatus." *The Theory of Criticism,* ed. Raman Selden. London & New York: Longman, 1988.

Balakrishnan, K. *Introduction to Hindu Religion.* Delhi: Publication by the Author, 1991.

Balibar, E. and Machery, P. "From Ideology and the State." *Modern Literary Theory : A Reader.* Eds. Philip Rice and Patricia Waugh. London: Edward Arnold, 1992.

Cronin, Richard. *Imagining India.* London: Macmillan, 1989.

Mehta, Gita. *Karma Cola.* New Delhi: Penguin, 1993.

Milner, Andrew. *Literature, Culture and Society.* London: UGL Press, 1996.

Narayan, R.K. *The Guide.* Mysore: Indian Thought Publication, 1972.

——, *The Bachelor of Arts.* Mysore: Indian Thought Publication, 1970.

Panikkar, K.N. "Outsider as Enemy." *Frontline,* 6 January, 2001.

Said, Edward. *Orientalism,* London: Penguin, 1978.

Selden, Raman, ed. *The Theory of Criticism,* London and New York, 1988.

Swindens, Patrick. "Hindu Mythology in R.K. Narayan's *The Guide.*" *The Journal of Commonwealth Literature,* Vol. 34, No. l, 1999.

7

Malgonkar's Balancing Acts of Gandhian Ideals in *A Bend in the Ganges*

SHIV KUMAR YADAV

Malgonkar's *A Bend in the Ganges* has received various shades of opinions as regards to its basic tone and tenor. For M. Rajagopachari it "stands out as an example of Malgonkar's insight into life,"[1] while for K.R. Srinivasa Iyengar it "reveals a sound historical sense [...]" and "experiments in artistically fusing the personal and historical perspectives in fictional terms."[2] In similar vein James Y. Dayananda opines that it deals 'with contemporary history especially the decade between 1938 and 1948;' and tells the story "of young men especially their growth towards maturity and understanding of the world" and it suggests "that an immense amount of research has gone into the facts straight."[3] But for G.S. Amur, this novel "is not merely to get down an objective record or to celebrate a set of passing values but to probe the ideology of ahimsa (non-violence) and truth which the Mahatma offered to the world, not only as a political expedient but as a philosophy and a way of life." The mood of the novel is defined by the epigraph which catches the prophet in an act of self-doubt and self-questioning "[...] can true voluntary non-violence come out of this seeming non-violence of the weak? Is it not a futile experiment I am conducting?"[4] Going through the author's note, one may feel tempted to suggest that Gandhi's 'sublime' success and 'ridiculous' failure occur in continuation; and, for Thomas Paine, "The sublime and the ridiculous are often so nearly related that it is difficult to class them separately. One step above the sublime makes the ridiculous, and one step above the ridiculous makes the sublime again."[5]

Malgonkar writes in his author's note, "What was achieved through non-violence, brought with it one of the bloodiest upheavals of history: twelve million people had to flee, leaving their homes, nearly half a million were killed; over a hundred thousand women, young and old, were abducted, raped, mutilated."[6] Despite having due justification for all the above observations, one can say that Malgonkar has thoroughly considered the complexities of the life, the time and the history and at the same time treated Gandhi's basic tenets Satya (Truth) and Ahimsa (Non-violence) as a political ideology in a fictional mode very safely and balancing way without being cornered by the Gandhian scholars.

Before entering into the Malgonkar's fictional Gandhi, it seems imperative to have a look on his personality. Gandhi, a continuously and conspicuously growing personality till his death, is still beyond comprehension despite the efforts made by innumerable thinkers, writers, critics and followers (if any). As "When he said, 'My life is my message,' he meant that he had delivered his message through his action-packed life,"[7] then definitely his conduct or action will come under scrutiny. And if we apply the Buddha's famous saying चेतनाहे कम्म वदामिष (Consciousness is an action), then we will have to know the consciousness of Gandhi revealed through action as well as speech to understand him thoroughly. But at the same time, Bhavbhuti claims लोकोत्तराणां चेतांसि को हि विज्ञातुमर्हति?[8] (Who, indeed, can claim to know the mind of the Great?). And it is more difficult to understand one who revises his perception frequently and thus invites the charge of inconsistency. Gandhi belongs to this category. Presenting 'his life as his message' does not absolve him from the charge of inconsistency as writings, speeches and conducts are inextricably related to each other.

Reacting to the charge of inconsistency, Gandhi writes in 1939:

> At the time of writing I never think of what I have said before. My aim is to be consistent with my previous statements on a given question, but to be consistent with truth as it may present itself to me at a given moment. The result has been that I have grown from truth to truth; I have saved my memory an undue strain; and what is more, whenever I have been obliged to compare my writing even of fifty years ago with the latest I have discovered no inconsistency between the two. But friends who observe inconsistency will do well to take the meaning that my latest writing may yield unless, of course, they prefer the old. But before making the choice they should try to see if there is not an underlying and abiding consistency between the two seeming inconsistencies.[9]

What one may perceive is that Gandhi believes in situation ethics—"the ethics based on the proposition that no conduct is good or bad in itself and that one must determine what is right or wrong in each situation as it arises'[10]—as his truth is evolutionary in nature and so relative. At the same time, he does not discover any 'inconsistency' ever, which suggests that his truth is absolute in nature. But further he advises "to take the meaning, that 'his' latest writing may 'yield' and again cautions 'to see if there is not any underlying and abiding consistency between the two seeming inconsistencies as if he never changed.'" But again at another place, he says. "Let Gandhism be destroyed if it stands for error. Truth and Ahimsa will never be destroyed [...]."[11] Definitely, here, he is referring to his own 'Ahimsa' not of the Buddha and others.

From this analysis, it seems that Gandhi oscillates between the 'relativism' and absolutism,' and this oscillation may give the impression that he strives hard throughout his life to attain the first and last objective of man on this earth—आत्मानं विद्धि (know thyself) as we know his experiments with truth. I am afraid that's why he says, "[...] Let no one say that he is a follower of Gandhi. It is enough that I should be my own follower [...] you are no followers but fellow students, fellow pilgrims, fellow seekers, and fellow workers."[12] It underlines the fact that his truth is only known to him. This is also "because of his unwillingness to follow a strictly logical route in coming to conclusions. He had a logical mind but felt that: 'Logic is a matter of mere intelligence, which cannot apprehend things that are clear as crystal to the heart. On the other hand, the intellect often believes in certain things, but if they do not appeal to the heart, they must be rejected.'"[13] Again one is compelled to accept him as a sole interpreter of his thought and action and an individual investigator of truth a true, disciple of the Lord Buddha, who said मउचराउनश्रउु (be a light unto yourself). Being his own light and finding his own axioms, Gandhi has got himself proved the most inspiring leader of the last century on this earth. One can hardly question the seven social sins of 21st century listed out by Gandhiji—

—Politics without principle,
—Wealth without work,
—Commerce without 'morality,'
—Education without character,
—Pleasure without conscience,
—Science without humanity,
—Worship without sacrifice.

Under this small backdrop of Gandhi's intellectual growth and Malgonkar's emphasis in the novel, this paper strives to examine the balancing acts of Gandhian ideals of non-violence and other tenets in the light of the complexities of social and political behaviours of an individual, who is essentially an admixture of human and subhuman qualities and the different collectivities of race, religion, creed and consciousness. In it, an effort has also been made to see how Gandhi passed even in his 'failure,' while his ideals are yet to become the Greater-Vehicle of Peace for mankind as Rabindranath Tagore once writes, "Perhaps he will not succeed. Perhaps he will fail as the Buddha failed and as Christ failed to wean men from their inequities, but he will always be remembered as one who made his life a lesson for all ages to come."[14]

The novel begins with the exposition of Gandhi's basic tenets—Satya (truth), Ahimsa (Non-violence) and Satyagraha and Swadeshi by his follower in his silenced presence but eloquent spinning wheel a symbol of non-violence, swadeshi, and dignity of labour. People are exhorted to boycott British goods and offer them to the fire. Here we find Gian Talwar's hesitation to offer his blazer to the fire and his fights against his 'irrational impulse' but the mob encouragement helps him to fling the coat into the flames. Tagore's objection to the 'boycott of British goods' is not so explicit but implicitly it is present. As Tagore writes in a letter to Gandhi: "This will not do either, for it is also of the outside. Your main motive is hatred of the foreigner, not love of country, as the boycott of Manchester, [...] had raised the profits of the Bombay mill-owners to a super-foreign degree."[15]

Very soon in the next chapter, "The Green Flash at Sunset," we witness the scathing attack on Gandhi's ideal of non-violence in presence of Gandhi's follower who believes in him just because "Even Nehru has become his disciple [...] the whole country."[16] Singh (Shafi Usman), a character of the novel, said, "Non-violence is the philosophy of sheep, creed for cowards. It is the greatest danger to this country."[17] So the basic tone of argument is very clear in the beginning: 'Non-violence,' an instrument of cowards or Brave? For Gandhi, 'the path of Ahimsa' is not for cowards, and for Shafi, non-violence is an instrument of cowards. Gandhi's Ahimsa results from high capacity of renunciation and sufferings which echoes the message of *Adi Granth*:

> Humility is my mace! To become the dust
> under everyone's feet is my dagger.
> These weapons no evil-doer dare withstand.[18]
>
> (*Adi Granth*; Sarath: M-5, 628)

Gandhi declares, "I have therefore ventured to place before India the ancient law of self-sacrifice [...]. The rishis, who discovered the law of non-violence in the midst of violence were greater genius than Newton. They were themselves greater warriors than Wellington."[19] Refuting the charge of being a coward, he writes, "I do believe that where there is only a choice between cowardice and violence, I would advise violence [...]. But I believe that non-violence is infinitely superior to violence."[20]

Again, he accepts 'Ahimsa' as a personal creed like the rishis of the past: "Ahimsa with me is creed, the breath of my life [...]. I placed it before the Congress as a political method, to be employed for the solution of political question [...]. As a political method it can always be changed, modified, altered, even given up in preference to another."[21] And again, we find his quite candid acceptance of non-violence as an expedient: "Yes, I adhere to my opinion that I did well to present to the Congress non-violence as an expedient. I could not have done otherwise if I was to introduce it in politics."[22]

Further, just before his assassination, he confessed in a private letter, "What I had mistaken for ahimsa was not ahimsa, but passive resistance of the weak, which can never be called ahimsa even in the remotest sense [...]. Hence the proper way to the present outburst of violence [...] is to recognise that the technique of unconquerable non-violence of the strong has not been discovered yet."[23] S.S. Gill writes, "It shows how till the end of his life he was craving to discover the Holy Grail of non-violence. And characteristically, he was blaming himself for his failure to acquire that 'soul force.'"[24] As he writes, "Ever since my coming to Noakhali, I have been asking myself the question, What is it that is choking the action of my ahimsa? Why does not the spell work? May it not be because I have temporised in the matter of brahmacharya?"[25] This certainly indicates that he was practising brahmacharya with a desire to have a theandric personality. Conceding his failure of non-violence in public domain, he does not concede 'any flaw in his concept.' And ultimately, assailed by doubts in the midst of the pre-Independence explosion of violence he asks himself: "May I not be living in a fool's paradise? Why should I ask people to follow me in the fruitless search? These are persistent questions. My answer is quite simple. I ask nobody to follow me. Everyone should follow his or her own inner voice."[26] Like the Lord Buddha and Kabir, Gandhi also realises that to get at the truth one has to investigate individually but honestly. But while demanding an unequivocal acceptance of his truth and ahimsa in public life, he does not accept the fact that "some actual force or developing power in the life of the times is needed before any ideal can exercise a practical effect."[27] And that's why G.B. Shaw visualises a Methuselah of A.D. 3000, may have a world without war, and nationalism.

After having outlined the growth of Gandhi's Ahimsa and his final dictum of मउचराउनश्रउु we find Malgonkar's 'anatomy of ahimsa'—a fine blending of resisting 'non-violence' as a final truth in every context and accepting it as the highest ideal for mankind to be achieved yet. Completely structured in historical perspectives, Malgonkar outlines the characters of his novel Debi, Shafi, and Gian in the distinct streams of philosophical, moral and political thoughts that are all pervasive during the Independence struggle especially after the advent of Gandhi. Debi represents the high principles and ideals of revolutionary groups who believe in leadership by example, sacrifice and commitment. Shafi, on the other hand, represents those nationalist and patriotic leadership of Muslims, who later on, turn separatists. Gian represents those hypocritic and morbid followers of Gandhi who are not only coward, opportunistic, unprincipled and parasitic in nature, but they believe in Gandhi just because 'only he can bring freedom to India.' Gian's growth in the novel typically represents the Gandhian followers. His effort of fighting against his 'irrational impulse' to offer his coat to the fire, drinking beer in slow sips in picnic, witnessing the murder of his elder as coward and murdering of elder's murderer with the same axe, despite having made promise "No man has the right to raise his hand against another, whatever the provocation. I shall never do it,"[28] showing hatred for Tukaram for his so-called, treachery, himself being a conman of Mulligan in Andman, collecting the money and photograph of Sundari and her husband, Gopal and then cutting the photo of Gopal, causing punishment to Debi later repenting for that, collecting gold coins from the 'khobri' of Ghasita, the Ramoshi, his selling of gold coins and later on the statue of Shiva by telling a lie about his relationship with Debi, and winning the emotional proximity of Sundari clearly show Gian's false personality.

Gandhi is aware of the hypocrisy of his followers and that's why he declares that he is his own follower and that is enough. Historical evidences are there about Gandhian followers (Congress leaders) who come to power in 1937-39. Regarding their corrupt practices, Bipin Chandra writes,

> Gandhiji began to feel that 'we seem to be weakening from within.' Full despondency, Gandhiji repeatedly lashed out in the columns of *Harijan* against the growing misuse of office and creeping corruption in Congress ranks. 'I would go to the length of giving the whole Congress organization a decent burial, rather than put up with corruption that is rampant,' he told the Gandhi Seva Sangh workers in May 1939.[29] Nehru too wrote to Gandhiji on 28 April, 1938: 'I feel strongly that the Congress ministries are working inefficiently [...]. They are adapting themselves for too much to the old order and trying to justify it [...].' We are sinking to the level of ordinary politicians who had no principles to stand by and whose work is governed by a day-to-day opportunism.[30]

Malgonkar after discrediting the Gandhian followers, who have link with Gandhi only through 'khaddar' and the 'Gandhian cap,' he explores Gandhi's ideals in the total context of life, as M. Rajagopalachari finds this novel as his 'insight into life.' For Malgonkar, it seems, "Life is contrast [...] life is ups and downs, light and shade, sun and cloud, opposites and opposites [...]. Life is no one way pattern. It contrasts all the way. And contrasts by law!"[31] And one has to find out one's choice of design, and "A man's choice (of words) [...] is conditioned by his experience [...]. To one, M.P. stands for Member of Parliament. To another it might mean major parasite. Depends on his experience."[32] Gian's justification for resorting to violence emerges out from his inability to ensure justice for himself within the existing framework. Debi, an embodiment of all Gandhian features, except being violent in the beginning, like high sense of sacrifice and commitment, capacity of suffering, high sense of discernment, strong belief in the unity of Hindus and Muslims (unlike Shafi and Basu, who turn to their sects), belief in the purity of love, not the purity of body, who is unable to tolerate the killing of a pup, turns 'violent' only after the soldier's attempt to rape his mother and ultimately indulges in violence against colonial injustice. We find similar parallel in history. Bhagat Singh, along with his colleagues, entrance into the vortex of revolutionary struggle was to avenge the death of Lala Lajpat Rai and in their attempt to kill the Police Commissioner, they assassinated the Deputy Commissioner. But the same Bhagat Singh declares: "Apparently, I have acted like a terrorist. But I am not a terrorist. [...] Let me announce with all the strength at my command, that I am not a terrorist and I never was, except, perhaps in the beginning of my revolutionary career. And I am convinced that we cannot gain anything through those methods."[33] Similar change, we find in Debi Dayal's perception: "He wondered whether all the exposure to what Gandhi had described as man's inhumanity to man had converted him to his doctrine of non-violence? Or was it just his feeling of revulsion against his fellow Indians, men like Shafi, the Brigadier and Gian Talwar, that had made his spirit curdle?"

He did not know the answer, the rights and wrongs were so inextricably mixed up; but he was conscious of some great change that had come over himself.[34] Visualising the immiment civil war, Debi comments: "It almost makes one think that non-violence is perhaps the only answer."[35] On the other side, Gandhi's helplessness regarding the non-acceptance of non-violence by public has been clearly deciphered by Basu:

> Non-violence! How can anyone be so blind? How can you go on striving for perfection and at the same time believing, it's already there? You can't change the human race overnight.

> Non-violence is merely a pious thought, a dream of philosophers. [...] Will he ever recognize that mankind is not prepared for true non-violence, will never be prepared [...] would you remain non-violent if someone threw acid at the girl you loved? Would Gandhi? [...] Non-violence is all very well, if the other party too plays by the rules. [...] Tell me what would non-violence do against brute force?[36]

Sundari, definitely a non-violent creature, also indulges in 'violence,' certainly an 'ideological violence,' only to give repartee to Gopal Chandidar, a faithless husband and, Gian Talwar, a false lover through the 'arrangement' she does on the beach and thus gets herself cured of her injured ego. She feels herself back after the 'beach incident.' "So this was her way of getting her own back, delivering the death blow to their marriage as she had once offered to destroy a puppy, ready to hold it down, squirming, to watch it wriggling in a bucket of hot water, as she was watching him now. She had always pretended that she had not seen Malini and himself that day; now, after all those years, she was telling him that she had."[37] To Gian Talwar she said in a terse tongue after the same incident of beach: "I asked you to come, merely to tell you how much I detest you."[38]

Malgonkar also sees the policy of non-violence like Gandhi, merely as political expedient as far as the people of India are concerned. At best, they had accepted it as an effective weapon against British power.[39] Malgonkar's balancing acts are quite evident, when he states clearly in the Author's note that "what was achieved through non-violence, brought with it one of the bloodiest upheavals of history."[40] But no where in the novel it is explicit that freedom was achieved through non-violence only, rather we find the question of Debi Dayal to Basu, "Do you think the Congress movement has been just as much of a failure as ours?" and gets reply like this, "It is an even greater failure. But will they ever admit it? [...]."[41] But Gandhi strengthens Malgonkar's position, by accepting the truth. To quote S.S. Gill, "Gandhi himself said, 'I see it as clearly as I see my finger:

British are leaving not because of any strength on our part but because of historical conditions and for many other reasons.'"[42]

M.K. Bhatnagar writes, "It is not merely ahimsa which is anatomized, and found wanting in certain respects; 'himsa' also comes to, in the final analysis self-destructive."[43] So, in Malgonkar's view, 'violence' or 'non-violence' as a principle or a creed cannot have absolute acceptance, rather it must be judged in the light of a more precious human value, and that is 'justice.' Malgonkar accepts that at an individual plane, one may succeed to ensure total acceptance of non-violence, as we find in Debi's confidence in Gandhi: "Personally, I don't think he would retaliate with violence [...] in his reply to Basu's question, 'Would you remain non-violent [...] if someone threw acid at the girl you loved?—would Gandhi?'"[44] But when one wishes to have its total acceptance at all the levels, then one will have to consider the values of Hafiz Khan, Ghasita, the Big House of Konshet, the rapist soldier as well as the State and the ignorance of Shafi Usman, Balbanbahadur, the Indian Brigadier in Burma and also the helplessness of Tukaram and Sundari, and many more things.

On the other side, we find Malgonkar's justification for other tenets of Gandhism—to hate evils, not the evil-doers, purification of character. G.S. Amur comments on the evolutionary character of Gian: "Gian may have jettisoned non-violence and truth, the great ideals, very early in his life but, what is remarkable, he survived the crisis and ultimately found his freedom in a purely existential discovery of the value of love which turned his falsehoods into truth and his weakness into strength."[45] But we find Malgonkar at his best in sketching the character of Debi Dayal, a 'positive protagonist' of the novel, as in him all virtues of Gandhism are quite visible in his highly transparent character. Truthfulness and courage to suffer for the cause and belief are the basic tenets of Gandhi and we find these characteristics in Debi Dayal abundantly and profoundly. Debi's love for Mumtaz, a woman from brothel and his view about Shafi—"Personally, I no longer feel any real hatred for the man. He's just like everyone else in India now, in one camp or the other"[46] clearly show 'Gandhi' in him. Gandhi is unwilling to choose follower as he is aware of the fortitude and confidence needed to be a Satyagrahi; but Malgonkar's effort is highly suggestive in portraying Debi Dayal's character, as he can only be a worthy disciple of Gandhi. It is not so surprising to find that when Gandhi feels dejected and just before Independence in June 1947 he says, "I ask nobody to follow me. Everyone should follow his or her own inner voice" Debi Dayal moves toward non-violence from violence and like Gandhi he is also assassinated. Debi's death unlike Shafi's during the Partition violence cannot only be viewed as the self-destructive nature of ahimsa, rather like Gandhi's, it also affirms that non-violence as a creed is futuristic in nature. It cannot survive the onslaught of the 'mob' until and unless the 'mass' gets enlightened. Gandhi passed the ordeal of his experiments with non-violence at personal level but his ideals are yet to become the Greater Vehicle of Peace (महायान) for mankind. Sri Aurobindo's comments regarding the idea of 'internationalism' can be helpful to explain the present state of Gandhi's ahimsa.

"The height and nobility of the idea is not to be questioned and certainly mankind sets its life upon this basis would make a better, purer, more peaceful and enlightened race than anything we can hope to have at present."[47] And finally Malgonkar's treatment of Gandhi's non-violence can be summarised in the words of Madge Micheels-Cynes: "Non-violence doesn't always work—but violence never does."[48]

REFERENCES

1. Rajagopalachari, M. *The Novels of Manohar Malgonkar*. New Delhi: Prestige, 1989.
2. Iyengar, K.R.S. *Indian Writing in English*. New Delhi: Sterling Publishers.
3. Dayanand, James Y. *Manohar Malgonkar*. Twayne Pubs., 1974.
4. Amur, G.S. *Manohar Malgonkar*. New Delhi: Arnold Heinemann, 1973.
5. *The Times of India*, Late City Edition. New Delhi, 13 December, 2001.
6. Malgonkar, M. *A Bend in the Ganges*. New Delhi: Orient Paperback, 1964.
7. Gill, S.S. *Gandhi, A Sublime Failure*. New Delhi: Rupa & Co., 2001.

8. Prabhu & Rao. *The Mind of Mahatma*. Ahmedabad: Navajivan Pub. House, 1967.
9. Iyer, Raghvan N. *The Moral and Political Thought of Gandi,* OUP, Paperback, 2000.
10. *Chamber's 20th Century Dictionary*, W.R. Chambers Ltd., 1983.
11. Iyer.
12. Iyer.
13. Iyer.
14. Gill.
15. *The Writings of Gandhi*, Ronald Duncan & Co., 1990.
16. Malgonkar.
17. Malgonkar.
18. 'Sacred Space,' *The Times of India*, Late City, New Delhi, 12 January, 2002.
19. Pandey, B.N. *A Book of India*, Rupa & Co., 1982.
20. Pandey.
21. Gill.
22. Gill.
23. Gill.
24. Gill.
25. Gill.
26. Gill.
27. Prasad, R.C. & Singh, J.P. *An Anthology of Indian English Prose,* Motilal Banarasidas, 1988.
28. Malgonkar.
29. Bipin, Chandra. *India's Struggle for Freedom*, Penguin India, 1992.
30. Bipin.
31. Iyengar.
32. Iyengar.
33. Bipin.
34. Malgonkar.
35. Malgonkar.
36. Malgonkar.
37. Malgonkar.
38. Malgonkar.
39. Malgonkar.
40. Malgonkar.
41. Malgonkar.
42. Gill.

43. Bhatnagar, M.K. *Political Consciousness in Indian Writing in English*. New Delhi: Bahan Publication, 2001.
44. Malgonkar.
45. Amur.
46. Malgonkar.
47. Prasad & Singh.
48. *The Times of India*, Late City Edition, New Delhi, 19 January, 2002.

8

Storm in Chandigarh: Crisis in Human Values

ABHA SHARMA

The crisis in human values in India is a by-product of the failure of the country's leadership in different areas of our fast-growing society. The most deplorable aspect of the present day socio-cultural crisis in India is that we have lost track of our long-standing Hindu tradition. That we find ourselves shaky and rudderless in the midst of tall claims of the Government, that we have made fast progress in different areas of our national life is an indication that something is radically wrong either with our policies or with our individual response to the fast changes that have crept into our society through industrialisation and modernisation. Nayantara Sahgal in her novel, *Storm in Chandigarh* has reflected upon the various aspects of the socio-cultural crisis in India after Independence.

The novel provides a peep into the various socio-political cross-currents in and around Chandigarh and New Delhi following the birth of the new state of Haryana, out of the territory of Punjab after nearly two decades of the partition of India in 1947. The chief character in the novel is an I.C.S. officer, Vishal Dubey who has been specially picked up by the much respected Home Minister—'the last surviving figure of the Gandhian era in public life,'—as the chief representative of the Central Government to look after the teething troubles of the new state of Haryana carved mainly out of the erstwhile Punjab state of the Indian Union. As far as the diverse strands of the crisis in human values are concerned, Vishal Dubey is the interpreter; and his being an ICS officer with sufficient education to his credit enables him to look at the crisis in India of his time, the period beginning from 1960s onward. Since in the post-Independence era, the crisis in human values has continued, the perceptive views of Vishal Dubey are very much relevant even in the new millennium. In the extract below, Dubey is seen absorbed in thoughts after his meeting with the Hon'ble Home Minister about the political and social affairs of Punjab and Haryana. He felt that the elements of violence exist in our national life in devious ways. At places the pervasive spirit of violence is hidden and at other places it is quite open, the sight of which puts a sensitive onlooker in dismay. This is how Vishal ponders over the widespread incidence of violence all over India including Haryana and Punjab.

> Outbursts of brutal, calculated violence had become a feature of the cities. There were too many in the congestion and chaos who had nothing to lose by violence, too many others who sat inert and indifferent, their sap sucked dry, watching it mount and ebb like some great tidal wave, waiting for them to engulf them. Passively waiting, as they waited for the rains, for the harvest, for the births of unwanted children, for death. Violence had become routine and expected. It was given different, names: indiscipline, unrest and disorder. It was dealt with each time—and forgotten.[1]

A Brahmin and educated in modern study-disciplines, Vishal Dubey had developed a subtle understanding of the peculiar social phenomena replete with devious forms of violence. He felt that violence was very much in the social atmosphere; and no part of the country was free from it. Even if the elements of violence were very much in pre-Independent India, these remained underneath because of the authoritarian English rule; but, after Independence, as the country adopted the democratic Constitution, the earlier elements of violence got seeded and spread getting more and more vocalised. This is the peculiar facet of violence in post-Independent India to which Vishal Dubey addressed himself. If one cares to look at the present-day violence in the country one would find that the elements of violence are very much in the air with the only difference that it has gone more complicated than what it was in the early phase of our Independence. This is primarily because the discontent has spread far and wide, influencing even our attitude to life. Our very subjectivity is coloured with it. On the analogy of Milton's observation, '*The mind in its own place, and in itself/can make a heav'n of hell, a hell of heav'n*,[2] one can draw an inference to say that violence has now started colouring even our subjectivity. Vishal Dubey refers to this aspect of violence when he says: "In this ministry one becomes a student of the subject. In a situation like we have now between Punjab and Haryana, we are faced with a violence of attitude. And that may, and often does, lead to the other kind. But at the moment there is this attitude that brooks no compromise and rejects all but one solution. These are people who have no feel for the periphery of a problem, for light and shade and the nuances in between. That is the source of their energy and, in a queer way, their integrity. It is useful to realize this before one tries to produce a solution."[3]

Violence is essentially an expression of strange feelings in man. It finds an outlet in different human beings differently. If India is a country of unity in diversity, it is equally valid to say this country is vast melting pot of different races and cultures whose descendants and followers espouse different religions. This is specifically so with the adherents of popular Hinduism; and they outnumber those who have really understood the mind enlightening ethic of the Upanishads, Vedas and the Bhagawad Gita. While violence in man is a by-product of various socio-economic distortions in society, it is often ignored even by the degree-holding educated people that the instinctual obstinacy in a large majority of population is a prolific source of violence. All types of violence perpetrated on women and girls from gang-rape to physical torture and shooting of the sex-victims are traceable to the widespread unregeneracy in our country. Violence is the real hub of the problem associated with the crisis in human culture. That is why Mahatma Gandhi decried violence.

In the above extract, it is stated: "These are people who have no feel for the periphery of a problem, for light and shade and the nuances in between." Nayantara means to upbraid the violence perpetrators because of their being stolid, unmindful of the nuances of life. Men without nuances are generally those who lack discrimination and sense of proportion. Such people are largely to be found all over India. The daily news about different incidents of violence is a woeful reminder that something is gnawing at the heart of India. Incidents of speechless mocking violence inflicted upon innocent women and children should make us astir; but the majority remains unstirred. And even if the molestation and body injury are done to any child, female or male, most of us are inclined to bypass the unfortunate news or at best, we make it a gossiping point, to be forgotten as easily as it is gossiped. It looks that Nayantara Sahgal is equally aware of this trait in the majority of our 'great' country when she writes: "Violence had become routine and expected. It was given different names: indiscipline, unrest, disorder. It was dealt with each time—and forgotten."[4]

In this extract the novelist has used the words 'dealt with'; it should be 'talked about'; then the real identity of the 'social scenario' comes dancing before one's eyes. We only talk about things and events and then say good night to the 'persona' of any sordid act of violence and moral depravity, waiting for the more and more sensational news. This is how our self-complacent people, employed either in the Government offices or the commercial establishment, spend their days of life-time with satisfaction unconcerned with acts of sputtering violence here and there in one city or another.

Political theoreticians nowadays are often fond of saying that the violent acts of bomb-throwing or different types of remote-controlled explosions are in main the handiwork of foreign agencies to destabilise the democratically elected government in the country; but if it is so, the question props up as to why the government leaders and the custodians of society fail to weed out such agents of violence in league with the foreign powers. The answer is that both governmental failure and social complacency are responsible for such a sorry state of affairs. Not to be able to check the seeds of violence is essentially the failure of our leadership.

Nayantara Sahgal is one of the few contemporary writers in India to be aware of the complexity of Indian problems. She knows it that according to some, India is a country of *rishis* and godly beings; but she has also questioned the falsity of holding to such a belief. Living should be intelligent and rational enough to link the causes to their effects; and if one tries to show his superiority on the strength of the mythological speculations of the remote past, he not only blackmails others with a modicum of rational understanding but also gets self-alienated from the reality. Unfortunately, a large section of our educated people hide their ignorance and deceptive ways of living behind the glorious stories of mythological heroes. Critically speaking, it is these people who are responsible for retarding the social awareness; and indirectly a kind of religious ferment whereby average man's capacity to discriminate between right and wrong gets weakened. It is in this criss-crossing frame of our mentality, the poorer sections of our people become mentally inert and sick so much so that they become willing tools of the foreign agents in such money-earning lines as narcotics-trading and women-trafficking. Violence is associated with such professions. Thus, we see that opposition to reform and lack of historical sense are responsible for the spread of violence—hidden and open both. Finally, the improvement in personal conduct of individuals and social progress is retarded. Vishal Dubey in *Storm in Chandigarh* echoes ideas on the burning issue of post-Independent India. Dubey felt that the incidence of violence with all its evils like narcotics trading, women trafficking, molestation and rape of women and children is ultimately linked to our having remained cut-off from the glorious tradition of the past. In this respect, the main problem is of interpreting the tradition; and here, the role of educated Indians like Dubey is long overdue. Unless the tradition is understood in historical terms, the mere reciting of the old tales in not going to be of any advantage.

Nayantara Sahgal would not associate with the routinised interpretation of our old wisdom. The past has to be understood in the context of the present as T.S. Eliot was to uphold.[5] It has a large measure of historical sense. In *Storm in Chandigarh,* Vishal Dubey was seized with this approach as a Brahmin. He was candid enough to say so, for the mind of most of us is governed by caste-values rather than the secular values to which, because of our Constitution, we pay lip-service. Vishal Dubey in explaining the research project topic "The role of Brahminism in our culture" to Professor Aldrich, the visiting professor from the New England university, said: "What I'm interested in exploring is the role of Brahminism specifically and whether it was a constructive role to play today, or whether the whole notion of aristocracy, that is, the quality a people evolves for itself, is outdated. Personally I don't think it is, but it has become ineffective. We seem to be in the grip of impotence, stuck for answers, because the most effective part of our inheritance isn't brought into play and made to provide the answers in ways that would suit our temperament."

> "The most effective part of your inheritance being Brahminism?" —Prof. Aldrich
>
> It is what we have considered 'quality,' said Dubey, and that is a product of the ages, of slow, profound development. It's the only thing that can't be copied or borrowed or mass-produced.[6]

On Professor Aldrich's positive comment: "Revolutions have to take place when living conditions become vulnerable, but even a revolution should not destroy a people's framework," Dubey said, "If we're going to avoid this here," tradition has to be upheld and used in a big, enlightened way. But it hasn't so far. We've got this superb ineffectual heritage supporting feeble issues like the preservation of cows, and we don't seem to be able to climb out of the stagnation onto the high road where the fresh air blows. We have the unholy trappings of tradition going on and on while the reality of it isn't there at all."[7]

While remaining bogged down in the trappings of non-essential issues like the preservation of cows, the Hindus in modern era have paid only lip-service to the essential teachings of Hindus enshrined in the holy books of Bhagavad-Gita, Upanishads and Vedas. In these sacred books man is enjoined to follow the higher morality of life of being worshipful to God and dedicated to the service of humanity for the sake of upholding the dharma. In terms of the teachings enshrined in the sacred books of the ancient religion of the Hindus, men and women were expected to be truthful and duty-bound to God and humanity through a dedicated life of sacrifice and austerity.

When Vishal Dubey assumed the duties of the Chief Liaison Officer of the Central Government at Chandigarh, everything was in mess. Nobody cared for the spirit of the dharma. Almost everybody who mattered in social life pursued his interest with impunity. The national interest was nowhere to be seen. Dubey found the situation unenviable:

> The map of India, once a uniform piece of territory to administer, was now a welter of separate, sensitive identities, resurrected after Independence. Psychology seemed to play as important a part in understanding them as did history, geography, and economics. Much more than facts and figures were required in coping with political rivalries that had now ceased even to make bargains. As long as a bargain could be made, work could go on. When that capacity wore out, only a collision was possible.
>
> In the new states, Punjab and Haryana, just carved out of the former Punjab, the quarrel over boundaries, water and electric power continued, intensified by the presence of both new governments in a common capital, Chandigarh, which each claimed exclusively as its own. And now Gyan Singh, Punjab's Chief Minister, threatened to demonstrate the strength of his demands by launching a crippling strike that would cover both regions.

> Dubey had the uneasy feeling that it was too late to consider persuasion [...]. In all these years there had been no open conflict between state governments though there had been disagreements. No one had yet had the will or the organization to risk an open threat. It was not surprising that the threat, when it came, had come out of robustness and prosperity.[8]

The bane of the contemporary Indian society is the spirit of divisiveness which is as pervasive as violence; and by virtue of these two evils, the successive governments at the Centre have maintained the fabric of Indian Union on the basis of authoritarian forces: police and military; and not on the basis of any cohesive feeling of nationalism. By and large most of us remain caste-ridden, provincialists or regionalists. There has been an extensive politicisation of our life, with the result, we think ourselves more on sectional lines than in terms of the spirit of national belonging.

To Vishal Dubey, human life seemed to ooze out of its inner kernel. The chanting of human values was only made for the sake of propaganda impact. Consequently, different types of dissensions have increased which has generated a climate of suspicion. A widespread spirit of alienation colours our altitude towards others. Necessarily, the incidence of mundane materialism has increased among all sections of our people. Vishal Dubey says:

> In his youth had used words like that freely and they had not had a hollow ring about them. Dedication, sacrifice, austerity. Each one now clanked timely with empty repetition. He never used them in his speeches any more. But he took them out, like valuable old coins no longer in use, and looked at them when he was alone. He was satisfied that they existed and had worth.[9]

Indian life is thus riven with dissensions and deceptiveness. Ancient values stand pulverised and forsaken. Mundanity in its grossest form is on increase. For the sake of petty gains, most of us are prepared to sacrifice the cherished human values. We have lost the inner spirit of being a human being. According to Dubey, much can be salvaged only if individuals exercise their 'vivek' or discriminating sense and act according to the light of reason within.

In conversation with Trivedi, another sophisticated character in *Storm in Chandigarh,* Dubey said: "[...] I've come to the conclusion that there's a higher morality than all that ([...] the glittering goods of mundane materialism). In fact, that's what I call it, the Higher Morality."

Trivedi quipped back: "Well, what's this Higher Morality all about? The wail of conscience in new garb?"

"It's more than that," Dubey sat forward eagerly. "It's a search for value, and an attempt to choose the better value, the real value, in any situation, and not just do what's done or what is expected."[10]

In her authorial comment on the conditions prevailing in the region, the novelist speaks about the immense worth of one's being committed in totality to the task in hand. Dubey was deeply absorbed in tackling the drought and its horrible impact on people. "What do you get out of it, Dubey? Trivedi had asked him. It—and everything else—might as well be left alone, the grain to wither, hope to die, unless you become part of the whole sorry mess and were driven to tackle it—not because it was your job and you were paid for it, but because it was yours, as everything you touched with tenderness became yours, even the maggots and sores, and the shrunken dreams and anguished cries."[11]

Yes, the novelist has a point worthy to be pondered, the crisis in the present-day human values can be greatly mollified provided the society throws up a dedicated band of individuals, like Vishal Dubey, at different places in the country to face diverse challenges of contemporary society shaken a great deal by the forces of violence, divisiveness and deception raising their ugly head in the horizon.

REFERENCES

1. Sahgal, Nayantara. *Storm in Chandigarh* (New Delhi: Orient Paperbacks) 5.

2. *Paradise Lost,* Book I.
3. Sahgal 7.
4. Sahgal 6.
5. Eliot, T.S. Tradition and the Individual Talent' *Selected Essays* (London: Faber & Faber, 1986) 13-15.
6. Sahgal 11.
7. Sahgal 11-12.
8. Sahgal l3.
9. Sahgal 15.
10. Sahgal 80.
11. Sahgal 82.

9

BHATTACHARYA'S NOVELS: THE PORTRAYAL OF POVERTY AND HUNGER

A.N. PRASAD

The works of Bhabani Bhattacharya depict the life of man in relation to society. Sometimes, they also portray the predicament of man in relation to himself and to destiny. All his works centre round the dictum "Art for the sake of life" or art must have a social purpose. Bhattacharya thinks that literature can have the main purpose of making mankind better by giving the truthful picture of society. This is what we find in almost all his major works like *So Many Hungers* (1947), *Music for Mohini* (1952), *He Who Rides a Tiger* (1954), *A Goddess Named Gold* (1960) and *Shadow from Ladakh* (1966). But a thorough perusal of his works also reveals the author's rich craftsmanship, his poetic and aesthetic presentation of a dry and harsh situation hunger and poverty and above all, his rich symbolic and connotative description.

The central theme of Bhattacharya's novels is poverty and hunger. His works also deal with disease, sufferings of the poor and the deserted, social evils, tensions and pretensions, caste politics, inter-racial relations, tradition and modernity and changing values of modern civilization. In brief, his novels present a microcosm of India. The author rightly holds the view:

> A novelist may well be concerned with today, the current hour or moment, if it is meaningful for him, if it moves him sufficiently into emotional response.[1]

There has been a great line of writers in Indian English writing who showed the theme of poverty and hunger, despair and desolation in their respective works. Mulk Raj Anand has beautifully presented a very realistic picture of poverty and hunger in the deserted lives of the untouchables—who are tyrannized by the upper caste people without any rhyme or reason. It is poverty which compels Bakha, the hero, to face many ups and downs, taunts and jeers. His other novel *Coolie* and *Two Leaves and a Bud* tell the same story of the poor and the downtrodden. The other great novelist who deals with the theme of poverty and hunger is Kamala Markandaya. Her works, *Nectar in a Sieve* and *A Handful of Rice* are the novels on the same theme. The truthful picture of the rural people who are bound to face the blows of natural catastrophes and also to the idiosyncrasies and injustice of the unscruplous men is beautifully projected in her novels. Here the romance between Ravi and Nalini does not run smoothly due to the steadily rising prices and so a handful of rice at that time could make all the difference between life and death. K.S. Venkataraman's *Kandan, the Patriot* and *Murgan, the Tiller* are the best examples of poverty-stricken villagers who are helpless victims in the clutches of landlords and cruel moneylenders.

The sense of adjustment and reconciliation between two diametrically opposed situations is the leading theme of Bhattacharya's novels. He never wastes his power of pen in delineating only the dream and fantasy of the fairyland, but rather his poetic genius is best expressed in the day-to-day life incidents and matters concerning the safety and security of the country especially the untouched general masses. He does not describe the metaphysical issue of life and death like Raja Rao. He also lacks the comic imagination of Narayan. But so far as the realistic picture of the natural and man-made crises are concerned, he is a superb novelist, even far better than M.R. Anand. Khushwant Singh generally leads us to the land of vulgar and obscene descriptions of pornography; but Bhattacharya's works never appeal to our baser senses. They, on the other hand, appeal to the core of our heart and arouse our sense of pathos and sympathy to the poor and the marginalised. As a matter of fact, Bhattacharya is not opposed to the sexual portrayal in literature as such. He is a great realist. So he cannot neglect it altogether. What he is really opposed to is the cheap description of sex or vulgar exploitation of sex. He has a very good opinion about the sexual portrayal of Hemingway and D.H. Lawrence. He observed:

> The flow of cheap, paper-backed, vulgar, low taste books revelling in sex descriptions cannot be welcome. I have a revulsion for them. But look at Lawrence. He creates a whole world of this much tabooed feeling and yet the descriptions are most beautiful and excel in their lyrical quality. Look at Hemingway and you will learn how sex can be a theme to write upon, without making it repulsive.[2]

Bhattacharya's first novel, *So Many Hungers* (1947) realistically deals with the theme of poverty engendered by Bengal famine in the early forties. It also flings satire on the cruel capitalists who create artificial food scarcity by hoarding rice. The title 'Hungers' has been connotatively used. It has two meanings—hunger for food and hunger for sex. Bhattacharya shows how the general people are starving to death for want of food and how, on the other hand, sex-starved soldier rapes the destitute rustic girl, Kajoli.

The book portrays the two diabolical forces of war and famine which sucked the blood of the poor. His harrowing account of a famine in Bengal and the joy of the profiteers and black-marketeers are very thoughtfully and beautifully projected, though a bit exaggerated and sentimental. Let us see an extract from the book:

> Corpses lay by the road, huddled together. Picked to the bones, with eyeless caverns of sockets, bits of skin and flesh rotting on nose and chin and ribs, the skulls peeked open, only the hair uneaten. A family group had sunk into sleep; and beyond the sleep-vultures.[3]

The description of the piteous plight of the general poor people is very suggestive and sympathetic. The story is told from the point of view of the starving farmers who go to Calcutta for jobs. There, too, they have to face many trials and tribulations, cares and anxieties to earn their bread. K.R.S. Iyengar rightly holds the view: "*So Many Hungers* is no doubt an impeachment of man's inhumanity to man, but it is also a dramatic study of a set of human beings caught in a unique and tragic predicament. The story has been effectively told and the tragic pathos of the real mass starvation described in the guise of fiction, moves the reader deeply. The novel describes a factual and vivid account of the most shocking disasters in history."[4]

Music for Mohini, the second novel by Bhattacharya presents the caste distinction and poverty and a reconciliation is suggested to fill up the gap between the low and the high, the rough and the sublime. It, as L.N. Gupta remarks, "blows up the citadel of old traditions and superstitions which menace India's progress."[5] As a matter of fact, Bhattacharya tries his best to mirror the modern India at that time in a very realistic and poetic way. *The Chicago Tribune* observes:

> India as presented by Rudyard Kipling, Rabindranath Tagore and others has become to us a multiple image. Now these diverse pictures are brought into focus by a native son. In a splendid novel that may rank with Pearl Buck's *The Good Earth*, Bhabani Bhattacharya gives us Modern India.[6]

The book deals with the story of a young city-bred girl Mohini who is married to Jayadev, a scholar and a writer with village background. As the story moves on, we see many disputes between the city and the village, between the literate and the illiterate. But in the long run, the author succeeds in reconciling the two different things into one. So, in a way, the book presents an idea of synthesis or adjustment. Though Mohini is bred and brought up in the lap of a city, yet she never hesitates to adapt herself in the village life in her husband's home. On the other hand, Rooplekha, the sister of Jayadev is married to a man of city. She like Mohini, succeeds in adapating herself in the city surrounding. She has to stand the critical store of the sophisticated. She has to give up her many village habits. She has to eat fish and meat. In this way, both the women characters want to bridge a gap.

But to adjust oneself in an entirely different atmosphere is not so easy. Mohini has to undergo many ebbs and tides in her husband's home. She has to struggle with the perversities of the stars, the jeers and taunts of an iron-willed widowed mother, the fierce resentment of Sudha, a beautiful and intelligent girl who failed to marry Jayadev because of her wrong fate line on her hand. S.C. Harrex, the Australian writer, rightly says:

> The main theme of the novel is the idea of synthesis, a profound union of today with yesterday, whereby the conflict between traditions and modernity will be resolved.[7]

He Who Rides a Tiger, the finest of all the novels of Bhattacharya deals with the theme of poverty and utter helplessness. It shows that any man who rebels against society cannot adjust himself and so he has to reconcile himself to it in the long run. Both *So Many Hungers* and *He Who Rides a Tiger* have the background and the detailed description of the Bengal famine of 1943 which rocked the foundation of humanity. Though there is a marked difference in the treatment of famine in both the novels, the common thing is that in both the works the common people are caught in the whirlpool of natural catastrophe. The rich are seldom affected.

The whole story revolves round the protagonist Kalo, a simple poor blacksmith of the village who wants to lead a very peaceful life. But, poverty and circumstances make him a changed man. He wants to jet his fury and resentment against an entirely cold and indifferent society which revolves on the two hinges of caste and cash. In Mulk Raj Anand's *Untouchable,* Bakha, the hero also suffers many trials and tribulations, tyranny and injustice. But unlike Kalo, he is a silent sufferer. Sometimes he, like a fuming tiger, wants to rebel against the caste-dominated society. But he is unable to do so as he is bound by the age-old norms of society. However, the case of Kalo is entirely different. He is so much terrorized and persecuted by society that he makes up his mind to teach a lesson to the upper caste people in society. He passes off as a Brahmin priest and by the fake miracle he becomes the most reverend priest. The fake miracle is nothing but a trick. He chiselled a piece of stone in Shiva's shape and buried it at the spot where the temple now stands. He placed some grams under the stone and began to water the earth. The gram underneath swelled and pushed the stone up to the surface. Thus, people watched the miracle happen. This way Kalo took the help of religion to give a good retort to society. Through this episode Bhabani Bhattacharya means to say that India is a country of beliefs and customs, traditions and superstitions. He also shows how the general people are duped through religion. He observed in this novel:

> Belief, in this country, could be likened to its mighty rivers. The swollen water burst the banks and flooded the countryside, destroyed lives, eroded the soil and went to waste, while great areas of dry corn land thirsted and crops failed; harnessed, put to proper use, the rivers could irrigate, produce power, add to the country riches. In the same way, the people's belief was a great force which could be guided in good ways, made creative. When this great force had ceased to go to waste, it would no longer be a curse, blighting lives. It would be the country's truest asset.[8]

In the very beginning of the novel, the novelist exposes the corruptions and belittling attitude of the upper caste men—who are in great illusion in giving value to the status of birth in preference to that of merit. The protagonist was wrongly punished for three years for stealing three bananas. He muses:

> What had he done to deserve this? Was this justice, fairplay? Was he no better than a common thief? His own savings, the fruit of hard work year on year, had, by a trick, become a fifth of its value. Who took the balance?[9]

It is interesting here to note that the hero's miserable situation is partly due to the indifferent society and partly due to natural calamities which racked him and other people of the village without any rhyme or reason. The natural catastrophe came in the guise of the plague in the entire Jharna town. Its havoc was so great that it rendered many people homeless and destitute. Kalo was among them. The entire Jharna town looks hungry and fearful:

> The plague washed up in fierce tides. Bengal was dying. Jharna was dying. Kalo sat idly in his workshop and watched the road. People were flying from the hungry town. Many were going to the capital city to seek a living. He watched her customers but none came. The people had exchanged their pots and pans, furniture and trinkets for fistfuls of foodgrain.[10]

The title of the novel, *He Who Rides a Tiger* is based on the ancient saying that, "He who rides a tiger cannot dismount." But, here the case of the hero, Kalo is different. He has the courage to dismount from the tiger in the hour of his critical juncture. Raju, the protagonist of R.K. Narayan's *The Guide* passes through the same problems in the temple of a remote village. He never exposes his reality. But Kalo pays attention to the cordial call of soul and develops his sense of wisdom and fortitude to face the critical situation and goes back to his original state so that he may identify himself to the society. It is consciousness that overtakes him in the last phase of his drama. Raju achieved humanity through his deep devotion to the cause of the villagers. But Kalo got that status by dint of the power of consciousness. He reveals his identity:

> But the need to kill the tiger grew because of a strength in him, a strength he had never known before. It was the strength which comes of seeing people as they are. He had looked deep into the faces of his superiors, inhabitants of a higher world whose very shadow had once struck him into abject humility.[11]

It is interesting to note that the story of the novel is full of irony and contrasts, antithesis and balance. Kalo is out to rebel against the cruelties and indifference of society. But, on the other hand, Lekha, the daughter of Kalo, is terribly afraid of the consequences of the whole history regarding her father's sudden transformation. About her character Dr Syamala Rao observes:

> She is wondering how to go back to the old futilities after this nine days wonder. She is out to rebel against her father. She speaks strange words that the way of struggle against fear is the true way. She has no craving for the good things of life. She is not for divine role. She is all too earthly, too human.[12]

The irony is in the description of the famine or plague. On the one hand, the poor people are suffering from hunger and poverty, the rich, the profiteers or the blackmarketeers, on the other hand, are busy in accumulating wealth by hook or by crook. The poor are hungry for corns, the rich for money and sex:

> Two great hungers had stuck the land of Bengal in the wake of war: the hunger for masses of people uprooted from the old earth and turned into beggars, and the hunger of the all-owning few for pleasure and more pleasure, a raging fever of the times. Uprooted women with their own kind of hunger, had to cool the raging pleasure-fever with their bodies.[13]

Mark here the irony and contrast. General masses are suffering from the ailment, fever. But the rich have their peculiar fever—fever for sex, money and other pleasures. Dr Ram Sevak Singh holds the view:

> Bhattacharya not only records the misery of the poor but the miseries of the rich also. The irony of situation very ably presents the ghastly contrast between affluence and poverty, power and helplessness, goodness and hypocrisy.[14]

Thus, this brief analysis of Bhattacharya's major fictions clearly reveals that he is a novelist with an aim. He wants to mirror the society with its various colours. Like Dr Johnson, his end of writing is to teach by pleasing. So far the description of the poor and the deserted is concerned, he is undoubtedly unequalled in the realm of Indian fiction in English. His truthful and poetic portrayal of the famine and plague is worth noticeable.

REFERENCES

1. Bhattacharya, Bhabani. *Indo-Anglian* (from the Novel in Modern India), ed. by Iqbal Bakhtiyar, 47.
2. Joshi, S. "An Evening with Bhabani." *The Sunday Standard* (April 27, 1969) VIII.
3. Bhattacharya, Bhabani. *So Many Hungers* quoted by K.R.S. Iyengar, *Indian Writing in English,* 413.
4. Iyengar, K.R.S. *Indian Writing in English* (New Delhi: Sterling Publication, 1962) 414.
5. Gupta, L.N. *Bhabani Bhattacharya—A Bridge between India and the West,* Hitavada, March 29, 1969.
6. Gupta 49.
7. Gupta 50.
8. Bhattacharya, Bhabani. *He Who Rides a Tiger* (New Delhi: Arnold Publishers, 1977) 181.
9. *He Who Rides a Tiger* 37.
10. *He Who Rides a Tiger* 15.
11. *He Who Rides a Tiger* 238.
12. Rao, Syamala. *Bhabani Bhattacharva's He Who Rides a Tiger* (Bareilly: Prakash Book Depot, 1988) 58.
13. *He Who Rides a Tiger* 53.
14. Singh, Ram Sevak. "Bhabani Bhattacharya—A Novelist of Dreamy Wisdom" (*Bhanasthali Patrika*, July 1969) 67.

10

Balan's Sense of Alienation, Dislocation and Salvation in Kasthuri Sreenivasan's *The Light from Heaven*

USHA RANI

Various threads of the narrative in *The Light from Heaven* portray the socio-psycho scenario of our contemporary society in very real and telling terms. The writer has explored and analyzed different aspects of our day-to-day life from various angles. As for instance, it entails a tough and traumatic struggle of a youth, Balan alias S. Balasubramanium Iyer, whom success eludes at every step in life. It delves deep into the multifaceted corrupt social environment, which leads to Balan's acute sense of alienation and dislocation from the mainstream of his native society. The text also reverberates a voice of protest against centuries old demarcations of caste and creed, which have been consuming the vitals of Indian society for ages together. Further, the novel also highlights and strengthens our faith in Indian philosophy against the backdrop of inner consciousness, theory of karma and moral strength. Simultaneously, the narration foregrounds the philosophy of selfless work, service to society leading to inner peace of mind, eternal bliss and ultimate 'nirvana' of the protagonist. These are some of the thematic concerns embodied through the texture of this novel. However, the present paper shall mostly focus upon Balan's (the chief protagonist) acute sense of alienation, dislocation and final salvation as embodied in this novel.

The recent developments, particularly in the field of science and technology, along with fast transitional changes in urbanization, globalization and mechanization have also brought in their wake a lot of maladies for human mind and soul. Materialistic and mechanical attitudes in the present social environment have further deteriorated bonds of human relationships. The centrality of falling and failing human values at all levels have resulted in excruciating pain of loneliness, traumas of broken and missing ties, acute sense of depression, and identity crisis. No doubt, the theme of alienation and dislocation has become very popular with many a contemporary writer of significance. Most of the contemporary literature, particularly in the post-colonial era, reflects upon these trends in quite a sizable amount, irrespective of the language they are writing in. Many of V.S. Naipaul's characters abandon their homelands and present post-colonial angst. Arun Joshi, Kamla Markandaya, Anita Desai, Salman Rushdie, Rohinton Mistry, Sunetra Gupta, Mahashweta Devi *et al.* have all presented many unforgettable protagonists who have fallen victims to these psychic tortures and sufferings in one way or the other.

The significant point to be noted here is that Kasthuri Sreenivasan in *The Light from Heaven* explores not only the social aspect of these human afflictions but he also digs deep into the mental, emotional and spiritual planes as well. At the very outset, the reader learns that Balan, alias S. Balasubramanium, is a very intelligent and hardworking boy. He possesses a scientific mind and he keeps on asking questions to his teachers. Very often, the ill-equipped teachers feel helpless to answer all his queries. Balan's father, Mr. Seshdhari Iyer, a staunch Brahmin by caste feels very proud of his intelligent son. Although financially they are not very well off, yet he is a staunch believer of honesty and sincerity. Balan has a great ambition to become a doctor since childhood, so that his inner urge to serve the suffering humanity can be materialized. Year after year he is promoted to higher classes with great distinction.

The main conflict in the novel arises when in spite of Balan's high academic record and wonderful personal interviews, he fails to secure a seat in any medical college around. On one pretext or the other, he remains out of the list of admitted candidates. Throughout his life, Balan repents about this failure without any fault of his own. The seed of resentment, despair and estrangement is sown in his heart at this young age of his life. Yet another shock erodes Balan's faith in the prevalent administrative system when he is unable to secure any suitable employment anywhere, once again, despite his merit and efforts. The unfortunate situation is quite suggestive of the dismal scenario of our social reality where youth, the future of any nation is denied the deserved opportunities. Great sense of frustration, depression and anger is bound to follow such people sooner or later. The reader learns that very often Balan's "[...] thoughts and anxieties kept him awake" (2).

Mr Iyer is going to retire soon; there is no other source of income; therefore, a job for Balan is very precious at this juncture of life; particularly when the anger and agony of failure in not getting a well-deserved medical seat is still fresh in his mind. But very unfortunately even on that front, he does not succeed. After great introspection and discussion with his fellows, Balan realizes that perhaps his Brahmin origin (the uppermost layer in the hierarchy of class system of Indian society that has had ruled over and exploited the other classes since ages together) is now being avenged indirectly, as after Partition the ruling power has come in the hands of newly empowered middle classes.

This realization changes the whole mind view of Balan. After deep brooding, he feels a soft corner for the subalterns and also gets annoyed over the fact that Brahmins have all along been treating their fellows very shabbily, just because they were born in high class families. He feels alienated from the society of his birth. Another fact that Balan resents greatly is that these Brahmins have always been chanting 'shlokas' and 'mantras' on every occasion from birth to death to impress upon the 'not so fortunate masses,' whom they considered even "Untouchables." But most of these reciters of mantras could hardly understand or explain exactly what these chantings meant. So much so, that many a time even his Sanskrit teacher failed to explain or answer Balan's queries to his satisfaction. This sorry state of affairs really speaks of prevailing hypocrisy and double standards of our social fabric. Balan rather feels more affiliated to these lower classes and he walks a step away from his own nativity.

This awareness of Balan further changes his mind view and he is driven more towards these other classes. Even the earlier agony of ill-treatment at their hands is also alleviated a bit. In addition, the situation rather proves a turning point in his life. The great beginning has been made and now he is on the lookout of ways and means to atone for the sins and atrocities committed by his ancestors on other classes. Here one is reminded of Willy Chandran's father, one major protagonist in V.S. Naipaul's *Half a Life*, who is a Brahmin by birth, shares the guilt of his ancestors. And to atone for their sins, he marries a lower caste girl and calls it an act of sacrifice and thus becomes a social outcaste. But the reasons behind that kind of realization were purely socio-political in nature, and in pre-Independent times. In Arun Joshi's *House for Mr. Biswas* too, yet another variety of alienation from the native society is presented. In this case the protagonist, Romi, a high class civil servant, prefers to die with the tribal girl rather than go back to his wife, family or his native society. In this instance, it is the sheer hypocrisy and double standards of the social life which drive an honest human being away from his own social environment. But here in the case of Balan we have this feeling of estrangement as well as dislocation in multiple aspects. Balan represents these feelings not only at the physical or intellectual level, but he further carries them at the emotional and spiritual planes also.

The four divisions of the novel actually present the four facets of Balan's identity and also the four layers of his consciousness. To begin with, this new phase of Balan's life, to express his mental anguish with his native society, the first stroke comes when in the wee hours of one fine morning, he goes to the river quietly, takes off his sacred thread (symbolic of his Brahmin origin), and throws it away into the river. The narrator informs the reader it was '[...] a symbolic act—act of definance against ceremony [...] rituals [...] devoid of meaning [...]' (3). But the reader experiences a bitter sting of irony that even when, '[...] he wanted to throw away the holy thread [...] (Balan) did perform the ceremony [...] did actually recite all those mantras.' This kind of behaviour on the part of the protagonist is also suggestive of his confusion and pathetic mental condition—he fears to accept what he believes and *vice versa*.

This shameful act of gross misconduct on the part of Balan, when discovered at home, creates a great furor in his family. The father of Balan, a very wise and prudent fellow, does not say much. He simply informs his son, thread or no thread, he cannot cease to be a Brahmin, any way. But his mother is very much annoyed with him. She often taunts him sarcastically, which Brahmin will marry his sister now, or who will give Balan his daughter. She condemns her son further, "You commit the worst of sins." Earlier too Balan had stopped using ash on his forehead.

This kind of abject treatment meted out to Balan at home, and his deep sense of introspection further alienate Balan from his family. Outwardly, though he remains quiet, he feels the sting inside. Poor Balan cannot help his father financially, though he earnestly desires it. He strongly craves to marry off his sister, Lakshmi, to a suitable boy as soon as possible. In the process, he is further driven away from his family and society both. Yet he loves his sister very dearly. So much so, that he is even ready to re-wear that brahmanic thread, if it could just help bringing a bridegroom for Lakshmi. Now he experiences great depression as well as self-reproach, Meanwhile, his father too has stopped talking to him. Any advice regarding his sister's marriage or any family matter is considered a provocative interference on his part. His father shouts, "[...] you keep out of all his [...] a disgrace to the family

[...] not fit socially, spiritually or even economically [...]" (33). And then silence reigned over the house for days together. His mother too is very much annoyed with her son. Balan suffers a great sense of shame and humiliation.

In this state of mental shock, fully engulfed in his grief, Balan reveals his longings and desires to his only friend, Jagan, who is a very practical fellow. Jagan's pleadings of not taking all these things seriously and not to feel perturbed prove futile. It appears that the time has been set ripe to take certain drastic decisions. With all his love for his family members on one side and the disgusting sense of humiliation, depression and total helplessness, on the other, the moment set for dislocation—physical, mental and emotional—too has arrived. His wailing mother and sister both try their best to ameliorate his pain a bit and pacify him but all in vain. His father too suffered in silence. Mother would scold and then immediately be very affectionate at the same time.

After the killing silence of many days, with a little baggage, a few rupees in his pocket and a very heavy heart, one morning Balan decides to leave his home. He finally breaks the ice and in a very assuring term discloses his decision to his father, "[...] I don't want to be a burden on you [...]. It is not my pride either [...] our paths have diverged (Balan tried to be honest). But I will not disgrace you [...]" (43). Then he picked up the small bundle "[...] gently pushed his sister aside (who tried to stop him), took one last look round the room and *walked out of the door*" (Emphasis mine). This moving out of the house symbolically represents Balan's going away from the known traditions, rituals, psychological protection, social security, his own people, the familiar surroundings and the total environment he had grown used to. In other words he was walking away from the familiar to the unfamiliar world around. And thus begins the second phase of Balan's alienation, with all confusion and no clear goals in mind. As he had not actual experience of life, he proves more vulnerable to the harsh realities outside.

In the process—face to face with life—whatever little provision Balan had made before leaving his home, is also stolen and all is gone. "The earth is my bed; (and) the sky is my blanket" (45), he comes to realize. Not a single penny in his pocket, he does not even converse with anyone for the fear of his identity being disclosed. Out and away from home, each new day brings a challenge for him. Many a time, "[...] the past keeps on haunting his mind [...] (his) mother's alternately fits of anger and affection [...] gloomy gentleness of his father [...] pleading and tearful eyes of Lakshmi [...] all gave him a dull ache" (44).

Physically worn-out though, his moral strength and his firm faith in his goal of atonement for the sins of his ancestors by actually living an untouchable's life (as he had confided in his friend Jagan, before leaving his home) help him survive all adversities. Meeting life face to face, now Balan realizes that deceit, fraud, hypocrisy and snobbery are the only realities of life today. Though his will power drove him along for some time, he could not go very far. Too tired, fatigued and shocked at the cost of survival, one day he collapsed in the shade of a tamarind tree. The depiction of social ills prevailing today, in the narration, are quite alarming and very much life-like. At this juncture of life, an old lady, Pappa, helps in lifting him, takes him home and looks after him with love and affection of a mother. Balan's shaking faith in life recovers, as it also highlights and reinforces reader's faith in the goodness of things and God's supreme power.

Balan tells the couple about his Brahmin origin, of leaving his nativity and also of his plans to live among the low-caste people and embrace their lives. Pappa's husband, Kuppan, though suspicious and unwilling in the beginning, does agree to Balan's proposal in the end and allows him to stay with them in his house, as his own son. Balan has to follow certain conditions, to which he agrees quite readily. Here Balan is looked after very affectionately, as the couple did not have any child of their own.

Actually living under such surroundings (unhygienic place, butchers performing their job in the open) people enjoyed their life with a recklessness that was "[...] impossible even in conception to a Brahmin [...]" gave Balan many a sleepless nights in the beginning. Learning to eat meat and then to "Arrack," was quite a tough time. At moments Balan "[...] experienced the inner universe of human consciousness—very forceful and dynamic and [...] free [...] a state of bliss" (90). Always acting "[...] always living on the fringe [...] great conflict inside [...]" identity crisis too persisted for quite a long period. But gradually his self-made decision, his inner enlightenment and above all the encouraging attitude of these people towards Balan, all help him greatly overcome all the initial adverse situations.

Here in *Sirumudi*, Balan learns that even these subalterns have their own hierarchy of sub-castes and classes in their society. Another painful fact that Balan observes is that even the treatment meted out to these people by the landlords and others at social functions is different according to their ranks. Even their serving and eating manners are different. Staying with Kuppans, Balan learns the art of designing, cutting, tanning and cobbling the shoes. His educational background is of great help to him in this new adventure. Occasionally, he experiences certain mystic revelations, and reaches a state of perfect trance. Balan is quite successful in accommodating himself in the new environment of life and he gets assimilated in this new society very well. To earn more as a shoemaker and help his poor foster-parents, now he wants to shift to another locality. After some arguments and promises, he is allowed to go but on the condition that this house will always belong to him. Thus, the second time Balan moves out of his home, but he is told, "Don't forget this home [...] Pappa wept" (79). With this, the third stage of Balan's estrangement from his native society sets in.

One more struggle begins afresh. Out of his earlier ordeals of penance, Balan has emerged more confident and successful too. On the outskirts of the village, *Kallupatti*, Balan sits under a tree with display of his shoes, sandals and working tools. Gradually, he becomes familiar with the people around and is soon embraced and warmly welcomed by one and all. His quality of education, his philosophy of karma, selfless service, eagerness to help one and all, and particularly, his devotion to duty make this high-class Brahmin a very efficient and admirable scavenger. In addition, his moral strength, his mystic powers, yoga, meditation and his pure heart endear Balan greatly to all and sundry. No one can say that he is of a different origin or he belongs to another society.

Balan's life in this village actually represents the epitome of Gandhian philosophy of Atma-shakti, Ahinsa and selfless karma. The narrator here seems to suggest that the fellow feeling of love and affection has got the supreme power of winning hearts. The more Balan absorbs himself in this community of scavengers, the cleaners of latrines, the more intense grows his sense of alienation and withdrawal from his native society. That is true of course, but the reader realizes that even now Balan's heart is filled with pity and remorse at times, when he thinks about his mother or sister Lakshmi. But his predefined goal and the principle of "karma" facilitate and enable him to live within the confinement of his foster kin.

Due to his loving behaviour, eloquent oratory, prudence and humility, every one around Balan loves him, respects him, nay, worships him. Finally, they make Balan their leader also, at the cost of Picchu, of course. At last Balan feels not only settled down in life, but he enjoys great peace of mind too. Perhaps now he realizes that his earlier apprehensions about his society were not true. The feeling of guilt no longer haunts him. He has not only come a long way away from his native environment, but has also fitted himself into this new fold of human and professional surroundings as well. Finally, with his marriage to another scavenging girl, Lachi, Balan feels, "[...] we belong to each other now—no one can separate us" (116). For the first time, since his quest began, Balan felt himself a real Untouchable. With this realization, Balan's journey of alienation and dislocation from his native society reaches its acme.

But exactly at that very time, all his earlier attempts to conceal his origin, education, and brahminic credentials are severely thwarted away just with one stroke of a news item. A report published in the newspaper about a missing person, with all the details mentioned, and signed by G. at the end resembles most of the details of Balan's life. Picchu, whose envy had always been hunting any such item to avenge himself on Balan, found an opportunity to discuss the matters with one and all. Actually Ganesh, Balan's friend, had been trying to know about Balan, as he wanted to inform him about his sister's marriage and his mother's death. The published letter from Ganesh "[...] rekindled his memories [...] emotions. He (even) shed tears for his dead mother and blamed himself for not having been there when she passed away [...]. He ought to have been there at least to light her pyre (he lamented) [...]. But could he go back? All his struggle till now seemed so unimportant. But he had gone through hell—through proverbial purgatory [...] and come out unscathed. Now Lachi as a wife and his child in her womb, his exile seemed to be permanent. [...] Going back had to be postponed for ever" (128).

Balan had no choice but to accept the truth. But fortunately, these revelations about his life prove providential, though Picchu had intended to be otherwise. The people around who were very affectionate till now start respecting him more than ever before. He has become their role model now, an avtar in other words and they can do anything to please him. And the reader is informed that Balan's tough struggle of life, his efforts of atonement, his sacrifice finally, did bear the fruit of eternal peace and bliss. Over night, Balan became famous and "[...] an unknown god to people."

As usual, under such circumstances, the news reporters and local politicians throng in, each one vying with the other to woo Balan in order to gain popularity and position. All financial and other helps start pouring in, though Balan does not feel inclined to earn any material gain. He rather realizes that the purpose of his atonement is over and thus feels a great sense of relief and satisfaction. Balan becoming a hero of the people, Picchu gets a real setback, which he cannot tolerate easily. Shocked with his failure to become leader of the people, one day, he stabs Balan in the dark, and almost kills him. Though Balan recognizes him but he pretends total ignorance about his assailant. This act of forgiveness makes Balan still further rise in the eyes of the people. He has become the Messiah, the great saviour. At the physical level his already serious condition worsens further and Balan is taken to a nearby hospital. There his friend Ganesh, his father Mr Iyer, sister Lakshmi and her husband all visit him. They want to take Balan to some better hospital, but Balan refuses to be moved. Instead, he is thankful to Picchu, for bringing this condition on him—the salvation, the final freedom from the cycle of life and death. He feels his mission in this world is over now. With his child (the seed of continuity) in the womb of his wife, Lachi, he is ready to make an exit from the world in a very contented manner. Lachi smiles through tears. Balan makes his last statement faintly, "[...] my work is finished [...] my living shall be an embarrassment [...]. Picchu has done a great service [...] forgive me for all the troubles father [...] I am glad you came [...]," and thus he breathes his last. Lachi refuses to go with his people, she rather declares—her place is by the side of her husband—whether dead or alive.

Balan's last rites are all performed by his friend Jagan with consultation of Lachi and her brother. On that very spot Bala yogi temple is established. Lachi in her own manner tries to spread the message of her husband, *i.e.* brotherhood of man and fatherhood of god. Jagan does the same in his own manner. Balan's soul rests in peace. Once again we find ancient philosophy of India gaining supreme ground on the path of repentance through atonement leading to final salvation.

Through the deep sense and torture of physical, mental, emotional and spiritual alienation and dislocation, Balan achieves salvation—Mukti—the ultimate freedom. Throughout, the writer seems to be suggesting that if the main philosophy of all the scriptures of the world—the fatherhood of god and brotherhood of men—is followed in spirit by each individual in his/her own capacity, it can very significantly and meaningfully prove a panacea for all the ills that our present world is suffering from.

NOTE

All quotes have been taken from *The Light from Heaven*, Penguin edition, 1990.

11

Coming Together: Shoes and the Seductions of Rational Love in Vikram Seth's *A Suitable Boy*

KERSTIN W. SHANDS

"Soyons réalistes: demandons l'impossible"

Vikram Seth's *A Suitable Boy* has been regarded both as a very Indian and a very European novel.[1] Many Western readers, not surprisingly, have seen this novel as a good introduction to India—or at least to those aspects of Indian history and culture that are conveyed through a narrative that, moving through an impressive array of dissimilar and disparate discourses, touches on historical, cultural, and religious issues ranging from the caste system, the Land Reform Act aiming to abolish the zamindari landowner system, the tensions between Hindus and Muslims, and the political struggles of post-Independence. Through the ramifications of the family trees of four high-caste families, the reader gains some insight into the cultural imperatives of the early 1950s, a time when preordained and astrologically auspicious forms of marriage were still stipulated or strongly recommended and a time when the new nation was undergoing dramatic development.

I moved into the 1,500-page narrative of *A Suitable Boy* as into a house. With all the idiosyncrasies of my own cultural identity, I responded to and interacted with the quirks and quandaries of Seth's characters. A mark of Vikram Seth's achievement is precisely this: his brilliant capacity to create characters who are as endearingly contradictory and lovably idiosyncratic as certain people in real life.

In its delineation of cultural identity and what post-positivist realists have called social location, *A Suitable Boy* continues the exploration of issues of pre-eminence in the novel as a genre: how our identities are found or formed in response to the difficulties of our lives and how we, in the struggle to forge selves and lives of our own, are empowered or restricted by the framework of family, culture, and religion into which we are born.

Questions of realism and identity are central in Vikram Seth's *A Suitable Boy.* If the Indian nation is moving towards full independence during the time span depicted, what about the characters in Vikram Seth's novel? To what extent are they acting out of dependence or independence, emotion or reason, realism or romance? What blend is seen as optimal on national, collective, or individual levels? How are Seth's characters restricted or empowered within their networks of family, culture, and religion?

Structures of domination and subordination affect our cultural identities and what post-positivist realism calls social location. As *Reclaiming Identity* argues correctly, moreover, "The significance of identity depends partly on the fact that goods and resources are still distributed according to identity categories" (Moya 8). One could turn that around and say that identities are distributed or that we are interpellated according to our relationship to the production of goods and the access to resources. Responding to the question raised by María Lugones and quoted by Michael Hames-García in *Reclaiming Identity*—'Who are our own people?,' I will offer the unrealistic yet necessary argument that it is only when *all* marginalized but epistemically valid voices are heard and when the sparks of passion and difference can ignite that the orchestra of emancipation can be heard in full and magnificent expression.

The organizing focus of my paper will consist of two "prisms" through which I will look at central motifs in Vikram

Seth's *A Suitable Boy*. There is the metonymic matter of marriage on the one hand, and the narrative of nation-building on the other. Through the marriage-making prism, I will look at the main characters, a mother and her daughter, each of whom stands in a different temporal relation to marriage (one is before marriage and the other is after) and whose experiences of femininity, womanhood, and motherhood extend backward in historical time. The nation-building epic is forward-looking and shows how individual identities and ideals matter for the development of the new nation of India. While it consists of many characters, I will focus on one, the suitable boy whose values are of crucial importance for both nation-building and marriage-making narratives. I will look at the interrelationship of these characters from a perspective of a theory-in-the flesh (with a term from Moraga, as cited by Moya) and a feminist criticism that, in the words of Rajeswari Sunder Rajan, "is not only produced within a post-colonial problematic" but that "radically reconfigures it in terms of its analysis of gender" (Rajan 4). Patterns of passion, power, and productivity inherent in social location will be shown to be determined by life stage and gender and framed by a normative nexus where emotion and reason, passion and realism (or rationality) are expected to blend and balance in the ordained measure.

Himansu S. Mohapatra and Jatindra K. Nayak have argued that, on a formal level, the post-colonial nation-building requires the kind of literary realism utilized by Seth in *A Suitable Boy*. I will look at another kind of realism: the economically, socially, and psychologically motivated kind of realism cultivated by several main characters in this novel. This is a realism rooted more in fear rather than in desire; a realism resembling resignation and rationalization; a realism that requests that the kind of passion and authenticity that threaten reified and atomized essentialist conceptions of cultural identity be sacrificed in the name of the survival of the same. It is the realism of the stultifying stability and security found in the repetition of capitalist productivity, that valorizes able-bodied and active people in their prime within a scheme of maximizing progress and development. Servants, old people, and, to a large extent, women, remain outside the public stage of production and profit. Just as the private is suppressed or subordinated in the public realm, moreover, sexuality, threatening the stability and security of sameness, must be channelled into accepted and controlled grooves.

Exploring various ways in which personal lived experience comes together with or collides with preordained cultural identity, Vikram Seth's novel shows how life stage, gender, and sexuality are primary factors determining cultural identity. From a perspective that sees connections between gender and social subordination, life stage and sexuality, I will examine how identity categories are valorized or marginalized in *A Suitable Boy*. As indicated in my title, furthermore, shoes turn out to be politically salient signals of cultural identity and significant symbols linked to the seductions of rational love in both marriage-making and nation-building narratives.

The Emotional Capital of Mrs Rupa Mehra

Let us begin with a look at the mother par excellence in *A Suitable Boy*, and, through this character, show the importance of life stage as intersecting with gender. Mrs Rupa Mehra is a vibrant, maddening, and engaging character. What sort of identity can she reclaim, re-evaluate, or rescue in terms of passion, power, and productivity?

Since "Realists," as Paula Moya writes, "contend that knowledge is not disembodied, or somewhere 'out there' to be had, but rather that it comes into being in and through embodied selves" (Moya 18), we may ask what "the materiality of the body" (Moya 92) means for Mrs Rupa Mehra. Mrs Rupa Mehra is an attractive widow who still mourns her husband eight years after his death. For Mrs Rupa Mehra, the pleasures of passion appear to be over. She attempts to focus obsessively on family matters and to eradicate all 'unrealistic' longings from her own life. Still, her sexual longings surface, explicitly—as when she laments that she will never again be held as a man holds a woman—and implicitly, perhaps, in the fixation of her vicarious desire on Haresh Khanna as a son-in-law. Mrs Rupa Mehra is a character who exemplifies how, in the words of Satya Mohanty, "gender relations and inequalities are played out in our most intimate relationships (including our relationships with ourselves)" (Mohanty 62).

Admittedly, since Mrs Rupa Mehra is not really old she is not really representative of 'old people.' A better example would be Miriam, the old servant in the house of Arun and Meenakshi Mehra. Miriam's "slow-moving back irritates Meeakshi" who sees her as "needlessly senile." T.C. is their private appellation for the ayah "and Meenakshi laughed with pleasure as she remembered the occasion over the breakfast table when Arun had turned from the *Statesman* crossword to say, 'Oh, do get the toothless crone out of the room. She quite puts me off my omelette.' Miriam had been the T.C. ever since" (65).

Nonetheless, since Mrs Rupa Mehra is seen as too old in crucial respects, her case is valid as a pointer to the importance of life stage, in particular as it intersects with gender, and for the ways in which we essentialize older people based on experiences they seem to share as members of an apparently static and unchanging social group, while we overlook the epistemic significance their identities may hold.[2]

Perhaps because "a realist theory of identity demands oppositional struggle as a necessary (although not sufficient) step toward the achievement of an epistemologically privileged position" (Moya 97) people in their prime—who can oppose and transgress and empower themselves—have, so far, tended to be privileged as examples in *Reclaiming Identity,* an anthology which, despite the attempt at a broad perspective, repeatedly lists race, gender, sexuality, or class as the politically most salient aspects of cultural identity. Even though "identities are subject to multiple determinations" (Moya 84), and "the role of multiplicity" is emphasized (Hames-García 102), the focus in post-positivist realist theory as delineated in this anthology remains fixed on people in their prime, on the movers and the shakers, in a way that is analogous to capitalism's evaluation of human beings according to their levels of activity and productivity, their doing and having over their being. Just as in postmodernist theory and criticism, the post-positivist production and marketing of ideas of identities has so far tended to be attracted to the spectacular and transgressive. However, since it causally determines our places in a capitalist scheme of production, life stage is in fact every bit as important as the above-mentioned fourfold aspects of identity. Despite or rather because of the limited scope for passion, power, and productivity and the unglamorous field of action, old age poses a theoretical challenge in pointing to one of the least obvious and most silenced of identities. Do alternative narratives or empowering paradigms exist for those who hold group membership in the category of old age? Or are we still mesmerized by the accomplishments of the lone heroes of today's bildungsromans and sagas of individualistic success who achieve their oppositional, anti-heteronormative, hybrid, or nomadic identities? In this respect, post-positivist realist theory could, however, be developed and applied also to issues of life stage.

As Satya Mohanty has written, "In analyzing identity-based politics, claims about the general social significance of a particular identity should be evaluated together with its accompanying assumptions or arguments about how the current social or cultural system makes some experiences intelligible and others obscure or irrelevant, how it treats some as legitimate sources of knowledge about the world while relegating others to the level of the narrowly personal" (Mohanty 63).[3] Mrs Rupa Mehra's experiences of her life-stage are indeed marginalized as obscure, irrelevant, and narrowly personal. She sees her own sexual longings, her anger at her husband's death, and her loneliness and vulnerability as a woman in a society that sees her as finished as a woman, as at the same time irrelevant and inexpressible.[4] Even though she is seen by Kalpana Gaur as her "good-looking aunt" and by Haresh as "very fine-looking" (600), as a mother and a widow, Rupa Mehra's identity is predicated upon giving to others before giving to herself, let alone requesting anything for herself from society. Suppressing her own needs and desires, she requests no rights for herself but moves around with her "three suitcases, filled with most of what she owned in the world" (148). The years after the death of her husband have been years of deprivation for Rupa, who makes her own birthday cards for friends and relatives since she cannot afford to buy them (42). Perhaps because she has little opportunity to improve her financial situation, Rupa is said to make "emotional capital [...] out of every possible circumstance" (3).

For Mrs Rupa Mehra's lived experience and social location, then, age, gender, and marital status are politically salient. Age, gender, and marital status determine her experiences and colour her choices as they curtail her hopes and possibilities. No oppositional struggle or epistemic reorientation occurs, and through a discourse of resignation and religious ritual,[5] Rupa Mehra channels her unacceptable desires into an imperial maternal authority and control over her children, governing them as if they were as anarchic an empire as her own sexuality.

The Premarital Rationality of Lata Mehra

What is interesting about Mrs Rupa Mehra is that she is an example of how one can be oppressed and oppressing at the same time. Within the structure of domination and subordination that the Mehra family inhabit, important aspects of Mrs Rupa Mehra's identity have to remain suppressed, at the same time as she oppresses others, such as her daughter, Lata.[6] "What was good enough for her mother and her mother's mother and her mother's mother's mother should be good enough for [Lata]," Mrs Rupa Mehra reasons, in particular as regards the realm of sexuality and marriage.

In spiritual matters, Mrs Rupa Mehra consults her heritage of wisdom, the Bhagavad Gita (although she finds that the "ancient wisdom so often proved unconsoling" [597]). When she is planning for Lata's marriage, however, Indian sources of wisdom are elided as she presents Lata with a supremely western, scientific manual of married love: Van de Velde's *Ideal Marriage*. In a gesture reminding one of Simone de Beauvoir's statement that even though "women's erotic capabilities are almost unlimited [...] marriage kills feminine eroticism in the effort to regularize it" (de Beauvoir 418), the mother hands this volume to her daughter, saying: "This book will teach you everything—about Men," adding that even other women in the family "had to have these experiences" (1453). In a language recalling a mechanic conveyor-belt productivity, the author of this book of graphs and cross-sections divides the "science" of "marriage" into

> "converse and averse types, and further divided these into the habitual or medial attitude, the first attitude of extension, the second attitude of extension (suspensory),
>
> the attitudes of flexion (favored, according to him, by the Chinese), the attitude of equitation (in which Martial described Hector and Andromache), the sedentary attitude,
>
> the anterior-lateral attitude, the ventral attitude, the posterior-lateral attitude, the attitude of averse flexion, and the posterior-sedentary attitude. Lata was amazed by the possibilities: she had only thought of one" (1453-54).

The distanced and disembodied, clinical listing of the possibilities of love-making parallels Lata's state of mind as she resigns herself to future fate as "the Bride of Goodyear Welted" (1455). She feels as if "she was someone other than herself. She felt [...] a curious, dislocated feeling [...] a sense that she was floating above her physical self and looking down at it from a height" (1454). Inspired by Clough, Lata arrives at the decision to invest in a "calmer, less frantic love, which helps you grow where you're already growing" (Seth 1420), which, given the contemporary framework of family, caste, and religion, makes sense. Although her impulse is to "run away" (1455)—she does not. Instead, she accepts the suitable boy.

In *A Suitable Boy,* potential husbands are compared and contrasted for their supposedly essential, unchangeable, and objective characteristics and evaluated according to how they fit into a supposedly stable grid of culturally stipulated criteria. Match-making, the manufacture of consent, and marriage, then, are central concerns in *A Suitable Boy.* Less obviously it is also the story of separation, loss, and divorce. Firstly, from the nation-building perspective in *A Suitable Boy,* the narrative is set in the years after India's 'divorce' from Great Britain and is as such a "story of the emancipation and empowerment of a colonial people" (Mohapatra and Nayak 194). Secondly, certain hints in the text suggest that marital arrangements enmeshed in structures of domination and subordination may not last, since enforced patterns of hierarchy obstruct rather than promote forces of creativity, vitality, and renewal.

Such forces of creativity, spontaneity, and vitality mark Lata's relationship with Kabir Durrani. She lives entirely in the moment when she is with Kabir. True, he may be romantic in seeing love as "all that matters" (at least at one point in the narrative, 184). However, it is significant that their first encounter takes place in the bookstore where Kabir observes and praises Lata's interest in both poetry and mathematics. Mohapatra and Nayak have argued that Kabir Durrani is "the unAustenian force in her life that momentarily disrupts logic and reason, giving [Lata] a glimpse of the heart of darkness, the abyss" (Mohapatra and Nayak 203). But Kabir is not really a dark romantic hero. If anything, his letter to Lata in Calcutta is too rational, matter-of-fact, and unemotional to set Lata on fire— when she has been ready to elope with him. In this letter, Kabir takes a long view into the future. He proposes to finish his education first, looking ahead to the Indian foreign service and Cambridge. Kabir combines realist and romantic strands and blends emotion and reason, although not always at the most right moment. When Lata wants emotion,[7] he gives her reason; when she wants reason, his emotions threaten her rational resolve.

The fact that the only really suitable boy in this novel, Kabir Durrani, is spurned and rejected suggests that atomizing and objectifying views of identity win out over relational views of identity as formed within and through inter-subjective and synthesizing spaces of authentic exchange. What is 'rational' in this case is the rule that prohibits inter-faith marriage. Kabir Durrani is a Moslem. Within both match-making and nation-building epics, then, Haresh Khanna, Lata's other main suitor and a good Khatri boy, possesses the required criteria.

Haresh Khanna's Shoes and the Seductions of Rational Love

The suitable boy in Vikram Seth's novel turns out to be Haresh Khanna—although not without a certain ironic twist. Haresh is a dedicated, focused, and practical man of action who works in shoe production, making it and himself a success story. Low-key rather than flamboyant, engaged but not empassioned, he enjoys an enviably even keel most of the time. Admiring the Czechs he works for since they are goal-oriented but looking down on Bengalis who, in his view, "do as little work as possible" (1224), Haresh Khanna—who is irritated by "Hamlet's indecisiveness" (649)—shares the Czech commitment to productivity, determination, and results. He even looks at the photo of Lata from a career angle of constant improvement, and writes to her: "It may tend to keep me more ambitious" (981).

While Haresh Khanna's shrewd ways of increasing production are good for the shoe factory, they could also be seen as an echo of relations between colonizers and slaves. Slaves historically had a tendency to sabotage work. Similarly, in *A Suitable Boy,* the workers in the shoe factory under Haresh are shown to lie about mechanical problems and to slow down production with their lazy, uncooperative attitudes. When Haresh understands that their behaviour is caused by their fears of losing their jobs if productivity increases greatly because of mechanization and standardization, he knows how to approach and appease the workers. Haresh Khanna is very much in accord with 'Fordist' or capitalist masculinist, paternalist, and patriarchal institutions. He represents the perfect blend of characteristics for the industrial world demanding "materialism, efficiency, largeness, mechanization, standardization, automation, mass production, mass consumption, mass democracy [...] uniformity, pragmatism, reformism, optimism, spontaneity, generosity, and openness" (Frank Costigliola, *Awkward Dominion*). In fact, Haresh Khanna is completely in line with those twentieth-century socio-economic and cultural ideals of rationalization and modernization that have been grouped under various umbrella terms such as "Americanism," Fordism, or Taylorism.[8]

While Haresh Khanna at one point is suspected of being a socialist, in the nation-building narrative in *A Suitable Boy* he represents, rather, a liberal, capitalist ideology. His to-to-lists and his correspondence to Lata are couched in an economic language of calculation, cause-and-effect, practical negotiation and exchange. Under "My Life," he lists: "Must catch up with news and world affairs [...]. Exercise: at least 15 minutes each morning: how to find the time? [...] Make notes of my five best and five worst qualities. Conserve latter and eradicate former" (650-51). If he cannot find 15 minutes for himself in the morning, one wonders how he will be able to make time for—much less love to—a wife, especially if the effect her photographed physiognomy has on him to increase his desire to work. The extreme dedication to work that Haresh evinces is not entirely positive, especially if we consider that Lata's father died from overwork in his forties leaving Mrs Rupa Mehra a widow (3).

Shoes, as suggested in my title, are important in *A Suitable Boy*. Shoes usually come together, in pairs, and in this book they also come together with rational love. When Haresh Khanna is depicted wearing co-respondent shoes, this is a subtle but significant signal. The co-respondent shoes are mentioned on several occasions (617, 627, 980, 1223) and are made much of by Lata for whom they indicate that something is missing in her relation to Haresh. Lata, who tries to convince herself that she should marry Haresh, is overcome by doubt and displeasure every time she notices his shoes. On one occasion, "Haresh noticed that Lata was looking at his co-respondent shoes with what appeared almost to be distaste" (1223). The co-respondent shoes suggest a discrepancy, a rift in the fragile premarital weave. Haresh's room, too, has a disturbing effect on Lata: "Everything was neat, tidy, smart—to Lata it appeared to be in extreme, almost disturbing, order. Even the volumes of Hardy on the small bookshelf were arranged alphabetically. The shoes standing on a shoe-rack in a corner of the room were polished to a glacial shine" (621).

Given the central significance in *A Suitable Boy* of the shoe symbolism—through which a whole cluster of issues concerning family, caste, social and political struggle is depicted—in a narrative ostensibly obsessed with marriage, it is disturbing, moreover, that the word co-respondent points to infidelity, separation, and divorce. A co-respondent is the "person cited in a divorce case as having committed adultery with the respondent" (Encarta).[9] The reference to co-respondents raises a suspicion about the suitability of the match between Lata and Haresh (and of shoes and rational love), a suspicion that is strengthened at the end of the novel. Lata looks at her new husband "for a second," after which she gazes out of the train window. Haresh is soon asleep, and in the final vignette Lata is seen interacting not with her new husband but with an old monkey (1473). Mohapatra and Nayak have seen this scene as "an image of exhaustion and listlessness after all passion is spent" (Mohapatra and Nayak 202). But it is worse than that: no passion has been spent between Lata and Haresh, and there are no indications that there will be any.

Conclusion

Just as in Europe, the roles of women and the views of marriage and divorce were beginning to change in the 1950s. At the time depicted, as referred to in *A Suitable Boy,* the Hindu Code Bill was "[aiming] to make the laws of marriage, divorce, inheritance and guardianship more rational and just, especially to women" (1104). In Seth's novel, we see vast differences between women in the cities and women in the villages and between Hindu and Moslem women. Even though highly educated professional Moslem women are depicted, such as the irrepressibly eloquent Begum Abida Khan, Moslem women, trapped in the zenana, are generally more oppressed than Hindu women. But the Hindu women also encounter contradictory messages, as when one of the father figures, Mahesh Kapoor, finds it acceptable that women strive for education and property rights but not that they use their education since their duties at home might be neglected (917).[10] Since, from feminist and anti-colonial points of view, it is possible to see analogies between the relations of domination and subordination in traditional marriage and the relations of colonizer and colonized, it is interesting that Seth has chosen to panoramically portray the 'coming of age' of post-colonial India through the motif of match-making and marriage, and *vice versa,* to depict nation-building through marriage-making metaphors.

As Satya Mohanty has argued, "The institutions of social reproduction and cultural transmission—schools, libraries, newspapers, and museums, for instance—are oriented to the dominant cultural and social perspectives. Much of their bias is often invisible because of the relatively benign form the transmission of cultural information takes: it seems utterly natural, part of the scheme of things" (Mohanty 65). To this list of "institutions of social reproduction and cultural transmission" we might add the institution of marriage, especially since, as Himansu Mohapatra and Jatindra Nayak have argued, "The nexus between desire, power and money is nowhere more sharply evinced than in the domestic, seemingly apolitical institution of marriage" (Mohapatra and Nayak 199). Vikram Seth's novel depicts how marriage is "oriented to the dominant cultural and social perspectives," held up as "part of the scheme of things," and naturalized from rationalist standpoints, or, with Michael Hames-García's term, made "transparent." While marriage in this novel concerns heterosexual couples joining in a sexual, social, and spiritual contract, it also corresponds to institutions that underpin normative syntheses on national levels whereby a discourse of rationality excludes, suppresses, or minimizes affectivity, authenticity, and sexuality in ways that may prohibit rather than promote progressive political development.

In part, Lata's decision to marry Haresh is an impulsive and ill-advised act of protest against the condescension and tyranny of her brother, Arun Mehra.[11] But her decision is also a capitulation and a resignation confirming a traditional, (British and imperial) conservative epistemology rooted in a rational western philosophy of restraint, discipline, systematization, and moderation that goes back to James Mill's (1817) *History of British India* and other works which argued for western knowledge and ideas of moderation (ideas that far from leading to moderation have brought us instead to an ever-accelerating conveyor-belt of over-production and pollution). However, even though, as Mohapatra and Nayak have argued, "the master narrative of nation-building requires this sort of utilitarianism," whereby "rationalistic 'sense'" wins out over "romantic 'sensibility'" and the "utile" over the "lyrical" the "dark, unAustenian pressures" cannot be entirely suppressed by "this rationalist ideology" (Mohapatra and Nayak 202).

On that note, one image that might sum up the marriage-making and nation-building movement in this novel is that of the female soul of *kundalini*—in Sanskrit the image of a snake or feather rolled up into itself and containing a strength and power, passion and difference, not fully used yet. In contradistinction to the forces unleashed by western capitalist productivity, this image evokes liberating energies of a different kind. In this novel, those energies have not yet unrolled.

NOTES

1. Mohapatra and Nayak see it as "a novel with anAustenian form and an Indian substance" (Mohapatra and Nayak 195).
2. Cf. epistemic privilege of 1950s housewives in Sweden—the repository of valuable knowledge.
3. Relying upon terms suggested by Hames-García, we might say that the interests of a life stage marked by activity, transformation, development are "transparent," while the interests old people are "opaque," and, if not "misrepresented," "misunderstood" in a process Hames-García calls "restriction" (Hames-García 104).

4. That gender is an important component in aging is obvious in that Mrs Rupa Mehra's father has remarried, taking a woman ten years younger than his daughter.
5. She fasts in memory of her husband each Ekadashi ["the eleventh day of each lunar fortnight] [39].
6. Similarly, Arun Mehra is part of a power structure where he is not at the top, and then he comes home to censure his brother's non-anglophile manner in ways that are oppressive.
7. "How can you write so coolly when you know what you mean to me and what I thought I meant to you" (498).
8. Haresh Khanna, then, I will suggest, is only a suitable boy in an ironic sense. The irony connects with the irony of the so-called civilizing mission of the British not only during continuing effects or internalizations of the anti-colonialist struggle in which Mahesh Kapoor has participated but also in the post-colonial effects to build a powerful and independent India.
9. It is a legal term referring to "one who is made a joint respondent with another in a suit; especially one who is charged with adultery with the wife or husband of the plaintiff, and made a party to suit for divorce" (Webster's 20th c).
10. Mahesh Kapoor's own wife is a "much-shouted-at" woman (18), and his daughter Priya is "married and virtually immured by her in-laws in a house" (18).
11. Haresh Khanna has little sense of social borders and hierarchies. His friendships cut across the usual social borders. To the horror of the upper-echelon socialites he invited a simple shoemaker, Jagat Ram, to his wedding. Haresh Khanna is in many ways a sympathetic and pragmatic sort of man who looks beyond the common ingrained social and religious grids. It is not Haresh Khanna himself who inflates his good Khatri qualities, moreover, but his self-appointed mother-in-law, Rupa Mehra. Haresh Khanna possesses the characteristics of Nehru, as they are ascribed to latter in this novel—a direct, hands-on, no-nonsense kind of engagement with the most central issues (equality, treating everyone with respect, honouring deeply felt and significant religious rituals). Like Nehru, Haresh Khanna is a man who is able to channel his considerable and democratic energies into work for improvement, development, and progress.

WORKS CITED

Costigliola, Frank. *Awkward Dominion:* American Political, Economic, and Cultural Relations with Europe, 1919-33. Ithaca: Cornell UP, 1984.

de Beauvoir, Simone. *The Second Sex.* 1949. Rpt. Trans. and Ed. H.M. Parshley. Bantam Books, 1970.

Hames-García, Michael. "'Who are Our Own People?' Challenges for a Theory of Social Identity." In Moya, Paula M.L., and Michael R. Hames-García,

Reclaiming Identity: Realist Theory and the Predicament of Postmodernism. University of California Press, 2000, 102-29.

Mohanty, Satya P. "The Epistemic Status of Cultural Identity: On *Beloved* and the Postcolonial Condition." *Reclaiming Identity,* 29-66.

Mohapatra, Himansu S. and Jatindra K. Nayak. "Farewell to Jane Austen: Uses of Realism in Vikram Seth's *A Suitable Boy.*" In Park, You-me, and Rajeswari Sunder Rajan, *The Postcolonial Jane Austen.* London and New York: Routledge, 2000, 189-204.

Moya, Paula M.L. "Introduction: Reclaiming Identity." *Reclaiming-Identity,* 1-28.

——. "Postmodernism, Realism, and the Politics of Identity: Cherríe Moraga and Chicana Feminism." *Reclaiming Identity,* 67-101.

Rajan, Rajeswari Sunder. "Austen in the World: Postcolonial Mappings." In Park, You-me, and Rajeswari Sunder Rajan, *The Postcolonial Jane Austen,* London and New York: Routledge, 2000, 3-25.

Seth, Vikram. *A Suitable Boy.* 1993. Rpt. New York: Harper Perennial, 1994.

12

Ironic Vision in Kamala Markandaya's *Nectar in a Sieve*

U.S. RUKHAIYAR

That Kamala Markandaya's *Nectar in a Sieve* is full of irony is a fact noted by almost all its critics. What is required, therefore, is to see in how many ways irony operates in the novel.

A close study shows that the entire novel has been conceived as a big piece of irony. Then there are secondary and tertiary ironies, which develop, sustain and repeat the keynotes of the novel and look like imagistic variations upon the central irony. Of all the various kinds of irony, *e.g.*, verbal irony, structural irony, Socratic irony, cosmic irony, romantic irony, dramatic irony, tragic irony, etc., this novel shows the use mainly of four kinds of irony *viz.* (a) structural irony; (b) dramatic irony; (c) tragic irony; and (d) cosmic irony, in a varying degree and often overlapping one another.

The first great irony in the novel lies in the very couplet by Coleridge that gives the title to the book. It says that work without hope draws nectar in a sieve. No doubt, it does so. But experience shows that very often work *with* hope too meets the same fate. A great part of our life is determined by destiny. Hence, if destiny is not kind to us, we have to fail, *with* hope or *without* hope. There are innumerable people who work hard all their life and that with all hope and still get nothing in return but only failure and despair. Further, it is also seen, especially these days, that no amount of hope can fetch anything until it is aided by manipulation, fraud or by the grace of God.

In this novel as also in *A Handful of Rice,* Kamala Markandaya shows how the wicked thrive while the honest remain languishing in the shackles of old values like honesty and integrity. In *Nectar in a Sieve* all the leading characters work hard throughout their life with all hope but only to reap despair and frustration. Nathan, his wife Rukmini, their daughter Irawady and all their children remain tossed throughout their life by the buffets of the cruel fate.

The greatest irony, or better say, the irony of ironies, in the book is the theme itself. It deals with the life of a typical poor Indian farmer in a typical Indian village. As all of us know, such a life is itself an irony. The farmer toils hard all his life but is always in debt, which he inherits from his ancestors. He works hard in scorching heat, chilly cold and heavy rains. Still he is not sure whether he will get anything out of the yield. The major share will be taken by the *zamindar* and we know how relentless he is. The farmer has to pay the zamindar's share even if there is no harvest on account of drought, flood or anything whatsoever. And, if he has no cash, he has to pay it by selling all his appurtenances, even the honour of his women. Thus irony is in-built or embedded in the very situation in which they are born and condemned to live. The irony becomes even more poignant when they realize that it is their fate, decreed by the Almighty God. (Here we get a glimpse of cosmic irony, often found in Hardy's novels especially *Tess*.)

Rukmini, the narrator, and leading character says about fear and despair, the fate of a common Indian farmer:

> Fear, constant companion of the peasant. Hunger, ever at hand to jog his elbow should he relax. Despair, ready to engulf him should he falter. Fear; for the dark future; fear for the sharpens of hunger; fear for the blackness of death. (79)

Similarly, about hunger she says:

> For hunger is a curious thing; at first it is with you all the time, waking and sleeping and in your dreams, and your belly cries out insistently, and there is a gnawing and a pain as if your very vitals were being devoured,

> and you must stop it any cost, and you buy a moment's respite even while you know and fear the sequel. Then the pain is no longer sharp but dull, and this too is with you always, so that you think of food many time a day and each time a terrible sickness assails you, and because you know this you try to avoid the thought, but you cannot, it is with you. Then that too is gone, all pain, all desire, only a great emptiness is left, like the sky, like a well in drought, and it is now that the strength drains from your limbs, and you try to rise and find you cannot or to swallow water and your throat is powerless, and both the swallow and the effort of retaining the liquid tax you to the uttermost. (87-88)

Both the above-quoted passages tell volumes about the story of the farmers' poverty and suffering as well as their helplessness. They seem to have reconciled themselves to them with a stoical resignation. But the irony is made more poignant by the addition of pathos to it and its rendering with images and symbols making it more vivid and telling. Fear, hunger and despair have been personified as gluttonous demons always out to devour us. At another place the narrator says:

> We live by our own labours.

But in the total structure of the novel these various kinds of ironies look like imagistic variations upon its keynote, adjusting its degree up and down as called for by the aesthetic needs of the book.

Then there is irony in the tannery. At the outset, it let hope in the villagers as the wages they got here were higher than those in the field. Kunthi says to Rukmini:

> The tannery is a boon to us. Have I not said so since it began? We are no longer a village either but a growing town. Does it not do you good just to that of it?

This observation seems to be based upon a superficial view of the things. Perhaps that is why Rukmini replies:

> "Indeed no," said I, "for it is even as I said, and our money buys less and less. As for living in a town—if town this is—why, there is something I would fly from

> sooner if I could go back to the sweet quiet of village life. Now it is all noise and crowds everywhere, and rude young and dirty bazaars and uncouth behaviour, and man thinks of another but schemes only for his money."

This observation comes out true when Nathan and Rukmini go to town. Rukmini says:

> For in the town there were the crowds, and streets battened down upon the earth and the *filth* that men had put upon it [...]. (115) (Emphasis added)

Now, the word *filth* carries overtones of various other kinds of filth—social, moral and spiritual. The town is full of thieves and pick-pockets; the town people confuse and misdirect the simple villagers who go there; street urchins take to evil paths out of starvation; even temple, that is, the seat of Lord Himself, is not free from sinners. A lame man is pushed aside in a rush in the queue. The food that is served there as *prasad* in the evening is labelled by some as alms to the beggars, and the receivers get derision and taunt.

But there is greater evil, the evil of prostitution, which has been stated in an ironical way:

> He (customer) has gained his relief, she her payment, he merges carelessly into the human through consigning her back into the shadows where she worked or to the gaudy streets where she loitered. (16)

But even more important is the author's comment on this evil:

> Of the thousands of men in the village, in the town, perhaps another village, another town, one man unknown is the father: of the vast range of manhood, who is to say he was not of the unsound, the unclean? (Pungent irony). What care or safeguard is there when the consequences of one's act are hidden from one's thankful (irony) eyes, and the woman is one of the many, soft, desired, lost, forgotten! (16)

Here irony has the sting of Swift and Voltaire. It is a slap on the face of all the white-collared hypocrites who are the chief, though hidden, patrons of the evil of prostitution.

Now, to add pathos to irony, Ira, daughter of Nathan and Rukmini, is also forced to join this profession to save her brother dying from starvation. This, incidentally, reminds us of a very beautiful passage in Bhabani Bhattacharya's novel *He Who Rides a Tiger*. A famine has broken out in Bengal. To slake the thirst of their belly, some ladies are selling their body to slake the thirst of the customers.

> Two great hungers had struck the land of Bengal in the wake of war: the hunger of the masses of people uprooted from their old earth and turned into beggars, and the hunger of the all-owning few for pleasure and more pleasure, a raging fever of the times. Uprooted women with their own kind of hunger had to soothe the other hunger, had to cool the raging pleasure-fever with their bodies.[1]

Earlier also Nathan says: "Better to starve where we were bred than live here. Whatever happens, whatever awaits us, we must return (167).

Rukmini also passes a fine comment, "Wide, wide world but as narrow as the coins in your hand. Like a tethered goat, so far and no farther. Only money can make the rope stretch, only money" (167).

Here the irony is still more poignant. But the cause is the same—hunger. Kamala Markandaya has hurled irony at the high-ups of the society to shake them out of their complacency and hypocrisy. The same has been done by Bhabani Bhattacharya. His irony is sharper.

Nathan and Rukmini's going to town in search of their sons has Hardian notes of despair. After facing a lot of hardships, they reach the residence of their son only to learn that he has left the town years ago leaving his wife and two children to starve. Hope turning into despair! This has echoes of Hetty's search for Captan Donithorne only to learn that he has left with a regiment for some place in George Eliot's *Adam Bede.* Disappointed and broken, Nathan says:

Nathan: "I came because I was *forced,* and believing that my son lived here. Now he has gone none knows

	where. I must return to my youngest son, he will somehow support us."
Puli:	"Are you sure?" said the ruthless child (Puli). "You are too old to keep travelling up and down."
Nathan:	"At least I shall be where I was born and bred. This city is no place for me, I am *lost* in it [...] (177)." (Emphasis added)

They contain verbal overtones. *Lost,* yes! Truly, he has lost his all—his son, his daughter's honour, and is now going to lose his life itself.

These lines contain a note of disenchantment or disillusionment. Nathan had already reservations against the town. He says he was forced to go there. And we know what he got there.

But the greatest irony is that, like a huge python, the town gradually sucks away the very life of Nathan. This is an example of dramatic irony.

In *A Handful of Rice* Kamala Markandaya recurrently conceives of the town as a jungle. A jungle also suggests bestiality. But it is difficult to say which is more predatory—man or beast. That novel also contains this irony. What Nathan gets here Ravi gets there, at least to some extent.

No less ironic is the life of Nathan and Rukmini's daughter Irawady. "She is endowed with beauty. It will make up for a small dowry—in this case" said the old Granny about her. She is married in the month of June, supposed to be a propitious season for wedding. Her parents spent all their little saving in her marriage keeping nothing to make their hut waterproof or to secure the land from flooding. Now, mark the irony. That year the monsoon broke early with an evil intensity such as none could remember before. This causes a lot of loss to the poor farmers. Now, how can we say that Ira's marriage was done in a propitious season for wedding?

Another irony. Ira's husband returns her to her parents on the ground that she is barren, and gets another wife. But the later course of events shows that it is not Ira but her husband who has the defect.

This desertion brings Ira humiliation, for in the rural Indian society, a barren woman is looked down upon by other women. But that is not the end of it.

Seeing her brother dying from starvation, Ira finds no option but to sell her body. By this means she gets money, buys drugs and saves her dying brother. She is forced to accept it as a profession. In this process she gives birth to an albino child. Now, this poses a serious moral question. Is Ira a sinner? From the conventional point of view, she may be. But would she have been innocent if she had saved her chastity and allowed her brother to die? There have been several works on this theme. The standard opinion is that it is the vicious social system that is the real villain. What were the so-called custodians of public morality doing when Ira's brother was going to die?

Incidentally, it reminds us of Hardy's observations when Tess was being violated by Alec. "But, might some say, where was Tess's guardian angel? Where was the providence of her simple faith?" And further: "Why so often the coarse appropriates the finer thus, the wrong man the woman, the wrong woman the man, many thousand years of analytical philosophy have failed to explain to our sense of order."[2] What were the guardian angels of Ira doing? What were the goddesses of chastity doing? Such questions have been posed by novelists like Dostoevsky. This irony gives jolt to the complacency and hypocrisy of our society. This shows what beauty and marriage in a propitious (?) season have brought to Ira. It is an example of cosmic irony.

Another scene in this novel sharpens this irony. We care a lot for the dead but little for the living. It is a common feature in the Indian society that when a person dies, we perform his *Shraadh* with all the rites and ceremonies. We have no scruple in taking loans for it. Even those who paid no heed to him when he was alive show unusual love and respect for him when he is dead. One of the reasons has been stated by the author herself:

> Once a human being is dead there are no people enough to provide the lost decencies; perhaps it is so because only then can there be no question of further recurring assistance being sought. (123)

In the same passage the author passes a sarcastic comment:

> A man might drift to his death before his time unnoticed, but when he was dead beyond any care then at last he was sure of attention [...]. (123)

Now, in the symbolic scheme of the things, the irony lies in this that we spend so much to perform the death rites of the Granny, but nothing to save the life of a child dying for want of medical aid and Nathan, who dies by overworking for the sake of bread. Such ironies come under the heading of structural irony.

Then there are some minor ironies in this novel. Let us look at the character of Kenny, the English missionary doctor. A lot has been written on East-West encounter in Indian fiction in English, or, for that matter, in the entire Indian writing in English. The English are usually referred to as callous people who oppressed us in all possible ways. But Kenny is an exception. He truly loves and respects the Indians. He gives sound medical advice. He takes interest in solving the domestic problems of Rukmini. This naturally creates suspicion among the village folk, a usual feature of a backward Indian rural society. People hurl taunt at Rukmini that she is having affairs with Kenny.

Now, the irony lies in this that the alien is kind while the native cruel. People, in general, and zamindars, in particular, are always out to oppress and squeeze us. But a foreigner is doing such a noble, philanthropic work with a missionary zeal.

The end of the book also contains a subtle irony, which may escape our attention because of its brevity, through succinct. When Rukmini and Puli reach home with the dead body of Nathan, her children do not know that their father is now no more. On such an occasion people beat their hearts and shed torrents of tears. But here we find nothing of the sort.

> Do not worry, Selvam said, "We shall manage." There was silence, I struggled to say what had to be said. "Do not talk of it," he said tenderly,' "unless you must." "It was a *gentle* passing," I said. "I will tell you later." (Emphasis added) (189)

Now, it is to be noted what Selvam means by saying "Do not talk of it unless you must." The first possibility is that he knows that his father is now no more and that his mother will now tell him to take his father's place. He has already said, two lines earlier, "Do not worry, we shall manage." But the word 'must' contains an ambiguity. Perhaps he means to tell his mother that such things are said only to those sons who do not realize their responsibility. Another possibility may be Selvam's suggestion to his mother that such things are to be suffered and not to be uttered; for uttering lessens the grandeur of tragedy.

But what about Rukmini's concluding remark: "It was a gentle passing. I will tell you later!" What does the word 'gentle' denote or connote here? In this context it is a bit unusual. First, it may suggest that Nathan died without prolonged illness accompanied by groaning and crying, without traction, without heavy use of drugs and without asking for long and arduous attendance from friends or relatives, etc. Thus, here 'gentle' seems to be a synonym of 'peaceful.'

But on the previous page there is a passage which would shed more light on this passage. Nathan dies:

> And so I laid my face on his face and for a while his breath fell soft and light as a rose petal on my cheek, then he sighed as if in weariness and turned his face to me, and so his *gentle* spirit withdrew and the light went out in his eyes. (188)

Now, here the word *gentle* qualifies 'spirit.' The meaning, then, would be that a gentle spirit has passed away (from an ungentle world, perhaps) and thus death has been to him a kind of deliverance. This world is not meant for gentlemen.

The real irony lies here. This is an irony on the entire system—both human and divine.

But equally remarkable is the fact, that, though bereaved, Rukmini and her son do not give up. Nathan says: "We shall manage." It reverses irony itself. The word *manage* has wide connotations. Here it suggests, perhaps, rebuilding. That way it is an irony on irony itself. Death may try to undo us. But we will not allow death to do so. We shall fight with it with a heroic fervour. We shall try to rebuild from whatever is left. Here irony melts into the grandeur of tragedy. The flow of life passes through the alternate rhythm of peace–panic–peace. So shows Beethoven in the Fifth Symphony. Hegel called it 'reconciliation,' which we may understand as life's temporary dissonance resolved into harmony. Nietzsche called it "the reaffirmation of the will to live in the face of death and the joy of its inexhaustibility so reaffirmed." It also recalls Hardy's famous observation that the business of tragedy is to show the sorriness underlying the grandest thing and the grandeur underlying the sorriest thing. Here we find the grandeur of sorriness. It is found in Tess. It is found here in Rukmini. This is a different kind of irony. Here irony itself has been challenged gallantly.

This novel has often been compared with Pearl S. Buck's masterpiece *The Good Earth*. They do have some similarities, no doubt. *The Good Earth* also shows a life of suffering and struggle; leaving the village and going to town in search of bread during a famine; and the trial of million kinds. Its hero Wang Lung ultimately returns to his village and asks his children never to leave the land. But Wang Lung, at least on one occasion, uses unfair means. A battle is going to be fought between soldiers in the town and the approaching enemy. When the wealthy people in the town fled, the poor began to loot their property. Wang Lung got some money by threatening a rich fellow. His wife O-lan looted some jewels. But in *Nectar in a Sieve* neither Nathan nor Rukmini does anything of the kind. They prefer to suffer with tragic dignity. That is their irony. It will not be an exaggeration to say that in the world today honesty itself is a piece of irony.

A more profitable comparison would be with the novel *The Tree of Man* by the Australian Noble laureate Patrick White. This novel is also a saga of hard struggle and harrowing sufferings of a farmer. Here also the hero Stan Parker dies fighting with the adversities. On his death the author says:

> Amy Parker (Stan's wife) did not cry much because she had often visualized this event [...]. Whimpering a little for those remnants of love and habit that were clinging to her. Stan is dead. My husband. In the boundless garden." (478)[3] (The phrase 'boundless garden' connotes far.)

Their grandson Elsie takes the death as it is, paradoxically though. He writes a poem on life. "Then death is faintly credible because it is still smelling of life" (480).[4] The last lines of the book are:

> So that in the end there were the trees. The boy walking through them with the head drooping as he increased in stature. Putting out shoots of green thought. So that, *in the end, there was no end.* (480)[5] (emphasis added)

(The last sentence contains volumes and volumes.)

Here also the message is that death is not the end of life. Life is eternal, ever-flowing. There will be connections and disconnections. But there can also be re-connections. We need not lose heart. Our job is to go on trying and trying and trying.

This is a peculiar type of irony. It is an irony on irony itself. It is a challenge to the omnipotence of the irony of fate. The novel ends on a note of hope.

This brief survey tries to show in how many ways irony operates in this novel and how deftly the author has been able to use it to enrich the form and content of the novel.

NOTE

All the textual quotations are from Kamala Markandaya's *Nectar in a Sieve*, Jaico Books, 13 Jaico Impression, 1990.

REFERENCES

1. Bhattacharya, Bhabani. *He who Rides a Tiger,* Arnold-Heinemann. First Indian Edition, 1977, Ch. 5, 53.
2. Hardy, Thomas. *Tess of D'urbervilles.* London: Macmillan, 1954 (Ch. XI, 93).
3. White, Patrick. *The Tree of Man.* Penguin Books, 1956, 478.
4. White 480.
5. White 480.

13

Fasting, Feasting: A Study in Desires and Dreams (Un)Fulfilled

USHA RANI

Anita Desai has been mapping and marking the literary landscape of Indian writing in English for the last four decades with great success. She is a remarkable painter of moods and wills, of minds and hearts. Her latest novel *Fasting, Feasting* (1999), short-listed for the Booker's prize, adds yet another laurel to the already established versatile genius of Desai.

In many ways *Fasting, Feasting* is a continuation of her earlier themes such as: the pangs of loneliness, the silence pronouncing louder than speech, changing trends in filial ties and psychological concerns. But in certain other ways this novel presents a striking deviation from her earlier works both at thematic level and the structural level. For the first time in the fictional world of Anita Desai, the reader experiences a complete family atmosphere prevailing over the world of *Fasting, Feasting*. In almost all her earlier novels, the protagonists had to suffer the limitations caused by only single parent; the other parent either being expired, or ailing or estranged or being totally ineffective. In this novel the very influential presence of both the parents Mama–Papa, side-by-side makes a complete whole—not only physically but mentally also. Throughout the pages of the novel they remain Mama Papa, always together. They are hardly addressed by their names as if this is the only role in which they are living their lives. They never talk of individuality or separate identity. They always have similar views, identical expressions and their decisions too are always the same whether aired by Mama or Papa—they both form a single identity.

The ever reminding iron swing in the backyard of their house is symbolic of the meeting point of the time past, present and future. The past is revived, present is lived and thought of; and even future plans are made while sitting together on that swing side by side. The silent moments, conversation, serious discussions and even disagreements are loudly hinted at while sitting on that very swing.

Comparatively speaking the number of protagonists spread over the world of *Fasting, Feasting* is very limited. Mama Papa with their two growing daughters initially and then a son's entry quite late into the family form the typical Indian family with traditional mind and modern living. A few close relatives; some friends and well-wishers; some servants, few neighbours, etc., do make their appearance now and then sometimes directly and at other times indirectly. But most of the other personae are merely presented through the coloured glasses of these characters in absentia.

The main concern of the present paper is to focus on one particular aspect of the lives of these protagonists, *i.e.*, the dreams and desires of these people and how far they succeed in realizing them. Here the word dream refers to all those happy expectations, desires and ambitions of life about which these people constantly think and strive to realize them. As hope springs eternal in human breast, the present researcher firmly believes that it is only our hopes and dreams about the future which make our present life look bright and cheerful. However tough and rough our present may be, this future phenomena of dreams and ambitions always lend it a substantial strength to sustain all the ups and downs of life. The characters of *Fasting, Feasting* too are not any exception to this general rule. They all have their own individual dreams and desires. In the journey of their life, some of these dreams are fulfilled; some others are partially realized and many more simply dash to the ground leaving behind long trails of woes and sufferings.

In the present paper I shall be mostly dealing with the main protagonists of this novel only, *i.e.*, Mama Papa and their three beloved children.

First I shall discuss the world of Mama Papa—a single identity in the context of this novel. They know each other well, understand each other and always dance to the tune of the other partner. The writer informs us, "Of course, there were arguments between them, and debate. In fact, these occurred everyday, at the same hour—when ordering meals for the day. This could never be done without heated discussions" (14). There are moments of disagreements too but they are often reconciled mutually. Being a typical Indian family, whole attention of Mama Papa moves around their children. Initially Uma and Aruna, two daughters, are the chief concern of their life. Not a moment passes when Mama or Papa does not need the help of Uma—their first-born daughter. Uma who is neither very beautiful nor even good at studies often disappoints them in their hopes and expectations. After Uma the parents wanted a son. So when the second child in the family was expected, they were very sure of being blessed with a son. They even named it "Arun" which was later changed to Aruna when a baby girl was born actually.

When the girls were quite grown up, there were expectations in the family of another child, which made "Mama's eyes swollen with crime as she lay across her bed and wept. Papa scowled his concern and embarrassment [...] "(15). Finally, the son arrived. "Arriving home, however he (Papa) sprang out of the car [...] shouted the news [...]. Papa, in his elation, leaping over three chairs in the hall [...] his arms flung up in the air [...]. "A boy!" he screams, "A bo-oy! Arun, Arun at last!" (17). How aptly the writer expresses the joy of the father at his long desired dream being fulfilled. Their joy knew no bounds. Now nothing else was as important as their son—Arun. Even Uma noticed "how Mama and Papa looked upon Arun with an identical expression" (31).

"Arun's birth did not mean that Mama Papa were finally separated into two entities—Mama Papa—not at all; rather

Arun appeared to be the glue that held them together even more inextricably [...]" [30]. Both looked after Arun very cautiously—over-caring the boy—everything was to be done in a proper order. What is to be given to the boy to eat and at what time—though it was a different matter that the boy felt suffocated under the pressure and showed his reluctance by not eating those very items which were most insisted upon.

The boy started going to the school and Papa's dream of sending his son abroad grew very strong. Papa insisted on in the realm of home and family—"the education for his son; the best, the most, the highest, tutors came in a regular sequence, an hour allotted to each, for tuition in maths, in physics, in chemistry, in Hindi, in English composition [...]" [118]. Papa did not expect Mama to understand the importance of sending Arun abroad to study—the value of a foreign degree, the openings [...] the opportunities. "Perhaps Papa's memories of studying under the streetlights and of the painful beginning in dusty provincial courts filled him with this almost manic determination [...]. Was he fulfilling through Arun a dream he had had there under the streetlights, or in the shabby district courts?" [121]. Uma tried to find out but, "How could Papa admit he had unfulfilled dreams? That he had done anything less than succeed, totally?"

Arun remained all the time busy with Papa's dream at the centre, living merely a mechanical existence, and his face lost all expressions. After hard work and efforts when the dream of foreign education was fulfilled and "the letter of acceptance finally arrived, Papa [...] collapsed from sheer exhaustion [...] (he) was not even able to rise to a celebration [...]. He lay back weakly on the swing, his face grey [...] (121). Mama was sorrowing at the thought of Arun going away [...]." "Arun too read the letter. Uma watched and searched for an expression, of relief, of joy, doubt, fear, anything at all. But there was none. All the years of scholarly tests had worn down any distinguishing features Arun's face might once have had [...]. Not the hint of a smile, frown, laugh or anything: these had all been ground down till they had disappeared. This blank face now stared at the letter and faced another phase of his existence arranged for him by papa. With Arun gone, Papa retired, life was (now) confined more than ever to the veranda, the swing, the intermittent exchanges, the gaps between them longer and longer" (122).

Mama's–Papa's dreams about their daughters, Uma and Aruna too were partially fulfilled. From the parents' point of view their desire to see their daughters well settled in their family life was not fully realized. Uma and Aruna, the two daughters growing side by side in the same family are yet poles apart from each other. Their desires and ambitions too differ greatly. The simple and plain Uma, not very beautiful to look at is a very homely child. She is always at the beck and call of her Mama and Papa. She is always busy with one or the other errand of her parents. Whereas Aruna, her younger sister on the other side is very smart, shrewd, arrogant and full of self-confidence. Uma completely lacks self-confidence. The dreams and desires of Uma too are very simple and yet they remain mostly unfulfilled.

As a small child Uma is very fond of her school and her teachers in the Convent Public School. Though Mama never approved of her daughter's education in a public school, her Papa wanted her to get good education. But unfortunately Uma never proved to be an intelligent child. Frequent offs from her school and busy routine at home never left sufficient time for her studies. As bad luck would have it, "there was not a thing Uma put her hand to that did not turn to failure [...] over and over again she failed [...]. Her record book was marked red for failure [...]. She wept with shame and frustration" (21). And when baby Arun arrived in the family it was again poor Uma's education that suffered a severe set-back. After the birth of Arun Mama could not attend much to the household work. It was Uma who had to supervise everything going on in the kitchen and around. Even attending to the needs of the guests was mostly her responsibility. In addition she had also to look after the needs of her baby brother. In spite of her failure in the exams and all other responsibilities, she still desired to continue her studies. But Mama who herself was not highly educated did not approve of it. "You know you failed your exams again. You're not being moved up. What is the use of going back to school? Stay at home and look after your baby brother [...] I need your help, *beti*, she coaxed, her voice sweet with pleading. Uma wrenched her hand free" (21-22). All her pleadings and requests to continue her school went in vain. Finally her desire of going to school and getting education remains an unfulfilled dream.

Another simple desire of Uma too remains partially fulfilled. One distant aunt, widowed Mira *masi* frequently visits their home while entouring religious places. Enjoying specialities with Mira *masi* was a sheer joy for Uma as a child. And going out with her to the river or to the temple lured her very much. But her Papa did not approve of it. Even then Uma perfectly enjoyed the trip to the river with Mira *masi* which "Mama and Papa themselves did not permit their children; saying it was too hot, too dangerous, too dusty, too diseased, too crowded—in every way inadvisable" (43). But Uma enjoyed it while she "tucked her frock up into her knickers and waded in with such thoughtless abandon" (43). Very often she chokes with laughter [...] she has tears in her eyes. They run down her cheeks. When Uma grows up, there are talks about her marriage among relatives. Her specially made photograph is also sent around. Like all girls of her age, she also dreams of a happy married life and a secure home. The rich clothes are bought, the jewellery is made to order and other fineries are prepared. The first ever suitor who comes to see her, feels more interested in her younger sister Aruna than in Uma. Great hue and cry is made at home about this. Uma too feels upset, though she doesn't express to others. After great efforts twice, the marriage of Uma was settled. The first time it broke off after the engagement ceremony. The father of the boy had taken the advance dowry in cash at the pretext of building a home for their daughter (his daughter-in-law). But when Mama Papa went to settle the date for marriage, they were informed that the boy had decided to go to Roorkee for higher education and was no longer interested in marriage as yet. It was however found later, that they had earlier duped another family too on the same pretext. The desire of Mama Papa to marry off their elder daughter first was realized after sometime when a party from another city agreed to Uma's marriage proposal. The auspicious ceremony was performed at home. The relatives came and everyone thanked Uma's stars. But this time when Uma reached her in-laws' house she got very suspicious of their behaviour. Later on Papa learnt that the boy (Harish) was already married in another city and had four children. It was only to save his ailing pharmaceutical factory that he had married Uma. Mama Papa were very annoyed. Papa went and brought Uma back. After that they never tried to settle her again. Papa always kept on regretting two dowries, which he had to provide for Uma's marriage, and yet she was staying with them without any home of her own. On this front they failed miserably. Thus the dream of Uma for her own sweet home dashed to the ground. She could not help, but reconcile with her fate and be busy in the day-to-day work. Another simple desire of Uma's eyesight being checked by a specialist is resented very much. In this very case, though unwillingly Mama supports her saying that her eye's hurt and she should get a check-up. But when Papa explains the botheration of going to Bombay, all the way involving so much money, she too surrenders. When Aruna is married and Arun has gone abroad for higher education, another phase of Uma's life begins. She is to take dictation from Papa to write letters to Arun. With Papa's retirement she gets busier. She hardly gets any time to go out or enjoy some private moments by herself.

When Mama Papa go out for any social meeting or at the club, she finds a few moments to herself but even these are disturbed by the unwanted entry of others into her room. She prizes these precious moments when she is all by herself—she wants to enjoy the collection of her greeting cards and Christmas cards, she wants to relish the collection of her bangles, jewelry and rich clothes of her wedding days. But even these little desires are not fulfilled very often. Mama Papa keep on intruding in her privacy. They don't like her going out—they don't like her shutting herself in her own room. Poor Uma [...] if she is invited by her favourite teacher for a cup of coffee even that is not liked by Mama Papa. "Coffee? Why coffee?" asks Mama.

"Uma grows violent [...] 'Why? What is wrong?' [...] 'Stay home and do your work—that is best.' Mama opines with an air of piety" (114).

Uma's all attempts to get little joy are smothered by Mama Papa or her stars. When Aruna goes to settle in the metropolitan city of Bombay, Uma hopes to visit her and also to get her eyes checked up there by a specialist. But even her younger sister throttles her hopes saying, "Do you know how much expenditure will it all cost?" No need to go to Bombay when the opticians here can do the best. She often keeps on bullying and threatening Uma on one pretext or the other.

Still desires keep on raising their heads in Uma's heart and the circumstances keep on suppressing them in one way or the other. One day Dr Dutt approaches Mama Papa with a job for Uma in her medical institution and is greatly welcomed by Uma. The very mention of a job for her was "So thrilling and exciting as if it was being launched into the space" (142). The sheer excitement at the very thought of moving out of the house and a job thrills her so much that half the glass of squash sloshed onto the tray which she is bringing for Dr Dutt. She had "even added on extra spoon of sugar in that glass." But lo! Mama Papa do not approve of it. They do not like girls going out for job. Their daughter will never need to go out for earning her bread and with this refusal they finally close up the chapter of Uma's ever being able to move out of her home. All her pleas and pleadings fall flat on deaf ears. Even her attempt to call Dr Dutt for help stealthily, when Mama Papa were away, is found out when they find on return their telephone unlocked. Her crime was found out. Papa kept on grumbling, "Costs money! Costs money! [...] Never earned anything in her life, made me spend and spend on her dowry and her wedding [...] spend till I'm ruined, till I am a pauper [...]" (147).

Was he being cruel to Uma or cursing his own stars and bad luck, the reader has to guess himself/herself?

The hope of Uma to ever see and enjoy the company of Mira *masi* in future is also belied. She has gone to the Himalayas—where she lost her "Lord Gopal" and discovered it too as Lila aunty explains to Uma, and with that she has lost all hope of ever seeing Mira *masi* in her life. Thus the reader realizes that Uma is deprived of even the little joys of life. Even a few moments of privacy in her own room; little time to watch her collection of cards of her childhood days in peace and tranquillity are snatched away from her and she is not even allowed to go out either for work or enjoyment. This attitude of Mama Papa forces her to live her life in a very dull and drab manner.

Aruna, the second daughter of Mama Papa is a very self-assertive, obsessive and arrogant girl from the early childhood. She spurns Uma's docility and slavish nature. She knows what she desires and also knows how to get her desires fulfilled. She is smart, active and full of self-confidence. She keeps her body and mind always fresh and active. Her perfect manner of walking, talking and social delicacies impress others very much. She would not do any household work, would go out with friends, and see movies too. She often bullies and threatens Uma at times.

While Mama searched energetically for a husband for Uma, families were already 'making enquiries' about Aruna. "There were so many marriage proposals for Aruna that Uma's unmarried state was not only an embarrassment but an obstruction [...]. Mama watched and wondered, Papa humped and hawed and scowled [...]" (85). Finally Aruna brought off the marriage—the wisest, most expedient choice—the handsomest, the richest, the most exciting of the suitors who presented themselves. "The wedding was a splendid one—not like Uma's drab, cut-rate affair [...] an event so chic—and untraditional as had never been witnessed before in the town." Aruna happens to be the only protagonist in this hour whose almost all dreams and desires are fulfilled. "Soon Aruna was whisked away to a life that she had said would be 'fantastic' and was [...] it was 'like a dream' (fulfilled)."

Even after her marriage she visited her Mama Papa along with her in-laws. She would dictate everything. Not only her parents and sister, she dominated her husband also. Everything had to be done and presented in a perfect order till they stayed there. Even when she came with her children—Uma had to look after the tiny tots and Aruna would remain busy with her friends and outings. She even suggested Uma to cut her hair short, to visit a beauty parlour off and on and also use perfumes and deodorants. [Once Uma expressed her desire to visit Aruna in Bombay on the pretext of consulting an eye specialist. Aruna at once snubbed her very rudely. It would involve lots of efforts and money too, and what is the use of all this loss.]

Arun, the third child of Mama Papa made his entry quite late into the family. He had been named long back though when the second child was born. But when it actually happened to be a girl it was changed to Aruna instead. There was great excitement and joy at the birth of a son in the family. Mama's position too was raised highly and it was poor Uma who suffered the loss of her studies at the pretext of looking after baby Arun. In an anxiety to rear him up, the best possible way—the best health, the best education, the best life they all grow over-possessive of the boy. What would Arun wear and what would he eat, it was all decided by Papa. And poor child—the more Papa insisted on giving him eggs and meat the more Arun spurned these things and he turned out to be a pure vegetarian, thus the first desire of Papa about Arun ended in a smoke. Arun grew up according to his parents' desires. Which school he would go, what subjects he should study, which tutors to be engaged, what times to study and what times to play were all dictated by Papa.

From very early life, the freedom, the selection, the choice of Arun had been smothered and he never could enjoy any dreams or desires. It was only a mechanical existence that he was dancing to the tune of others, particularly Papa. Through Arun Papa wanted to fulfil his own desires and dreams of higher education and a foreign degree and a bright career. Arun became simply a means to provide satisfaction to Papa. When Arun was over exhausted with his tutors, studies, entrance exams and finally got admission in a foreign university—Papa too collapsed with exhaustion. Arun was disposed of to a foreign land.

In an alien land Arun stood bewildered. The cross-cultural problems cropped up. He had never seen so much freedom and so much stress in his own land. The poor child, who always had been dictated terms to, was to stand on his own feet now, had also to make his own decisions. Mama and Papa are busy in weaving their own dreams about Arun in a foreign university while Arun finds himself in a very critical situation there. His letters—eagerly awaited at home—are very small, formal and always complaining about the food there. Uma feels such letters could have easily been written from any local university too.

During summer break when the hostel is vacated, Arun's boarding arrangements is made with an Indian family settled there, The Pattons. Mr and Mrs Pattons welcome 'Ahroon' to their home. They try their best to make him feel comfortable but Arun feels very awkward. Mrs Patton tries to be over-caring, over friendly and even overbearing, which Arun resents in his heart. She often asks him 'I'm not fat—am I, Ahroon?' 'Or young,' she adds, 'am I? Ahroon? [...] Hi! Come and enjoy the sun? [...] the very idea appals Arun, if it means the bearing of flesh in public. He has never seen so much female flesh before [...].'

He does not know any cooking and Mrs Patton tries her best to prepare Indian food but that does not help Arun. He hates non-veg. all the time and Mrs Patton cooks only non-veg. at home. Even the Patton's children don't like his intrusion into their family. And Arun too passes his time with great difficulty. Finally the vacation is over. He goes very hesitatingly to Mrs Patton, 'I—uh—brought you some presents. I'm leaving now, Mrs Patton! [...] the semester starts tomorrow, [...]' I am packed. 'Please take these things—my parents sent them for you,' he lies, 'hoping they will never guess what happened to their gifts [...].' 'Why Ahroon' [...] this is just beautiful. Thank you, thank you [...]. He withdraws quietly [...].

Poor fellow, he did not even learn the meaning of any dream or desire and simply lived a mechanical existence.

Of course, the other characters in this novel such as Anamika, Mira *masi*, Ramu *et al.*, too have their share of dreams and desires and ambitions but as stated earlier, the main concern of this paper revolves around the close-knit family of Mama Papa and their three children.

NOTE

All quotes have been taken from *Fasting, Feasting*, Vintage Edition, 2000.

14

A Clash between Male Chauvinism and Existential Concerns in Anita Desai

DEVIKA

Anita Desai occupies a very specific position in Indian writings by female writers. Writing had a great fascination for her and she plunged into this art at the tender age of seven. Success became acquainted with her at the arrival of her maiden novel *Cry, the Peacock,* published in 1963. *Clear Light of Day* (1980), *The Village by the Sea* (1982), *In Custody* (1984), and *Fasting, Feasting* (1999) fuelled her into the arena of fame. In a long career spanning over couple of decades, Anita Desai like all the writers throughout the globe, is not far behind in her endeavour to unravel the imbroglio in which human beings are caught. In her pursuit to find out the true meaning of existence she makes her characters her mouthpiece. Her characters are beset by the existential dread to such an extent that all of them directly plunge into this abyss to get at least an inkling of the affairs of life. The question 'What does it mean to exist?' sets them at fire with the varying intensity. The uneasiness of *how* comes much later and remains in background. Like Robert Browning, she gets deep into the psyche of her characters and unscrambles their true nature lacerated by the forces of self, family, as well as society. She continues oscillating between two extremes, that is, her fascination for life and her infatuation for death. Her concerns with the issue of life and death put her in the tributary of those writers who show the existential anxiety and are on their way to trace the meaning of *existence*. Anita confesses, "Writing is my way of plunging to the depths and exploiting the underlying truth. All my writing is an effort to discover, and to underline and convey the true significance of things" (Dalmia 4).

She attempts to portray in her works the complexity of themes—Indian sensibility, the quest of self-assertion, and the status of women in this patriarchal social set-up. Her omphalos theme is the existential predicament embedded in the social milieu where males and females are shown in contrastive terms—males being the ruler, females being ruled over. Her protagonists get swayed by this problem of loneliness, alienation, and pessimism. But existential concerns are quite different in Anita Desai; she weaves her web which includes only "the mad or bad [...], the shocking, the sordid or the obscene" (Grene 1). Her chief concern is human relationships.

In her works existential conflict sprouts from self's craving for the fulfilment. Moreover, her female characters are beleaguered by males as well as the norms of society finalized by them. The struggle of her characters gets a distorted shape because of this shift in focus. In her very first novel, *Cry, the Peacock* Anita Desai astounds the readers by the neurotic behaviour of her heroine Maya whose integrity is fast dissolving under the pressures of so many things, especially because of her marriage with a person of not emotional but intellectual sensitivity. Crumbles of the dilapidated relationship are brought to the fore with the incident of the death of her dog, Toto:

> And I thought of the long journey of the dead from birth into another, the brave traversing of mute darkness, the blind search for another realm of lucidity in the midst of chaos. And I looked down again, and fingered one softpetalled flower, a white one. Small white Toto, whining a little out of fear, his futile barks dying away into a hopeless silence. Small white Toto, small white corpse into the blaze of the sun abandoned. 'I shall miss him so—Gautama!' I cried then, the confession tearing out of me in a stormy rush and even as I wiped away my quick tears, and wept more, I cried to myself, what is the use? I am alone.[1] (Desai 24-25)

Maya regards this incident as cataclysmic whereas for Gautama it's a natural incident because death is an intrinsic part of life. For Maya the line between realism and illusion gets extenuated; she feels free to put the blame on her husband for all the vicissitudes. She feels the pangs of isolation pushing her towards defunct part of life, which she does not want to lead. The distressing conflict between external and internal forces accentuates her sufferings. It appears to Maya that her life is shaped by males; when unmarried, her father had remained the source of strength to her as she says:

> As always happened to me, it was after my most anguished moments that a piece of truth fell into my exhausted mind—the truth [...] my gentle father who would have said to me, with assured and reassuring calm, 'It will all be well, it will all be well soon, Maya.' He had often to hold me in his arms, or, when I was smaller, wash the tears from my face, and repeat those mesmerizing words to me in his deep tones. (59-60)

After the death of her mother her father has brought her up as a toy princess in a toy world. She has had a sumptuous feast of life and is never exposed to life but always kept away from it. She forgets the prophecy of that albino astrologer that either she or her husband will die in the fourth year of her marriage only to remember it in the fourth year of her marriage. The novelist attempts to establish the queer psyche of her protagonist by showing her over-sensitiveness. Married to Gautama, she gets no satisfaction or fulfilment in her relationship because she thinks her husband is emotionally indifferent to her. She feels sexually starved, emotionally enervated, and intellectually overfed; she expects emotional and physical satisfaction in her married life but gets cold intellectuality and insensitivity from her husband. Maya's longing for sensuous pleasures gets neglected to such an extent that she is befuddled. Her emotional demands are always quelled by the analytical approach of her husband. As for love is concerned, it seems to her that he just makes her feel disgusted with herself for not making an impact on him despite her beauty. Her unrequited love drives her crazy and she is forced to feel terribly appalling on this account; she wishes her husband to make her the centre of attention and think only about her:

> But then he knew nothing that concerned me. Giving me an opal ring to wear on my ringer, he did not notice the translucent skin beneath, the blue flashing veins that ran under and out of the bridge of gold and jolted me into smiling with pleasure each time I saw it. Telling me to go to sleep while he worked at his papers, he did not give another thought to me, to either the soft, willing body or the lonely. Wanting mind that awaited near his bed. (9)

Maya is desirous of leading a contented life, taking in her stride all the pleasures that a marriage offers. Her longing for all these pleasures remains unfulfilled because of her husband—be it physical pleasures or the desire to see a dance because she thinks that it's the job of her husband to provide her all the pleasures. Despite her frustrations she rarely finds herself blessed with even an iota of any realization that could bring her any satisfaction; she remains tethered to the fragmentary life with her husband. She expects her husband to do things for her whereas she does not exhibit the composure of her friend Leila who selflessly serves her tuberculosis-affected husband. Her life becomes grimy and grubby. Harassed by her unfulfilled desires she continues roaming directionless filled with all the negative emotions reaching nowhere.

She feels angry to realize that she is dying in tits and bits. First her father has shown her the path and now it's the turn of her husband to treat her like a kid and lead her ahead. No doubt, she is stupefied when Gautama tries to tell her: "You are a grown woman now, Maya, no light-headed child. You must not allow yourself to grow so upset about these things [...]. There is nothing constructive in your misery, after all. Besides, your life is your own, so different from theirs—your world completely separate" (76-77). The same message her father had wished to convey to her that she should learn to face life on her own sans banking on others to support her every now and then:

> One must—and he dropped his voice—'accept.' In his eyes there appeared a vision of the life he had accepted when he had inherited it, with its luxuries and its responsibilities, its demands and inhibitions [...]. But then he turned to smile at me, there was all the pain of parenthood upon his lips, chastening and subduing. 'Is that so difficult to see. Maya?' (62-63)

However, she fails to understand what her father and husband want her to understand and continues suffering because of her loneliness. Gradually, her angst corrodes herself. The 'poor Maya' (104) remains upset but is contented to stink; realization does not depend only on physical activities. She roughly tries to get involved in the inner journey that can show her some light of awakening but the intangible affairs of life crush her spirits.

Though Maya is given a mythological name, she hardly stands as the incarnation of those glorified values; she is shown as a common woman who like all normal human beings is caught in the labyrinth of life. She is not totally secluded from the social or familial ties of her life. Instead she is entangled into the complexity of affairs so much that she finds it hard to snap these ties and helplessly continues to be smothered. The injustice and humiliation she faces sound vague because except accusing her husband and longing for her father's company, she does nothing creative that could lead her ahead on the path of realization. Instead she plunges deep into stygian glum to accuse males and the society set by their whims and norms.

Like many other characters of Anita Desai who are always shrouded in the pale of gloom looking at life from a distance where life seems quite out of their reach, Maya feels the same kind of uneasiness as she longs for breaking the shackles but tries in an awkward way to come out of her carapace that is hindering her view of life. Her present sort of existence haunts her to the brim of insanity but virtually her quest for something more real and more substantial is so lackadaisical that it lacks the power to push her towards some enlightenment. Existence itself seems vague to her because it seems to her that she is deprived of the involvement into the affairs of life by her husband. She expresses her wish to see the Kathakali ballets:

> 'I want—I want,' [...] 'to see the Kathakali dances. I have heard of the ballets they have in their villages [...]. And the dancers are all men, [...].' The masks they wear—you must have seen them? And their costumes. And the special kind of music. And it is all out in the open, at night, by starlight—and perhaps they have torches. (42-43)

When she wants to go to the South to see the performance of Kathakali dancer, her husband wants her to wait till the troupe comes to Delhi. She wants to go there to make her life a bit active and she wants Gautama to help her enjoy the ecstasies of life. Gautama doesn't tread on the path of life along with her; to make the matters worse she is deprived of the greatest bliss on the part of woman, *i.e.*, being a mother. Her barrenness also indicates that she is not a complete woman; she misses the contentment and bliss of motherhood, another death of one of her parts.

The institution of marriage is considered the root cause of all the dilemmas, which may sound plausible but lacks conviction when only marriage and males are held responsible for the vacuum prevalent in the lives of women. Anita tries to study the inner life of her characters but she never allows them to forget about their social and familial ties. Similarly Maya suffers because she is supposedly bound to lead her life with a person who seems to her ignorant of the fine feelings so common to women. She hinges on the age-old tradition that a male can save her soul "Father! Brother! Husband! Who is my saviour? I am in need of one" (112).

Males seem to stand in between her and her destination. Instead of considering her life and marriage a journey she considers it a game and gives her piece of mind when she utters: "One of us will win, the other must lose" (131). It is male characters in her works who give a reasonable view of life; they seem to understand life in a better perspective. Her husband makes it clear when he says: "Life is a fairy tale to you still. What have you learnt of the realities? The realities of common human existence, not love and romance, but living and dying and working, all that constitutes life for the ordinary man" (132). Through Maya, Anita tries very hard to give the touch of ferocious assaults of existence but falls short of the reader's expectation when she presents a world that is incomplete and fragmentary full of nothing but vagueness. Her leading characters are almost sick of life; they are highly sensitive to the point of distortion and solitary to the point of being neurotic. She deals with the inner trauma of human beings in her novels, an attempt never attempted before her, but does not convince because of her blind accusation of males. In her very first novel she gives the right to her protagonist to blatantly lambaste the males for her miserable plight.

She wants to live life and considers her husband a hindrance as per the fulfilment of her desires and dreams are concerned. She considers her tie with her husband the root cause of all her miseries; existence to her is merely related to her relationship with her husband. Like a woman wronged by her husband she puts all the blame on her husband and though unconsciously, she probably wishes to kill her husband to remove him from her life because she feels that it is he who always stops her from living life the way she desires. Here the existential concern is merely related to the males in her life. Ultimately she does what she has always desired, that is, she kills her husband so that he can't meddle with her life any more:

> And then Gautama made a mistake—his last, decisive one. In talking, gesturing, he moved in front of me, thus coming between me and the worshipped moon, his figure an ugly, crooked grey shadow that transgressed its sorrowing chastity. 'Gautama!,' I screamed in fury, and thrust out my arms towards him, out at him, into him and part him, saw him fall then, pass through an immensity of air, down to the very bottom. (208)

Though her life comes to an end yet her journey remains incomplete because her realization remains materialistic and nebulous. Concerned as Anita is with the inner world, her arena includes travails and turmoil, apprehensions and uncertainties, obscurities and shadows, joys and sorrows, ups and downs, impasses and imbroglios, confusions and mysteries, etc. in the life of her characters against discriminating social set-up. Their grapple with vagaries of life brings forth their struggle to find out their identities. Her attempt to delineate the inner turmoil against social backdrop has largely expatiated the thematic horizon of Indian works but her lacunae spoil the worth of her attempt as is clear from Dr S.P. Swain's observation regarding her work:

> Her major novels tend to disappoint the reader due to their one-dimensionality, turning the characters wooden and insensitive. They are not kaleidoscopic in their thematic projection. In most of them there is a repeated and droll harping on the isolation of the self. However, they are deeply moving in their existential and socio-psychic import. Microcosm of man's endless struggle for survival, they voice the anguished ennui of the caged bird that symbolizes the modern man. Emblems of remonstrance and psychic protest, they strive for the protection and preservation of their dignity and self-esteem in a patriarchal society. (Swain 1999: 253)

The same type of stream is evident in the life of Sita, the heroine of *Where Shall We Go This Summer?* She is fed up the way she leads her life; along with other innumerable forces she finds her husband and the institution of marriage the root cause of all her problems. The inability on the part of her husband to understand her and her stance of life disturbs her to such an extent that she plans to move away from her husband to lead life independent of him. However, her husband fails to consider it a very good decision because he feels that she is getting averse to her responsibilities:

> She had escaped from duties and responsibilities, from order and routine, from life and the city, to the unlivable island. She had refused to give birth to a child not fit to receive the child. She had the imagination to offer it an alternative—a life bewitched.[2] (139)

She goes to the island that promises her an idyllic existence but her hopes of golden life get thwarted there. She gets befuddled by the lack of facilities there. She comes back with her husband not because she has realized something sublime or her husband has started thinking the way she wishes him to be but because in the absence of certain luxuries she is wont to, she cannot live there. Her existential quest gets blurred because she finds her husband standing in between her and her journey—a belief that lacks conviction. Her estrangement from her husband does not initiate her on an inner journey. Even when on her own she feels out of joints and instead of moving ahead she undertakes a spiral route, only to tread on the trodden path.

In *Where Shall We Go This Summer?* Anita tries to show the anxiety of Sita who suffers because of her biased attitude towards life. Like Maya she is also over-sensitive and finds herself confined in the urban life after leading a carefree life in rural area under the aegis of her father. The artificialities, fast pace, and harshness of city life nauseate her to such an extent that she longs to go back to the island where she has cherished all the delicacies of rural life and where she thinks her roots are. After being taken away from her sister and father she senses the void in her life. Lack of roots makes her insecure as well, and she finds everything wrong with the attitude of her husband:

> He had nothing more to give her, or he was just unaware of her needs and demands. He raised his hand and stroked Karan's hair with a gentleness she herself ached to attract, and stared at him, bored into him with her eyes, wanting and not being given what she wanted. (132)

She wishes acceptance from her husband but her expectations are rather too high like Maya. Both the ladies wish their husbands to treat and pamper them like their fathers whereas both the males are pragmatic in their approach leaving no space for idiosyncrasies. But the ladies fail to realize this and continue accusing their husbands though the intensity varies.

Sita hates her husband for not understanding her and dislikes her kids for being like their father—practical and insensitive. The way she starts reacting to the situation around her even puts her kids off. When she starts shooting the crows with the pop-gun of her son to save the innocent birds from falling a prey to the crows, her daughter notices her doing so and finds it quite disgusting:

> Menaka, coming home from a visit to a friend, stopped on the balcony to stare at the odd figure of her mother standing at the rails, firing Karan's pop-gun at the furious band of crows. She watched for a while, in astonishment, then pressed her lips together and went away without asking for an explanation—her mother had before arranged, created wilfully such acts of drama purely, Menaka maintained, to embarrass her family. This, she thought, closing her bedroom door, was another. (26-27)

She is set off by the type of existence human beings lead: "They are nothing [...] nothing but appetite and sex. Only food, sex and money matter, Animals" (47) but what does she herself do to do something better? She goes to the island with two of her kids but finds life unbearable there because she also needs the comforts of home that she does not find there. Her escape to the utopian island leads her nowhere and finally she returns with her husband to the city. However, Anita Desai does not allow her characters to undertake the spiritual journey that shows them the path to sublime enlightenment as well as lofty realization. She allows her characters to move only in a restricted sphere from where they cannot move out, no matter however hard they try.

In fact, she presents a world in which wronged women are desperate to assert their liberty and individuality. They want to establish themselves as individuals without any support from males or rather they consider only males the root cause of their plight. Her female protagonists strongly react against chauvinistic males as well as patriarchal society—in which they exist. Whatever injustice is meted out to them, they shout very loudly in rather harsh terms; in their endeavour they fail to present a convincing portrayal of the affairs. The dilemma of identity crisis becomes a hollow cry in her works because the treatment given to her characters is somewhat short of conviction. The world she aspires for in her works is hazy and the harmony though desired desperately is seldom achieved as Suman Bala and D.K. Pabby (2002) in their introduction to *The Fiction of Anita Desai* express similar views:

> The world of Anita Desai's novels is an ambivalent one; it is a world where harmony is aspired but often not achieved; and the desire to live life fully with proper zeal and love, clashes, at times violently, with the desire to withdraw and keep inwards. Instinct, emotion and passion appear to be strangers in the world of sordid daily routine.

However, in *In Custody* and *Baumgartner's Bombay,* she spares women the atrocities meted out to them by males; here Anita has made males the protagonists and tries to depict existential concerns from their point of view which even sounds convincing. But her latest work again focuses on the same kind of life—making women victims and males superior and ultimate authority. It suggests that she is moving in a circle only, highlighting the sufferings of women at the hands of males. Her latest novel *Fasting, Feasting* is no exception.

Fasting, Feasting is supposed to be a very sensitive story unveiling the human values through her characters, namely, Uma, Aruna, Arun and the Patton family. The first part covers the life of Uma and her family whereas the second part deals with the life of Patton family; the binding link is Arun. Uma is the pivotal figure who sees life in its iridescent sheen and observes how others live through it. In the first section Uma presents life the way she perceives; her parents lead life of twins not because they love each other to such a great extent but because the father has completely overshadowed the mother though it is a pity that he himself had nothing specific to cling to. "MamandPapa, MamaPapa, PapaMama. It was hard to believe they had separate existence, that they had been separate entities and not MamaPapa in one breath"[3] (Desai 5).

Anita quite deftly puts her vision of life in which though woman does not remain in the background yet she is quite lacklustre when put beside male. Her father rules over her mother in a subtle way where he leaves no space for her mother except the mundane affairs. He makes her his spokesperson for those affairs, which he considers trivial enough. Important matters are always to be decided by the father. When one speaks the other remains quiet because one speaks for both:

> If Papa gave his opinion of their local member of parliament or the chances of the government in the next election, Mama said nothing because he had spoken for her too. When Mama spoke of the sales at which she planned to buy towels or of the rise in the price of silver that made her wonder if it was time to sell her plate, Papa made assenting grunts because his thoughts were one with hers. Their opinion differed so rarely that [...] there was no point in appealing to the other parent for a different verdict: none was expected or given. (13-14)

If there is difference of opinion at all then their stand is decided keeping in mind the matter; if it does not affect Papa much then mother is given the liberty to decide but if it is something important then Papa is to decide and Mama is expected to stick to it. Her father's right to decide on the part of her mother to give birth to the baby who may turn out to be a boy because he wants a boy is given preference; it bothers him the least whether his wife desires that late pregnancy or not. "He (Papa) had not only made her his wife, he had made her the mother of his son. What honour what status [...]. She had matched Papa's achievement, you could say, and they were now more equal than ever. Was that love? Uma wondered disgustedly, was this romance?" (13).

Her mother is forced to lead a life that suits her father; her decisions are brushed away when it does not suit the whims of her father. The father remains the hub of all the activities and when the son is born he becomes the focal point of the life of his parents. His father more than his mother wants to fulfil all his dreams through his children and especially his son. Consciously or unconsciously Anita Desai holds man responsible for all the vicissitudes that occur in the life of females, as is clear from her depiction of Uma's father. Her heroines or the females in her works suffer because of this male element in society as is clear from the life of Uma.

The role of nature and society is very dim in her works; society just disappears into the thin air after setting her characters into a specific situation. Hereafter her characters lead life accordingly independent of the forces of society. More or less she points her finger towards males who lead a privileged life wholly denied to females. However hard Anita may try, she finds herself inextricably intertwined in her concept of gender bias, which spoils her worth as a writer. Uma, the heroine of his latest novel, is always denied in her life whatever she longs for or wishes to obtain, be it her desired lover Ramu, the world of nuns, or the gamut of knowledge and ultimately she is forced to lead a life which denies her any freedom except the boundary of household.

Uma is shown as a simple girl cherishing the desire to lead a life that fascinates her. She is bestowed with nothing in her life and ultimately is forced to lead a life amidst the four walls of the house. She is an utter failure as per the norms of society are concerned; she never masters the art of housekeeping; she is very plain looking girl; and above all in the case of her marriage she is held responsible for bringing disgrace to the name of her family. She suffers a lot because of males in her life as marriage proposals are concerned. The very first suitor shows interest in her younger sister, Aruna. Second time she gets engaged but the male snips off the ties. Ultimately she is married off at the third attempt only to realize that her husband is already married. After being humiliated by so many males she stays always with her parents and marriage is never thought of again.

Next in turn is her father; when alone and wronged, she needs the support of her parents but she just does not get it from even her parents, those who should support and encourage her at the every cross of life. The proposal to work at a local hospital comes as a whiff of fresh air but is whisked away by her parents because her father considers it below their dignity to let his daughter work somewhere. It is none of his concern to think of his daughter's welfare; only marriage is considered the noble way of living for women by her parents. Whatever others think of her, she is provided with the ability to see through the affairs of life and displays the sensitivity to comprehend them also: "The tightly knit fabric of family that had seemed so stifling and confining now revealed holes and gaps that were frightening" (86).

Her sister Aruna presents a complete contrast to Uma; she hasn't required instructions for carrying herself with élan or about the cooking stuff or anything else in her life; "instinctively, she knew" (85) except the most important thing in life, that is, how to live and enjoy life without giving way to trivial things. As her stance makes it clear she leaves no chance to live according to the standards of life set by her parents. "As was to be expected, she took her time, showed a reluctance to decide, played choosy, but soon enough made the wisest, most expedient choice—the handsomest, the richest, the most exciting of the suitors who presented themselves" (100). She is considered lucky in comparison to Uma because she has everything in her life that is considered important in society but Uma realizes that she is leading an insipid life which has nothing substantial inside it:

> Was this the realm of ease and comfort for which Aruna had always pined and that some might say she had attained? Certainly it brought her no pleasure; there was always a crease of discontent between her eyebrows and an agitation that made her eyelids flutter, disturbing Uma who noticed to it. (109)

Marriage is considered an end of the road for girls whereas Arun is given altogether different treatment. Proper care is taken of him until he becomes a full-grown male, strong enough to take the reins in his hands. He is never allowed to go astray and his father husbands the choices he is supposed to make in his life. Arun does not like non-vegetarian food much to the chagrin of his father. Nor does he display the mannerism of elite, dashing all the hopes of his father to ground, which his father can't bear at all. "Papa was deeply vexed" (33). Neither is he blessed with an athletic physique as he is always in the grip of diseases like mumps, measles, chickenpox, bronchitis, malaria, flu, asthma, nose-bleeds, etc. His life gets crumbled under the pressures of books though he makes one of his father's dreams come true when he wins a place at an East Coast College in the US. Uma helplessly watches the proceedings. It is only she who understands the essence of life; she senses that like Aruna, Arun is also not able to hold things in his grasp:

> She [Uma] watched and searched for an expression, of relief, of joy, doubt, fear, anything at all. But there was none. All the years of scholarly toil had worn down any distinguishing features Arun's face might once have had. They had left the essentials: a nose, eyes, mouth, ears [...]. There was nothing else—not the hint of smile, frown, laugh or anything they had disappeared. (12)

But the treatment meted out to him is for altogether different reason. The parents want him to be blessed with good manners, physique and intelligence so that one day he becomes strong enough to handle his responsibilities in a better way. They are just trying to make him a good and promising male who will one day be the head of the family.

Right now, he finds solace into isolation from the tumult of life and feels contented to remain away from glaring gazes. He has his share of realization as Uma has hers though of different nature and depth. "[...] he had at last experienced the total freedom of anonymity, the total absence of relations, of demands, needs, requests, ties, responsibilities, commitments. He was Arun. He had no past, no family and no country." Being a male member he is allowed to enjoy this freedom. When he goes abroad to study his father arranges for him to stay with Pattons so that he may have the comforts of home. Here, he is given the same kind of treatment that sets him off as his father does when he is with his parents. Mrs Patton showers love on him to such an extent that Arun starts feeling uneasy and is reminded of his family:

> Arun was overcome by the sensation of his family laying its hands upon him, pushing him down into a chair at his desk, showing a textbook under his nose, catching that nose and making him swallow cod-liver oil, spooning food into him, telling him: Arun, this, Arun, that, Arun, nothing but [...]. (175)

Anita Desai seems to suggest that there is no escape from the affairs of life. Ladies have their share of responsibilities and males have their share of rights. When Arun goes abroad he feels relieved because he hopes that the change of place may change the nature of life as well. The realization is quite poignant for Arun when he starts feeling that it remains the same everywhere:

> No, he had not escaped. He had travelled and he had stumbled into what he had known at home; not the real thing which was plain, unbeautiful, misshapen, fraught and compromised—but the unreal thing—clean, bright, gleaming, without taste, savour or nourishment. (185)

Gradually Arun commences realizing that there is no escape for anyone, be it his family or some other one. Like his family, Arun notices, Pattons also lead life the same way pestered by somewhat similar anxieties. Mr Patton reminds him of his father, especially when he is disturbed; then Arun notices "[...] his father's expression, walking off denying any position, any challenge to his authority [...]." Their health freak son, Rod is just the opposite of Arun, insensitive to the needs of his mother and indifferent to his sister's problems. His sister Melanie is the reflection of Arun's sister Uma who frets and fumes because she is not given the required attention and her anguished soul cries, "[...] against misunderstanding, against inattention to her unique being and its hunger, merely splits and froths in ineffectual protest" (214).

Being a novelist who is concerned with the existential problems Anita succeeds to create the aura but fails to clarify it. Her characters do not gratify the whims of the readers; they lack conviction as is clear from the case of Mr Patton, Mrs Patton, Rod as well as Melanie. Similarly, Arun's father, mother, and his sister Aruna do not leave an indelible print on the mind of readers except Uma who has realized that life is this way only:

> When she had plunged into the dark water and let it close quickly and tightly over her, the flow of the river, the current, drew her along, clasping her and dragging her with it. It was not fear she felt, or danger. Or rather, these were only what edged something much darker, wilder, more thrilling, a kind of exultation—it was exactly what she had always wanted, she realized. (111)

Uma who is considered the disgrace of the family is the only character in this novel who has the realization of the affairs of life; she may have failed as a daughter, as a sister, as a student, as a cook, as a lady, but she wields the most desired thing in life, that is, realization. She is blessed with the vision to comprehend the complexities and perplexities of this inexplicable affair, that is, life. As Anita Desai puts it "the murky water catches the blaze of the sun and flashes fire" (156).

To recapitulate, Anita Desai attempts to limn the existential concerns that are so common to humanity. She chooses her characters that are under stress and tries to peep inside their psyche and come up with an explanation of their actions. All her characters have existential pangs and they are on a spree to find out the root cause and reach at some sort of realization to complete their cycle of search of life. But in her works this existential journey is spoiled by the advent of males into the lives of females and the shift mars the impact of her existential concerns. The male characters act as a stymie in the women's process of finding their self and reaching at some sort of realization. In Anita's fictional world it is the males who rule over these women; they hold the reins of all the females in their family and this spoils the efforts on the part of women to find out on their own the core of life. Instead of being concerned with their journey into one's inner self, the women in her works are obsessed with only one thing, that is, how to get out of the clutches of these males or this institution of marriage. The clash between Anita's existential concerns and male chauvinism in the society assuages her intensity as a writer because this presentation somewhat falls short of conviction.

NOTES

1. All the subsequent references for *Cry, the Peacock* have been taken from the same edition of the book hereafter cited, within the text along with page numbers.
2. All the subsequent references for *Where Shall We Go This Summer?* have been taken from the same edition of the book hereafter cited, within the text along with page numbers.
3. All the subsequent references for *Fasting, Feasting* have been taken from the same edition of the book hereafter cited, within the text along with page numbers.

WORKS CITED

Bala, Suman and D.K. Pabbay. Eds. *The Fiction of Anita Desai.* New Delhi: Khosla Publishing House, 2002.

——. "Introduction." *The Fiction of Anita Desai.* Eds. Suman Bala and D.K. Pabbay. New Delhi: Khosla Publishing House, 2002.

Bhatnagar, Manmohan K. and M. Rajeshwar, Eds. *The Novels of Anita Desai: A Critical Study.* Delhi: Atlantic Publishers and Distributors, 2000.

Bhatnagar, Manmohan K., Ed. *Feminist English Literature.* New Delhi: Atlantic Publishers and Distributors, 1999.

Dalmia, Yashodhara. "An interview with Anita Desai," *The Times of India,* 29 April 1979, 4.

Desai, Anita. *Cry, the Peacock.* New Delhi: Orient Paperback, 1980.

——. *Fasting, Feasting.* London: Chatto & Windus, 1999.

——. *Where Shall We Go This Summer*! New Delhi: Orient Paperback, 1982.

Grene, M. *Introduction to Existentialism.* The University of Chicago: Chicago UP, 1950.

Oliver, Pamela. "Victims and Survivors in the 'Sugar-Sticky Web of Family Conflict': A Reading of Anita Desai's *Fasting, Feasting.*" *The Novels of Anita Desai: A Critical Study.* Manmohan K. Bhatnagar and M. Rajeshwar, Eds. Delhi: Atlantic Publishers and Distributors, 2000, 247-55.

Rao, B. Ramachandra. *The Novels of Mrs Anita Desai.* New Delhi: Kalyani Publishers, 1977.

Swain, S.P. "Note of Existentialism in Novels of Anita Desai." *The Novels of Anita Desai: A Critical Study.* Manmohan K. Bhatnagar and M. Rajeshwar, Eds. Delhi: Atlantic Publishers and Distributors, 2000, 164-71.

——. "Tradition and Deviation—A Study of Anita Desai's Novels." Manmohan K. Bhatnagar, Ed. *Feminist English Literature.* New Delhi: Atlantic Publishers and Distributors, 1999, 253-79.

15

The God of Small Things: A Note on Roy's Sociological Imagination

ASHWINI KUMAR VISHNU

The God of Small Things is a "moving novel."[1] Critics across countries are bedazzled by its virtuosities as also shocked by its daringly telling tone. I'm not going to iterate host of those opinions here as my intention is to be as much unembellished and forthright in my approach as possible. I should, however, mention the name of Professor C. Wright Mills here whose book *The Sociological Imagination* has provided me with a particular tool for an assessment of the novelist's narrative skill.

Imagination plays an integral role in all artistic endeavours. Aesthetes and theorists down the ages have acknowledged its agentship in man's conscious responses to the world: visible and invisible. Doubtless to say, it has affixed the place of pride among other faculties that make a person an artist; an artist, a skilled craftsman; and a skilled craftsman, an authentic voice for times to come. Many things can be said in this line. At this juncture, appropriate as it will be, let me say a few things about the sociological imagination.

According to Professor Mills, the sociological imagination is "a quality of mind that seems most dramatically to promise an understanding of the intimate realities of ourselves in connection with larger social realities. It is not merely one quality of mind among the contemporary range of cultural sensibilities—it is the quality whose wider and more adroit use offers the promise that all such sensibilities—and in fact human reason itself—will come to play a greater role in human affairs."[2] It is "the capacity to shift from one perspective to another—from the political to the psychological; from examination of a single family to comparative assessment of the national budgets of the world; from the theological school to the military establishment; from considerations of an oil industry to studies of contemporary poetry. It is the capacity to range from the most impersonal and remote transformations to the most intimate features of the human self—and to see the relations between the two."[3]

It is not too difficult to infer the inmost meaning of Mills' words. What he means to say is that the sociological imagination is that active principle in mind that undergirds all cultural sensibilities. Nothing concerned with the individual and the world, out-circumferences it—be it science, philosophy, psychology, politics, theology or the welter of routines like waste disposal. It is that potent dimension of mind that capacitates an artist to absorb, analyze and reincarnate the physio-social, the bio-social and the psycho-social environment of man.

For Roy-like authors of our times, the importance of the sociological imagination may be well-estimated. The serious pursuers of literature do not need a fanciful entertainment only. Instead, they do require a big picture of themselves and the world, wherein they can believe and within which they can come to understand themselves. If a work fails to disturb their complacency and orientate them to realize afresh cultural as well as social meaning, it, along with its author, is sure to suffer its doom. Arundhati was probably pretty aware of the fact while writing the book, as she has revealed in an interview, "For me the structure of my story, the way it reveals itself was so important [...]. I really took a lot of care in designing the structure of the story, because for me the book is not about what happened but how what happened affected people."[4] A close reading of the novel validates her statement. The post-sixties India is scanned on micro as well as macro-structural levels. Ayemenem becomes a transforming world-in-miniature that is torn in dissensions: individual as well as collective, emotional as well as instinctive. All this, let us dwell on a few issues of current relevance and see to what extent the novel captures the mood of the day.

The novel is spun on the very fabric of social stratification we are having for several centuries. Despite institutionalized watchwords: Equality, Liberty and Justice to all citizens for years; the Democratic India is still reigned over by four-class system. Worse than ever the latest shift in politics unashamedly encashes caste and community card to reap maximum benefits. Even the most progressive of democrats, irrespective of their political party or ideology, are unwittingly perpetuating social inequality, religious intolerance and racial discrimination. The Indian people at large are still moaning under the unshruggable burden of the Chaturvarna pyramid. Protective discrimination, in seemly form of reservation, is perennially there to worsen everything. Arundhati has shown a very fine sense in enlivening the whole scenario with discreet correctness. Velutha, the prodigal Paravan, becomes her spectrometer for the purpose. He displays diverse colours of her experience in varied wavelengths of caste-feeling. The novel reveals that in all walks of life he suffers stock scorn and segregation of the upper caste people. The 'touchable' workers in Paradise Pickles sniff at him because "according to them, Paravans were not meant to be carpenters" (77). The guardian of law and justice, Inspector Thomas Matthew and the 'crusader of the Oppressed,' Comrade K.N.M. Pillai wilfully shake hands with each other to favour the false FIR lodged against him by schemy Baby Kochamma, merely for the reason that all of them are touchables and Velutha is untouchable. Comrade Pillai doesn't even mention that Velutha is a member of the Communist Party. At another place the Comrade is seen discussing with Paradise Pickles' owner Chacko, the matter of Velutha's dismissal from his Touchable-like job:

> But see, Comrade, any benefits that you give him, naturally others are resenting it. They see it as a partiality.

> After all, whatever job he does, carpenter or electrician or whatever it is, for them he is just a Paravan. It is a conditioning they have from birth [...]. Better for him you send him off [...]. (279)

Caste-consciousness is so pervasive in Indian society that the 'pure' and the 'high' try all sorts of tactics to flaunt their superority. The maid-servant Kochu Maria puts on Kunukku in her sewn-up earlobes just to impress on others her Touchableness:

> Kochu Maria couldn't stop wearing her kunukku because if she did, how would people know that despite her lowly cook's job (seventy-five rupees a month) she was a Syrian Christian, Mar Thomite? Not a Pelaya, or a Pulaya, or a Paravan. But a Touchable, upper-caste Christian (into whom Christianity had seeped like tea from a teabag). Split lobes stitched back were a better option by far. (170)

Baby Kochamma, on homecoming of Margaret, talks to Sophie Mol of Shakespeare's *The Tempest* "to announce her credentials to Margaret Kochamma. To set herself apart from the Sweeper Class" (144). Even religious conversion fails to lift the dispossessed lot up to an esteemable status. Irrespective of religious affiliation the underdog remains as fallen as ever in the dog-eat-dog society:

> When the British came to Malabar, a number of Paravans, Pelayas and Pulayas (among them Velutha's grandfather, Kelan) converted to Christianity and joined the Anglican Church to escape the scourge of Untouchability. As added incentive they were given a little food and money. They were known as the Rice-Christians. It didn't take them long to realize that they had jumped from the frying pan into the fire. They were made to have separate churches, with separate services, and separate priests. As a special favour they were even given their own separate Pariah Bishop. After Independence they found they were not entitled to any Government benefits like job reservations or bank loans at low interest rates, because officially, on paper, they were Christians, and

> therefore casteless. It was a little like having to sweep away your footprints without a broom. Or worse, not being *allowed* to leave footprints at all. (74)

Similarly the Constitutional mandate of India provides particular attention to women under Articles 14, 15 (1) and 15 (A)(C). It is maintained emphatically that the State shall not discriminate against any citizen on grounds of sex along with any other ground. All citizens are told to regard women and not to do anything derogatory to the dignity of women. Special provisions are made through Five Year Plans in order to strengthen and mobilise this long-submissive section of society. The reality, however, is rather scary. Women still remain objects to be appropriated, possessed and bargained in male domain. Contemporary consumer culture has further devaluated the status of woman. One can see around their victimization and exploitation more than ever. Under various crowns of power, freedom and glamour she is, in fact, being machine-tooled to play custom-designed roles. *The God of Small Things* very pointedly portrays women's fate inside and outside Indian home and hearth. Mammachi, Ammu, Baby Kochamma, Margaret, Rahel are cases in point. Mammachi's pickle-making job earns Pappachi's jealous frowns instead of favour. He greatly resents the attention she gets in the society for her skill in it. Far from assisting her in buying, weighing, salting and drying of limes and tender mangoes "every night he beat her with a brass flower vase" (47). She is overtaken by his black moods and sudden bouts of temper. Ammu is also a victim of her Asst. Manager husband's routine drunken violence. The repelling man even feels no trace of shame or guilt or morality when his English Boss Hollick makes an indecent deal with him. Hollick demands Ammu to sleep with him and the fellow agrees and goads Ammu to gratify the Boss. Ammu's so natural declination draws his fury and she is thrashed black and blue. Her partnership in Paradise Pickles further illustrates the status of corporate woman in India:

> Though Ammu did as much work in the factory as Chacko, whenever he was dealing with food inspectors

> or sanitary engineers, he always referred to it as *my* factory, *my* pineapples, *my* pickles. Legally, this was the case because Ammu, as a daughter, had no claim to the property. (57)

Chacko, the Oxford avatar of the old zamindar mentality, a self-proclaimed Marxist, misses no chance of exploiting his women employees:

> He would call pretty women who worked in the factory to his room, and on the pretext of lecturing them on labour rights and trade union law, flirt with them outrageously. (65)

The fate of divorced women too is brought to the fore. Comrade Pillai's pronunciation of the word as "Die-vorced' confers mortality to Rahel. Divorcee Margaret is no more than a whore in Mammachi's eyes. Baby Kochamma's attitude towards deserted Ammu is typically Indian:

> She subscribed wholeheartedly to the commonly held view that a married daughter had no position in her parents' home. As for a *divorced* daughter—according to Baby Kochamma, she had no position anywhere at all. And as for a *divorced* daughter from a *love* marriage, well, words could not describe Baby Kochamma's outrage. As for a *divorced* daughter from an *intercommunity love* marriage—Baby Kocharrlma chose to remain quiveringly silent on the subject. (45-46)

Kochamma's stance encompasses a wide world of apathy for such women.

The novel also gives a thorough insight into children in our society. Children, being the most vulnerable group, require supreme priority on all levels: civil, social, cultural, political, etc. They need utmost support in bad times as well as in good times at familial, national and international fronts. Article 39 in our Constitution pledges to provide children opportunities and facilities to develop in healthy, free, and dignified way. It also asserts their protection against all sorts of exploitation. Even ogling the child in a sexual manner is a punishable offence in Indian Penal Code, along with various other forms of visual, oral and tactile sexual abuses. Psychologists overtly maintain that disorders like nightmares, depressions, anxiety, extreme inhibitions, low self-esteem, suicidal inclination, etc. are but outcome of the traumatic childhood. Such psychological deformities are easily escapable if a concentrated attention is paid on the matters related to child welfare. It is, thus, responsibility of parents and society as well, to adhere to the principle of "First Call for Children." Through Rahel and Estha, Roy has drawn our attention on related affairs. They are the type not very uncommon to find in our immediate vicinities. The twins are living with Ammu and her family as their father is in separation with Ammu. Here, they undergo diverse pressures, taboos, condemnations. Nobody in the family shows serious concern for them. In a way they are growing upon the cold aloofness and eccentricities of the seniors in the family. The sad, Father Mulligan-less Kochamma resents them in their faces:

> In the way that the unfortunate sometimes dislike the co-unfortunate, Baby Kochamma disliked the twins, for she considered them doomed, fatherless waifs. Worse still, they were half-Hindu hybrids whom no self-respecting Syrian Christian would ever marry. She was keen for them to realize that they (like herself) lived on sufferance in the Ayemenem House, their maternal grandmother's house, where they really had no right to be. (45)

Their willingness to love and to be loved rises manifold whenever they come across glimpses of boundless affection like Chacko hugging and hugging, kissing and kissing his step-daughter Sophie Mol. Their state is

> like a pair of small bewildered frogs engrossed in each other's company, lolloping arm in arm down a highway full of hurtling traffic. Entirely oblivious of what trucks can do to frogs. (43)

Ammu wants to educate them in a way so that they could face harsh realities of the world boldly. She tells them the story of Julius Caesar to prove that "You can't trust anybody. Mother, father, brother, husband, best friend. Nobody" (83). It is only

Velutha who provides them love, care and company they need so badly. But his subsequent brutal death in custody leaves one more everlasting scar on their memory, in turn leaving them unconnected, alone, alienated from all humdrum life. Arundhati has been sociologically very sensitive while recording even the slightest stirs in their life.

The novel, to summate, is a fine piece of the exactitude of Arundhati's recording consciousness. Everything is keenly observed, deeply felt and carefully constructed. Be it the breast-tapping policeman, electrocuted elephant, Doctor In and Doctor Out plate, fathers playing sublimated sexual games with their nubile teenaged daughters or yellow bullfrogs cruising the scummy pond for mates—nothing seems foreign to the sensibility of an Indian reader. Use of the stream of consciousness technique has made the novel amazingly effective. Aided with Roy's fervent linguistic devices, its force has increased many times. Look, for example, this Cochin Harbour Terminus scene—

> Scurrying hurrying buying selling luggage trundling porter paying children shitting people spitting coming going begging bargaining reservation checking.
>
> Echoing stationsounds.
>
> Hawkers selling coffee. Tea.
>
> Gaunt children, blonde with malnutrition, selling smutty magazines and food they couldn't afford to eat themselves.
>
> Melted chocolates. Cigarette sweets.
>
> Orangedrinks.
>
> Lemondrinks.
>
> CocaColaFantaicecreamrosemilk.
>
> Pink-skinned dolls. Rattles. Love-in-Tokyos [...]. (300-01)

Constant flashbacks and fast forwards lend a peculiar, cinematographic character to the novel. Nothing falls apart contextually. All qualities assorted together, the work evidences that Arundhati is not just the princess of prose, but the proud possessor of sociological imagination in the true sense of the term. The proof comes from her own words, "If you're a writer, you tend to keep those aching eyes open. Everyday your face is slammed up against the windowpane. Everyday you bear witness to the obscenity. Everyday you are reminded that there is no such thing as innocence. And everyday you have to think of new ways of saying old and obvious things. Things about love and greed. About politics and governance. About power and powerlessness. About war and peace. About death and beauty. Things that must be said over and over again."[5] *The God of Small Things*, quite in line with her statements, acknowledges the condition of the world around us and that too without any distortions and aberrations. It may be hoped that in future too, Arundhati would keep alive this awareness and give us such brilliant pieces of writing.

NOTE

All numbers in brackets refer to the pagination of Arundhati's *The God of Small Things*, New Delhi: Indiaink, 1997, edition.

REFERENCES

1. *Frontline,* 14 November, 1997, 33.
2. Mills, C. Wright. *The Sociological Imagination.* New York: OUP, 1972, 15.
3. Mill 7.
4. *The Week,* 26 October, 1997, 46.
5. "The Cost of Living," *Frontline,* 18 February, 2000, 65.

16

WOMEN NOVELISTS OF THE POST-COLONIAL INDIA

VEENA SINGH

Indian writing in English has acquired a great significance in recent years, not only in India but all over the world. A large number of Indians use the English language as a medium of creative expression. Salman Rushdie rightly observes:

> One important dimension of literature is that it is a means of holding a conversation with the world. These writers are ensuring that India, or rather, Indian voices (for they are too good to fall into the trap of writing "nationalistically") will henceforth be confident, indispensable, participants in that literary conversation.[1]

In the fifty-two years of independent India, we have progressed in many fields, in the field of writing too there has been a great flowering, and the contribution of Indian women writers, specially novelists, is really remarkable.

Fiction is one of the most powerful and characteristic expression. It is the latest of literary forms to be evolved, and the most dominant in the twentieth century. Writers like Kamala Markandaya, Ruth Prawer Jhabwala, Anita Desai, Gita Mehta, Gita Hariharan, Namita Gokhale, Bharati Mukherjee, Nina Sobal, Shashi Deshpande, Uma Vasudev, Shobha De, Kalindi Sen Gupta, Arundhati Roy and Manju Kapoor through their writings, very successfully and skilfully, capture the Indian ethos. At the same time they show their deep insight into human nature, and their understanding of day-to-day problems.

They deal with the various themes of clash between tradition and modernity, identity crisis of their protagonists, Indian woman's quest for independence, the East-West conflict, freedom struggle movement and the traumatic effects of Partition. Their books portray the complexity and different colours of life in India. In more recent years, a generation of talented women writers have emerged. They have their own different styles, but these writers share one common characteristic : that is in their hands, the English language becomes refined and they use it effortlessly.

Ruth Pawar Jhabwala is the first woman novelist of India who won the prestigious Booker Prize in 1975 for her novel *Heat and Dust.* Her other novels are To *Whom She Will, The Nature of Passion, Esmond in India, The Householder, Get Ready for Battle, A Backward Place, A New Dominion, In Search of Love and Beauty, Three Continents* and *Poet and Dancer.* Jhabwala has lived in India and given to her experience of life and society in this country an artistic expression. Khushwant Singh calls her an "adopted daughter of India." Her knowledge and awareness of the Indian character, the Indian family system, the Indian society, and the Indian sensibility assume greater significance. For her an approach to India's basic conditions is to accept them. She writes mainly about urban India that she knows at first hand. Her novels like *A Backward Place* portray the lower middle class with sympathy and understanding. *The Nature of Passion* dramatizes the clash between two families or two individuals in the family in the context of the present-day changes in the urbanized India. Jhabwala is also critical of the validity of the westernised Indians' attitude to their country. Her highly acclaimed novel *Heat and Dust* examines the reasons and truths beneath the clash between the English rulers and the Indian subjects. The action is set against the background of the decadent British Raj. Olivia, a rebel falls in love with a nawab which results in her alienation from her own people. The nawab who was to be removed by the British for the mismanagement of his state stands for everything in India that was designed to repel and baffle the colonizing British. Harry's dislike of India is at variance with Doughlas' cool and steady love and Olivia's sympathetic interest in India. She visits the cemetries of the British families with generations of service in India. In *Esmond in India* Shakuntala's plight is presented with compassion. Her parents, brother or lover cannot do anything for her. She has to redeem her bruised heart and her broken life, and learn diligently to work out her salvation in her own way. Jhabwala's writing is marked by irony, humour and sympathy. K.R. Srinivasa Iyengar describes:

> The pathetic rootlessness of the foreigner in India and the tragic-comic rootlessness of the Indian who has become too westernised to feel at home with his own people, the singular drama of confrontation between the old and the new, the alien and the native, the national habit of constant glorification of our Great History, and our sustained denigration, of the present, all invite Mrs. Jhabwala's amused attention and precise observation, but there is no malice or even deliberate distortion in the portraiture, and there is the touch of compassion that humanizes even the most ironic situation or the most satiric portrait.[2]

The theme of East–West clash is taken up by Kamala Markandaya in her novels like *Possession* and *Nowhere Man.* Jhabwala and Markandaya have an impressive corpus of fiction to their credit. In *Possession* the scene shifts from India to England and America, and again back to India. The novel is concerned with clash of wills, the confusion of cross-purposes and the unleashing of passions. The formidable Caroline Bell, "Rich, divorced and well-borne" has spirited away the Tamil rustic boy Valmiki and made a painter and paramour of him. She would possess him if she could. But she has to reckon with her rivals, her antagonist Swamy under whose protection Val had been before the coming of Caroline, Ellie with her nightmarish memories of a Nazi camp, the girl Annabel, and the pet monkey Minou that Val is so fond of. Ultimately Swamy wins to the discomfiture of Caroline. Caroline represents western materialism, and also the domination of feminism. In *Nowhere Man* Srinivas is caught in somewhat same dilemma of clash between East and West, he is the 'nowhere man,' a rootless, with no sense of belongings. "No more, he said to himself: I can endure no more. I am quite worn out. So he withdrew himself and rested."[3] Markanday's other novels are *Nectar in a Sieve, Some Inner Fury, A Silence of Desire, A Handful of Rice, Two Virgins* and *The Coffer Dams.* Her first novel *Nectar in a Sieve* has been compared to Pearl Buck's *The Good Earth.* The writer deals with different themes in her novels like quest for identity, the spiritual realism, feminism, unfolding of passion, the rural and urban economics. Her latest novel *The Pleasure City* sums up all these themes successfully.

The women writers of today conceive the relationship of man to his surroundings in new and realistic terms, and face the challenges posed by the influx of western ideas. Though writing in particular milieu of middle class society of India, they transcend the narrow confines and their books explore the individual's experience of his/her uniqueness in his/her power to transcend the given. They do so with the unusual perception of reality. A remarkable feature of these writings is their understanding of human life and its predicament.

Anita Desai is one of the best living authors of English, today. Her novels are studies of her protagonists' psychological development. Her novel *Clear Light of Day* was nominated by the 1980 Booker prize. *In Custody,* her best novel, is about the decay of Urdu language and its literary culture. She depicts the dying past through two brothers, one is the poet, the last, boozing, decrepit-custodian of the dying tradition and the other his younger brother Deven, 'a wimp' who is the central character of the novel. Desai's hold on English language is noteworthy. *Clear Light of the Day* is the story of Tara who is not weak-willed or defeatist. Like Tara, Aditi in *Bye Bye Blackbird* is engaged in the struggle with her own self. *Fire in the Mountain* which won National Academy of Letters award and Winfred Hollt Memorial Prize, is about her protagonist's dilemma caught in an identity crisis. Nanda Kaul is like Henerik Ibsen's heroine who walks out of her "Dolls House." Married to a Vice-Chancellor in Delhi, she seeks freedom from her mundane existence. The husband's extramarital affair compels her to reflect on her situation, though she does not want to create a scandal because of her middle-class morality. She comes to Kasauli in search of freedom from her cluttered and choked past. But she cannot completely reject her roles as wife and mother, and so accepts her granddaughter coming to live with her. The action, setting and characters of Desai's novels are set against the background of middle-class urban milieu. Her novel *Baumgartner's Bombay* describes the impressions of a German tourist, Mr. Baumgartner, of life in Bombay and Calcutta. Here is an India seen through the eyes of a foreigner. The novel is also a comment on human relationships and human predicament. Desai, in her novels, is concerned with her protagonists' psychological development and their eternal quest for freedom. Her novel *Fasting, Feasting* is the story of Uma's hopes and despair in her journey of life.

Uma Vasudeva explores the inner struggle of her characters in her novels *Song of Anusuya* and *Shreya of Sonagarh*. Her emphasis is not so much on the external forces as on the quest of their own self. Her Sherya is a woman who is a traditional wife and daughter-in-law, but finds love outside her marriage. Love transforms her and liberates her from many inhibitions, but she wants to strike a compromise between her family and love-affair. *Song of Anusuya* probes deeply into man-woman relationship. Jagan the central character of the novel emphasises the importance of sex in a relationship. He muses:

> The feeling of love was a distraction, I thought, a sort of emotional ferment aroused by another human being. Intimacy with that human being would doubtless result in some supreme physical moments, but those moments would be secondary, a by-product of an otherwise secure personal relationship.[4]

An important point to be noted is that in the works of these women novelists, woman emerges as an individual challenging her existential survival. They aim at catching the whole woman alive in terms of feelings, intellect and emotions. Namita Gokhle's Paro in her novel *Paro: Dreams of Passion* seeks her identity in sexual freedom. Like Gustav Flaubert's Madam Bovary, D.H. Lawrence's Lady Chatterly and Herman Hesse's Kamla, Paro symbolises female will. She represents a woman who yearns for completion and refuses to be consumed by the monstrous schematization of the male dominated institution. In her other recent novel *God, Graves and Grand Mother,* Gokhle tells the story of young Gudiya, her mother and her formidable grandmother, highlighting a woman's position in the modern world. The novel is remarkable for its searching scan of life in the downwardly mobile class of the Indian metropolis. In a ductile circumspective tone, the writer exposes the humorous underbelly of merchandized religiosity; and looks at the squalidity of poverty with unsentimental urbanity.

Shobha De, on the contrary, depicts urban upper middle class society. The very titles of her novels like *Starry Nights* and *Socialite Evenings* convey a picture of fashion and glamour. It is a society where sex and materialism have acquired significance. Amrita Aggarwal in *Strange Obsessions* is an aspiring model, young, beautiful and confident. She is trapped in an unsavoury situation, but is able to free herself from the clutches of her lover and tormentor Meenakshi. For De, the sexual exploits are the expressions of the free woman, symbol and prototype of emancipation and individuality. Bharti Mukherjee's Hannah Easton, in her recent novel *The Holder of the World,* discovers her sexuality in the arms of Raja Jadav Singh. Hannah, a puritan from Massachusetts becomes the Raja's mistress and transforms herself into Salem Bibi. There are hints of feminism but Mukerjee's novel has a sense of history which holds the book. Her earlier novel *Jasmine* is about cultural dualism of East and West. Her protagonist *Jasmine* caught in this clash tries to come to terms with herself.

Many of the women novelists of India today do not depict their women according to a strict traditional code. Shashi Deshpande's Jaya in *The Long Silences* is another such character, who seeks fulfilment outside her marriage. A typical middle class, middle-aged housewife in Bombay, Jaya seeks liberation from mediocrity in self-expression. She ventures to break out of her long silences and to express her urges and desires in her autobiography. Nina Sibel's *Yatra* is about the 'yatra' of a woman faced with the dilemma of choice. Krishna not knowing about her paternity, goes in search of her father. Disillusioned with her own marriage, she attempts to assert her individuality by becoming a leader. Hers is the 'yatra' from home to the world.

These Indian women novelists have successfully projected the urges, dreams and desires of Indian woman, in particular, the middle-class housewife who refuses to be suffocated by her environment. They depict woman in the context of the contemporary world, as an individual with freedom of choices. However, their canvas is not limited to women only, they depict a wider cultural scene, and the problems and difficulties, joys and sorrows of human beings which have universal significance.

Gita Mehta is another such writer who has carved a niche for herself in the field of writing. Her novels *Raj* and *River Sutra* brought her fame. *River Sutra* depicts contemporary India. The river here is the river of life in which flows the essence of truth. Mehta's earlier novel *Raj* is about the transfiguring experience of her protagonist in post-colonial India. Gita Hariharan's novel, *The Thousand Faces of Night* won the Commonwealth Writers Prize. Some other important names in this field are those of Bapsi Sidhwa, Sara Guleri, Kiran Desai and Kalindi Sen Gupta. Like many other twentieth century novelists, these women writers consider search for identity the first and foremost condition of living. Iyengar remarks: "Women are natural story-tellers even when they don't write or publish. And in India we have seen how the marvellous Tarulata (Toru Dutt) wrote both a French and an English novel before she died at the age of 21 in 1877. Other women writers too have since made their mark in Indian fiction in English."[5]

Among the women writers of the 1990s, the most renowned name is that of Arundhati Roy. Rushdie remarks: "The Keralan writer Arundhati Roy has arrived to the accompaniment of a loud fanfare. Her novel *The God of Small Things,* is full of ambition and sparkle, and written in a highly wrought and utterly personal style."[6] This Booker Prize winner novel created a storm in the world of writing at the fag end of the century. For Roy the transition from script writing to novel writing is important because novel writing gave her more freedom. The visual imagery used in the novel is internal, what happens in head or heart. The imaginatively created world of *The God* [...], the events taking place in the lives of people appear before our eyes and we become part of it. It is a novel about life in its small ironies and human beings we may come across in our day-to-day life. To use Roy's own words, "It is a book about human sustenance." It is deeply rooted in the cultural ethos of South India. Here we have love affairs, marriages, divorces, the questionable Christian morals, hints of incest, wild passions, the dying feudalism, references to Kerala history, the Marxist movement and the civil disobedience movement. The Paradise Pickle is the symbol of the small world in Ayemenem House packed with all kinds of 'masala' for preservation. The House is the symbol of the old, the worn out and the traditional. Everyone returns to the house; Chacko comes back with the machines for pickles after his marriage to Margaret. Rahel who drifted into an unsuccessful marriage with Larry McCaslin, gave up her job to return to the house. Her twin brother Estha who was sent to the father after the funeral of Sophie Mol, returns after 23 years. Ammu, the mother of Estha and Rahel, is a 'rebel' like the author herself. She is a divorced daughter from inter-community love marriage. When she comes to the Ayemenem House she is looked down upon by the people of her society including her brother Chacko, who considers her and her twins a burden to the family. Ammu yields to the allures of Velutha, the carpenter. Their passions run wild. But Velutha is beaten up, and Ammu dies at the "die-able" age of 31. The cremation was attended by no one from the family except Chacko and daughter Rahel. The author here gives the minute details and a vivid picture of this family saga and the house microscoped in time.

Manju Kapoor's novel *Difficult Daughters,* a 1999 publication, imaginatively reconstructs the historical events around the time of Partition. Written with absorbing intelligence and sympathy, *Difficult Daughters* is the story of a woman Virmati torn between family duty, illicit love and the desire for education. Virmati realizes that "It was possible to be something other than a wife [...]. No, she too had to go to Lahore, even if she had to fight her mother who was so sure that her education was practically over."[7] Virmati, a young woman born in Amritsar into an austere and high-handed household, falls in love with a married man, a professor, her neighbour. She does get married to the professor but cannot escape the wrath of her scandalized family or the pain caused by the irritable lines of Partition and by the battle for her own independence. Another name which needs to be mentioned is that of Jhumpa Lahiri, who won The Pulitier Prize for her collection of stories, *The Interpreter of Melodies.* Her stories depict the diverse aspects of India's culture.

These women writers of the post-colonial India portray life in all its depth and complexity in their novels. They have poignantly conveyed the predicament of people who are engaged in the struggle not only with their circumstances, with their limitations and failure, but also with their own self. The novelists show a deep insight into human nature, and at the same time they catch the epiphanies of life in their work. They view life with a keen perception, sharp sensibility, an acute sense of observation and a fine sensitivity. Their achievement is recognized not only in India but in the world.

NOTES AND REFERENCES

1. Rushdie, Salman. *The Vintage Book of Indian Writing* (1947-97). Vintage 1997, XV.
2. Iyengar, K.R. Srinivasa. "The Women Novelists," *Indian Writing in English.* New Delhi: Sterling Publishers, 1983, 460.
3. Markandaya, Kamala. *Nowhere Man.* Sangam Books, 1975, 252.

4. Vasudev, Uma. *The Song of Anusuya*. New Delhi: Vikas Publishing House, 1978, 10.
5. Iyenger 435.
6. Rushdie XXIII.
7. Kapoor, Manju. *Difficult Daughters*. Penguin Books, 1998, 17.

17

Nationalism in Pre-Independence Indian Poetry in English

RAJENDRA P. LOKHANDE

1.1 Introduction: The Indian Renaissance

The emergence of the Indian English literature in the early nineteenth century was a significant aspect of the Indian renaissance. There set in a movement in this country towards a new life and new thought that is generally characterised as the renaissance in India.

In the study of literature, one has to follow the course of socio-cultural factors which shape the sensibilities of the writers in that period. As far as India is concerned, the entire phenomenon has to be related to the great Renaissance which came in the nineteenth century in the wake of the western impact. One of the greatest consequences of the western impact on India was the awakening of national consciousness, the rediscovery of her cultural heritage. The great poet Sri Aurobindo describes the Indian renaissance as 'less like the European one and more like the Celtic movement in Ireland, (1972: 397). He defines it as "the attempt of a reawakened national spirit to find a new impulse of self-expression which shall give the spiritual force for a great reshaping and rebuilding." In Ireland, this was discovered by a return to Celtic spirit and culture after a long period of eclipsing English influences. In India, the course of renaissance led to new self-identification with ancient cultural heritage. This awakening of India, as

Jawaharlal Nehru observes, was 'twofold': "She looked to the West and at the same time she looked at herself and her own past" (1961: 330-31). In the rediscovery of India's past, some of the early officials of the East India Company played a significant role.

While Englishmen were rediscovering India's past, the gradual spread of English education and western ideas brought forth a band of earnest Indians who drank deep at the fountain of European learning. The general awakening began with the introduction of English education. Besides this, the pressure of a superimposed European culture made the reawakening inevitable. The idea of liberty came through Renaissance and thereby determined the future of India. The renewed interest in the ideas of political liberty and nationalism was the unmistakable fruit of western education.

The introduction of the British educational system by the rulers in 1814 may be regarded as the main cause of modernisation of Indian elite. It marked the beginning of Indian renaissance as it brought Indians in contact with the western culture. One of the most important elements of this renaissance was a dramatic change in the attitude to cultural life of India. The new intelligentsia represented by Raja Rammohan Roy, Dawarkanath Tagore and Baidyanath Mukherji advocated the cause of English education in India as they realised that it could inspire people to rational thinking, individual freedom, self-identity and would bring the spell of modernization in life through western science and literature. This new socio-cultural situation led individuals to assert, for the first time, their full identity as independent, self-made in the colonial society. With the introduction of English education in different parts of the country, several English educated Indians started using English as the medium to express their ideas. Indian English literature was the meritable result of this excitement. Rammohan Roy's essay *A Defence of Hindu Theism* (1817) may be regarded as the first original publication of significance in the history of Indian English literature.

Besides English education, Christian missionaries played a significant role in enhancing the spirit of Renaissance. The Christian missionaries set up printing presses all over the country and published cheap versions of Bible in the Indian regional languages. The socio-religious organisations like Brahmo Samaj, Arya Samaj and Prarthana Samaj revived the cultural past of India and aflushed the Indian minds for national spirit.

Thus, the revolutionary fervour of Rammohan Roy and his associates, the educational enterprise of the missionaries and the adoption by Government in 1835 of Macaulay's scheme of modern education through the English medium contributed to the generation of the spirit of nationalism and the creative expression was the natural outcome of this.

1.2 Indian English Poetry before Independence

Many of the young men who received the blessings of a dynamic education in the new schools were fired with the ambition to put India once more on the cultural map of the world. They yearned to make their seemingly dumb country articulate once again. This meant naturally that they should themselves write, either in English or their own mother-tongues. They should write in English so that they could easily compel the attention of their English 'masters' and also reach their own countrymen in different linguistic areas. Indian English literature was born out of this excitement.

Indian English poetry had its humble beginnings in this environment of growing craze for English education and English literature. The Renaissance period gave tremendous fillip for self-assertion and the first attempt was made in 1830 by Kashiprasad Ghose. His *The Shair and Other Poems* brought the flavour of local tradition in Bengal. Henry Derozio and Michael Madhusudan Dutt were his contemporaries. To this period belonged Lai, P., Rajagopal and Hasan Ali who had only mediocre poetic abilities. It was in the poetry of Derozio that early Indian English poetry found its finest efflorescence of beauty and genius.

Along with the contemporary socio-religious situation, the forceful writing of Rammohan Roy was a shaping influence on the body of Indian English poetry. H.M. Williams observes: 'His (Roy's) influence extends through the Dutts, Tagore, Sarojini Naidu and on Sri Aurobindo Ghose' (1987: 1). Further he says: 'This continuity I find strongly related to the development of Indian self-awareness and national aspirations' (1987: 1). As he points out, the cultural response to the challenge of British rule resulted mainly into 'cultural nationalism' and Indian English poetry was the bold expression of this.

In its historical perspective, Indian English poetry reveals three main stages in its growth and development. These three stages may be indicated as—Imitation, Indianization and Individualization. Though these are transition phases of Indian English poetry, the common thread that links them together is the Indian sensibility. In the first transition phase, the sensibility is weak. In the second phase, it is exhaustive and in the third, it is precise, rich and truly indigenous. The growth of national character of Indian English poetry seems to justify itself, indeed, this way.

These three stages, in a way, are complementary to develop the perspectives of different periods of Indian English poetry.

The growth of nationalism in India and its reflection in Indian English poetry may be traced through different periods.

M.K. Naik (1989: 7-114) divides the history of Indian English poetry into four periods. They are:

1. Indian poetry from beginnings to 1857,
2. Indian poetry from 1857 to 1920,
3. Indian poetry from 1920 to 1947 and
4. Indian poetry from Independence and after.

The great revolt of 1857 makes an important turning point in the colonial history of India as does the year 1920, which is generally regarded as the beginning of the Gandhian era in the struggle for Independence. Likewise, 1947, the year of Independence is important as the beginning of our history as a nation.

These phases encompass the socio-political development in India which naturally gets reflected in literature regenerating nationalistic spirit. And so, they would be quite useful in discussing 'nationalism' in Indian poetry in English.

Nationalism

The course of nationalism in pre-Independence Indian poetry in English can be determined by different aspects of nationalism. Indian nationalism manifested itself in various stages in its growth. Naturally, the various aspects of nationalism are the direct outcome of the growth of nationalism in general. The various aspects can be enlisted as: the search for identity, the glorification of the past, the social and reformative zeal, the patriotic fervour and the political aspect of the struggle for freedom.

The Search for Identity

The act of self-assertion can be perceived as anti-colonial in spirit. The renaissance spirit cultivated through English language and literature awakened the Indians for self-assertion or self-identification. What did prompt the poets for self-assertion? It is the process of cultural colonisation of India started in the early nineteenth century that motivated the Indian poets for self-assertion. The enslaved consciousness in the Indians slowly withered away with the touch of renaissance and for the first time they realised their cultural identity.

The Christian missionaries depicted Indian society and religion in a derogatory manner to promote proselytization. A very dark picture of inferiority of the Indians in every field of life was painted, be it religious, social or about scientific progress. Indian culture was looked down upon and the superiority of British culture was advocated to impress the Indian mind. This biased propaganda of the Christian missionaries was a challenge which was counter noted by rediscovering India's glorious past and cultural heritage in English language.

This cultural challenge was faced effectively by the Indians. In their zeal to show that they are by no means inferior to their rulers, they then make a search for their own identity and try to affirm it. And this is the first stage of the assertion of national identity. The derogatory attitude of the rulers incited the Indian elites to assert themselves and the Indians, educated in the new system of western education through the medium of English started eulogising Indian tradition and culture. They found in the English language an excellent medium of rediscovery and creative statement.

This act of self-assertion or self-identification led the Indians to distinguish their manners and customs, religious and social institutions and culture and civilization. There are a number of poems depicting Indian customs and manners and folk-tales, mythological tales and legends. This aspect of nationalism very boldly asserted in the poetry of Toru Dutt, Sri Aurobindo, Rabindranath Tagore and Sarojini Naidu. To generate pride in being an Indian was the motivating force behind these creative writers. The act of self-identification rightly promotes pride and unity amongst the Indians in the colonial period. So the search for identity in the religious and cultural past is nationalistic and at the same time Hindu in spirit. Hence, the act of self-assertion can be perceived as a Hindu nationalism.

Hindu Nationalism

The act of self-assertion or self-identification is an off-shoot of Hindu nationalism. In the second phase 1857 to 1920, the search for identity is wholly imbued by Hindu nationalism. The poets like Toru Dutt, Sri Aurobindo, Tagore, Sarojini Naidu and others have specifically explored the rich tradition of Hinduism through their themes and characters. Hinduism is the watchword of their poetry. So it is necessary to understand the concept of Hindu nationalism.

Hindu nationalism has been defined as a feeling of pride in the ancient glory of the Hindu culture and tradition. It discards the western ideas and is solely inspired by Hindu culture and tradition. It is believed that the Hindus are bound together by most sacred and most enduring bonds of a common Fatherland and common Holyland. Hinduism accepts the authority of Vedas which are foundational scriptures of Hindus. It is not dogmatic or authoritarian religion. Hinduism, as a faith, is indefinable, amorphous, many-sided accepting to all men. Mahatma Gandhi defines it as the search after truth, a religion of truth. Hinduism is a relentless pursuit after truth, a religion of truth. Whatever the word we may use, Indian or Hindustani for our cultural tradition, derived from the Indian philosophic outlook was the dominant feature of Indian culture and even social development.

All these features strengthen the spirit of Hindu or Indian nationalism. Though the terms Hindu nationalism and Indian nationalism seem different, it is not easy to separate them. They are not competitive but complementary phenomena.

Indian English poetry of the period 1857 to 1920 gives an ardent expression of Hinduism. To generate the spirit of Hindu nationalism, the contemporary socio-cultural factors are responsible. The revival of Hinduism was at its peak and the zeal of social reforms was subsided. The contemporary socio-religious organisations like Brahmo Samaj, Arya Samaj, Ramakrishna Mission influenced the character of Indian English poetry. All this contributed to the promotion of Hinduism and that was the need of time.

With the dawn of twentieth century, the nationalist movement in India became more agitational. With the partition of Bengal in 1905, the extremists dominated the political scene. The moderates who dominated the Indian National Congress believed in the development of liberal, secular nationalism. They sought inspiration from the western countries. But the extremists led by Tilak, Aurobindo, Bipin Chandra Pal and Lala Lajpat Rai and others sought to rely on aggressive Hinduism. The nationalism of the extremists had a religious tinge. Sri Aurobindo, Bipin Chandra Pal, advocated spiritual type of nationalism.

This account of Hindu nationalism is useful in the discussion of the poetry confined to the period—1857 to 1920.

The Glorification of the Past

The second aspect of nationalism is the glorification of the past or the discovery of the past. Behind the glorification of the past lies the spirit of the regeneration of the nation. The people of a country are enthused by this spirit generally in the first stage of the development of nationalism. The search for the glories of past is a sort of an endeavour for self-assertion and this appears in the first stage of development of national spirit in the country. Thus, the assertion of the self of the nation through the historical past has the purpose to arouse political and historical consciousness of the nation and achieve national unity. The poets were influenced by this renaissance spirit. They idealized the country's historical past and her inspiring heroes and thereby promoted the feeling of nationalism and patriotism. The aim is to generate self-confidence by national assertion and inculcation of pride in Indian heritage.

This aspect of nationalism reflects in the first and second phase of Indian English poetry.

The Patriotic Fervour

The patriotic fervour is the direct outcome of the Bengal renaissance. It is a kind of self-assertion which has a purpose to awaken the people for freedom and patriotism. The sense of patriotism develops generally amidst the oppressed subjects of a country and a complete development of this sense leads to a struggle for total freedom. The sense of patriotism also arises at the time of war or when the new awakening dawns in the form of knowledge.

With the dash of renaissance, the Bengali elites were influenced by the European literature of revolt. This new literature germinated in them the zeal of patriotism and the ideal of political liberty. This made the Indian elites to explore the ancient and historical past of India. They ransacked history to find out the high ability and heroism of Indians in the political and military fields. This blooming patriotic zeal influenced the character of contemporary Indian English poetry. The poets idealized the valour of king Porus, Prithviraj, Shivaji,

Baji Prabhu and Tara Bai to promote the sentiments of patriotism and freedom in the Indian minds which were caught in the decadent phase. In some poems, the patriotic fervour is born out of the concern for human liberty. In others, there is direct assertion of freedom but it is conceived on romantic plane.

Thus the patriotic zeal is the part of Indian renaissance.

The Social and Reformative Zeal

The social and reformative zeal developed in Bengal as one of the offshoots of national consciousness. The English education and western culture made Bengalis keenly conscious of the retrogressive effects of the superstitious customs that were prevalent in the society and the dogmas issued by the Hindu shastras. This consciousness gave birth to several religious and social reforms. The very people who extolled India's glorious past and cultural heritage were bitter critics of prevalent evils in the society. This was not double thinking but two aspects of the same phenomenon of national assertion. The mighty reformers like Raja Rammohan Roy, Derozio, Vidyasagar brought about drastic changes in social customs. The efforts at social reform always involved religious reform. Enlightened Hindus became aware that only such a reformation in religion should bring real progress to India. They had no concept of nationalism as such but zeal was nationalistic in spirit. And this zeal enhanced in the country through reformative societies like Brahmo Samaj and Arya Samaj.

The growing demand for social reform exerted its influence on the poetry of the contemporary period. Indian English poets like Henry Derozio, Kashiprasad Ghose, B.M. Malbari and others have given expression to this spirit with the purpose of purging society of its harmful practices that in the name of custom are only causing harm, is also a national process. So this zeal can be treated as one of the aspect of nationalism.

The aspects discussed above rightly bring to notice that the first expression of Indian discontent and the assertion of nationalism were not mainly political but strictly cultural. Naturally, Indian English poetry can be studied as an emblem of cultural nationalism. According to K.R. Minogue, this is the first stage of nationalism. It is time of casting around for a cultural identity.

The second stage is the centrepiece of nationalism; it is the time of the struggle for independence. And this spirit is understood as the political aspect of the struggle for freedom.

The Struggle for Freedom

The period 1920-47 is considered as the Gandhian age or the period of struggle for freedom. The entire period of near three decades of the Gandhian age was one of far-reaching changes not only in political scene but in all areas of Indian life. This was an epoch-making period of Indian nationalism.

Gandhi activated the mass of people all over the country for the ultimate goal, *i.e.* freedom. This activization of people came through various movements launched by Gandhi. The movements were more political strategies realised through nationwide agitation and protest.

India's freedom struggle under the leadership of Gandhi assumed three distinct features—attainment of Swaraj, use of truthful and growing progress towards constructive nationalism and mass movement. The story of Gandhiji's movements from the Non-Co-operation of 1920 to that of the Quit India Movement of 1942 confirms this fact.

Indian national struggle after all is an expression of the people's dissatisfaction with the foreign rule. The collective awareness of suffering broke out as Gandhiji launched systematic movements. The aspect of freedom struggle is the outcome of all these movements. Gandhiji launched the first countrywide Non-Co-operation Movement on 1st August, 1920. The movement created an unprecedented awakening, the most important feature of which was that it had converted Indian nationalism 'from middle class movement to a mass emotion' (Spear 1961: 359). The movement proved to be a first experience of warfare which initiated the people into a new faith and new hope, and inspired them with a new confidence in their power to fight for freedom. The second mass movement was launched in March

1930 to practise civil disobedience. The Salt laws were made focal point. This movement differed substantially from the earlier Non-Co-operation movement, though the goal remained the same. 'The first was passively, the second was actively, revolutionary. The first hoped to bring government to a standstill by withdrawing from the administration; the second sought to paralyse government by mass performance of specific illegal acts' (Spear 1965: 351). Among these acts, the one that captured the imagination of the people was the illegal making of salt. To break the Salt laws electrified the entire civilized world. The Salt satyagraha roused India to action as never before. Another ten years later come the third and last satyagraha campaign of 1940 which after the historic 'Quit India' resolution of 9 August, 1942, led to violent underground revolutionary activity. The British Government arrested all the top leaders of the Indian National Congress. The people launched the movement according to their understanding of the situation. The Government's repressive policy added fuel to the fire, the enraged people took to the destruction of government's property which included the burning of post-offices, railway stations, the cutting of telegraph wires and tampering with railway tracks. There were huge demonstrations of thousands of workers and college and school students carrying the tricolour flag armed with nothing but non-violence, people ready to carry out Gandhi's call for "Do or Die." This massive upsurge made the movement so formidable that the government took to brutal repression. Soon after the World War II, the political, economic imperatives of the day compelled Britain to concede independence to India on 15 August, 1947.

Thus the aspect of the struggle for freedom quite rightly reveals through the national movements. This political aspect generated an all-pervading national consciousness.

In cultural sphere, Gandhian thought and the Quit India Movement provided an immense creative impetus to contemporary literature. But in case of Indian English poetry, the impact of Gandhian whirlwind produced no outstanding poetry of any kind. However, the poets like Armando Menzes,

Humayun Kabir and V.N. Bhushan reacted with the spirit of Quit India Movement and thereby promoted the spirit of freedom.

In short, these aspects are the theoretical grounding through which the pre-Independence Indian English poetry can be assessed for the spirit of nationalism.

1.2.1 Indian Poetry from Beginnings to 1857

The pioneers of Indian English literature were the elite who assumed the role of interpreting the ethos and culture of India to West through creative literature. Poetry naturally came first and it was associated with the cultural renaissance in Bengal where the assault of English on the citadel of Indian culture first took place. It was here that literary awakening dawned. It was here that Indian English poetry underwent the sweet pangs of birth.

It was the period of renaissance which English education brought about. M.K. Naik comments: "It was a period when English education and western ideas had begun to act as a great liberating force in a country which had been suffering from political instability for about a century and from social fossilization and intellectual stagnation for even much longer" (1984: 10). Raja Rammohan Roy vigorously championed the cause of English education and accelerated the Indian psyche to challenge the cultural aspects of colonialism. Roy paved the path for self-assertion through English to integrate Indian culture and to make inquiry into socio-religious practices. This was the first stage of the germination of the spirit of nationalism. It influenced the creative expressions, especially Indian English poetry.

The first group of poets—Henry Derozio, Michael Madhusudan Dutt and Kashiprasad Ghose, the pioneers of Indian English poetry—asserted the spirit of nationalism as part of national awakening. Obviously, the assertion of the self was to search for cultural identity and thereby to confirm national identity or Indian identity.

THE POETS

I. Henry Derozio

Derozio (1809-31) is generally regarded as the first Indian to write English poetry. Half-Indian, half-Portuguese, Derozio was wholly Indian in spirit and aspired to be India's national bard. He was one of the earliest nationalists in the country and that he considered himself a true Indian. His love for India is revealed in several of his poems from the collection *Poems* published in 1827. Besides self-assertion, the patriotic fervour is quite loud in his poetry. This teacher-poet believed that the best solution to India's problem was speedy westernization. This fiery nationalist asserted his love for India in the hope of social and cultural revival.

The urge for self-assertion gets manifested in the poems like "The Harp of India," "To the Pupils of the Hindu College" and "Song of the Hindustan Ministrel."

The search for identity is quite apparent in the sonnet "The Harp of India." It expresses Derozio's pride in the glorious past of India. Here Derozio identifies himself with India's great poetic tradition. He boldly asserts his Indianness:

> [...] thy notes divine
> May be by mortal wakened once again,
> Harp of my country, let me strike the strain!
>
> (Derozio 1980: 1)

India's great poetic tradition refers to 'Veena' and not the 'harp.' Here the sense of musical instrument 'harp' has association with the symbol of 'Veena.' The harp refers to India, the great country whose riches and potentialities lie inert and undiscovered under a foreign rule. It also refers to India's poetic or artistic tradition which, after centuries of glorious manifestation, now lies dormant. This spiritual association with the Indian culture brings the sense of Indianness.

The harp of India had sweet music that enchanted the world in the past. Derozio's passionate urge is to revitalise the divine chords of the harp. But the condition of the harp is—

Neglected, mute, and desolate art thou,
Like ruined monument on desert plain.

It clearly suggests that the cultural degeneration of India continued up to the beginning of the nineteenth century. The harp is pictured as one whose music had been brought out by many worthy hands but which now lies abandoned for want of talent. Those who had plucked its strings in the past had won many laurels but they are no more. If poor mortal hands such as his own can awaken the divine music which lies in it dormant, he would indeed be happy to strike the chords. Distressed at the sight of this unstring harp, silent on a withered bough of history, the poet wants to revitalise its chords into an immortal harmony.

Derozio's dear India is presented in the symbol of harp which figures forth the rich cultural tradition. By striking the notes of it again, the poet wants to bring cultural revival in India. It was also due to the impact of Indian renaissance which brought an awakening of national consciousness that stirred the poet for self-assertion.

Though the sonnet exhibits the sense of loss, at the same time the poet is eager to locate his self in the poetic tradition of India continued from Vedas and Upanishads. He yearns to make his dumb country articulate once again. Here K.R. Ramchandran Nair (1987: 49) asserts: 'The poem is lyrical refurbishment of the faded image of India by recalling her ancient glory.'

The harp represents the cultural ethos of India and the glorification of its past identity inspires us for the regeneration of the nation. Moreover, the self-identification of the poet with the cultural continuity of India strengthens the sense of nationalism. The poem is a bold assertion of the cultural identity of the colonial India.

Derozio's patriotic fervour is born out of his concern for human liberty. The goals of the French Revolution and the teachings of the great Raja Rammohan Roy inspired Derozio in his involvement with the ideals of liberty, equality, justice and social progress. As a teacher he had enthused students with liberal and rational ideas. In poems like "Freedom to the Slave," "Greece," "Address to the Greeks" and "The Greeks at Marathon," Derozio glorifies man's urge for liberty and desire for breaking the chains that enthral him.

In early nineteenth century Bengal, the growing demand for social reform exerted its influence on the creative minds of the time. The early creative minds like Derozio, Kashiprasad Ghose, B.M. Malbari and others enriched the character of social and reformative zeal through their poetry.

Derozio was against slavery, both mental and physical. During the few years that he was a teacher, he tried and succeeded in inspiring his students to cast aside their mental slavery, to look at life afresh in the light of reason and not to accept blindly any custom or belief howsoever ancient. He was truly a rebel leader, who dreamt of men and women free from the bondages of ignorance, blind faith in tradition and of religious superstitions.

This reformistic bent of mind of Derozio's attracts the attention of critics. V.K. Gokak (1985: 23) remarks: "The championing of Indian widow starts with Derozio." C. Paul Verghese (1971: 7) comments: "Derozio's ardour for social reform shows itself in this poem, The Fakeer of Jungheera." John B. Alphonso-Karkala (1970: 41) points out the reformistic element: "[...] Derozio attempts to tell a long tale [...] exposing the social evil of Sati."

The zeal for social reform gets an ardent expression in Derozio's most ambitious work "The Fakeer of Jungheera" (1828). The main thrust of the poem is to expose the social evil of sati, the custom of widows burning themselves on the funeral pyres of their husbands. It was a cruel and painful medieval custom, continuing till the fourth decade of the nineteenth century, practised by the Hindus under the sanction of their religion. The social reformer, Rammohan Roy raised his voice against this custom and later in 1829, Lord William Bentick declared it as illegal.

Derozio, being a reformer, naturally the social zeal to eradicate this evil practice gets its bold assertion in the present poem. The poem rightly projects the first phase of Indian nationalism, *i.e.* national awakening.

II. Kashiprasad Ghose

Three years after Derozio signalled the birth of Indian English poetry, the first volume of verse by an author of pure Indian blood appeared: *The Shair or Minstrel and Other Poems* (1830) by Kashiprasad Ghose (1809-73). He continued Derozio's efforts to write on Indian subjects. He wrote several poems on Indian festivals which were meant for his British and Eurasian readers. His poetic creation was totally under the influence of the British Romantics and naturally his 'shair' being Scott's 'ministrel' in an Indian garb. So, there is little originality either in the form of the poems or in their themes. Despite this, he is considered as a pathfinder for Indian English poetry.

He has the distinction of being the first Hindu to write original English verse. His *The Shair and Other Poems* published in 1830 which after passing through the hands of critics blamed for the lack of originality. John B. Alphonso Karkala (1970: 43) comments on this verse collection as: 'These immature verses, lacking originality and sincerity only indicate to what extent he was influenced by the minor love poets of the late Elizabethan age.' M.K. Naik puts: "This 'Shair' being obviously Scott's 'Minstrel' in an Indian garb, slightly dishevelled as a result of the arduous voyage across the seas" (1984: 210). Though these charges are levelled against his poetic achievement, and considered him as a minor voice, some poems in this collection do reflect the Indian ethos and bring the sense of Indianness.

The poems like "To a Dead Crow," "The Shair's Farewell Song" and "The Boatman's Song to Ganga" bring the sense of an ardent love of Indian culture.

III. Michael Madhusudan Dutt

After Derozio and Kashiprasad Ghose, the tradition was carried a step further by Madhusudan Dutt (1827-73). His long poem *The Captive Ladie* published in 1849, rightly brings the nationalistic feelings as it draws its sustenance from the historical past of India. *The Captive Ladie,* Madhusudan's best known English poem, was written while he was working as a journalist and was first published in the columns of the *Madras Circulator* and *General Chronicle.*

The poem is an outcome of the renaissance spirit ushered in India. The glorification of the heroic deeds, valour of Indian kings further strengthen the renaissance spirit and with it the nationalistic feelings. This is what we expect in *The Captive Ladie.*

A nation, says Renan is a spiritual principle constituted by two things, "one is the possession in common of a rich legacy of memories; the other is actual consent, the desire to live together, the will to continue to make the best use of the invisible heritage received" (in Gokak 1979: 76). This legacy of memories in case of India is more rich and grand one. M.M. Dutt through *The Captive Ladie* opens the historical legacy of India and generates national pride among the Indians.

H.M. Williams rightly remarks: "*The Captive Ladie* is a narrative poem on a subject taken from Indian history interspersed with references to Hindu myths and legends" (17). Basically this is a love poem where history is strongly blended with love.

The poem deals with one of the most popular legends of Indian history, that of Prithviraj, the king of Delhi, who ruled in the eleventh century, just before the beginning of a series of Afghan raids into India. The subject of the poem is the jealousy and rivalry for supremacy in northern India between Prithviraj and Jai Chand, the king of Kanouj. When the latter celebrated the time-honoured 'feast of victory' almost all the contemporary princes, with the exception of Prithviraj, accepting Kanouj's overlordship, attended the feast. Highly incensed at the refusal of Prithviraj, the king of Kanouj ordered an image to be made to represent the absent chief. On the last day of the feast, Prithviraj and his followers, entering the palace in disguise, carried away not only the image but also the Princess Royal, whose hand he solicited in vain. The fair princess was, however, retaken and confined in a solitary castle from which her lover effected her escape and married her. The king of Kanouj never forgave this insult. When Mohammed of Ghazni from Afghanistan invaded Prithviraj's kingdom of Delhi, Kanouj sternly refused to aid his son-in-law in expelling the foe, who soon after crushed him also. Unsupported Prithviraj could not stop the Afghan invader; his kingdom was sacked. But before the Muslims could enter the city next morning, Prithviraj and his captive princess killed themselves by mounting a funeral pyre. This is how the course of events runs through the poem.

This glorification of historical past has aim to enrich the spirit of renaissance in India. By reawakening the minds of the Indians through this historical consciousness, the poem regenerates national spirit among the Indians.

Through this poem, M.M. Dutt shows the valour and heroism of Prithviraj of whom Indians can rightly be proud, on the other hand, the mean jealousy of the king of Kanouj which paved the way for the eventual Muslim conquest of India. Thus, along with the motive of inculcating pride in India's cultural heritage among the Indians, there is an added motive of instructing the western readers about India's heritage, culture and social values. He reminds his countrymen the glory and greatness of their ancestors, to draw their attention to the direct cause of their fall, and to show the evil of disunity, amongst them and to create the spirit of valour in their mind.

Memory of the historical past promotes the love of the motherland and patriotism. This is clearly disclosed in this poem.

IV. Shoshee Chunder Dutt and Hur Chunder Dutt

After Michael Madhusudan Dutt, the two minor voices of Bengal *viz.* Shoshee Chunder Dutt and Hur Chunder Dutt explored the glorious past of India to regenerate national confidence among the Indians and thereby to promote the spirit of nationalism and renaissance.

Shoshee Chunder Dutt (1825-86), in his collection *A Vision of Sumeru and Other Poems* (n.d.) asserts the legendary and historical past of India. There are some poems in this collection which manifest the glorious past of India; but the poem entitled "Sivajee" gives strong assertion of Indian nationalism. The spirit of Indian nationalism is asserted through the heroic deeds of Shivaji.

The poem is set on the well-known historical incident that took place in 1666 at Agra when Shivaji visited the great Moghal Emperor Aurangzeb in his court. This incident is the subject of the course of narration in the poem. After the death of his father Aurangzeb made his first public entry in the Agra Fort and decided to celebrate his fiftieth lunar birthday which fell on 12th May. As Shivaji was expected to reach Agra about the same time, it was arranged that his first audience with the Emperor should take place in that Durbar on 12th May. Aurangzeb was then at the height of his glory.

This historical incident intensely appealed to the poetic sensibility of Shoshee Chunder Dutt. The renaissance spirit ushered in India created national zeal in the Bengali elites, which in turn, made the elites to delve into the historical past of India thereupon to strengthen the national awakening. This sublime historical past generates pride among the Indians.

The historical consciousness operates in the poem as:

> They led him to the stately hall,
> Before the royal throne,
> Where, towering in the pomp of power,
> The tyrant sat alone;
> And knights and nobles stood around.
>
> (Gokak 1985: 68)

The entry of Maratha Jagirdar Shivaji in the court of royal status of Aurangzeb brings the flavour of Moghal empire. He made salutation and offered nazar to the Emperor. But Shivaji could not receive smile from Aurangzeb. The self-respect of Shivaji was afflicted. The poet brings the humiliation of Shivaji as:

> Now mock'd the valiant Sivajee
> with cold respects and sneer.

He was a Maratha Jagirdar and he deserved his royal status which was deliberately mocked in the court. He was made to stand in the row of third-rate nobles of the empire. He could not bear their servile scorn. He was totally heaved with anger. Being a symbol of heroism, with great respect, the poet reveals:

> He was not born to shame.

This clearly brings message to the Indians in the nineteenth century who were under the mental slavery of British. The self-respect of Shivaji regenerates the spirit of nationalism. Here Shivaji stands for dignity, self-respect. Here the humiliating treatment was not restricted to Shivaji as a royal person but the great Jagirdar of Maratha. Through Shivaji the whole Maratha spirit was humiliated.

This glorification of the historical past promotes patriotism. The poem records the heroism of Shivaji who did not submit to Moghal emperor Aurangzeb despite all physical tortures inflicted upon him. Shivaji stands for self-respect, freedom, strong will, courage, valour and heroism. Thus the glorification of heroic figure shaped by time naturally accelerates the spirit of nationalism.

Hur Chunder Dutt's "Tarra Baee" recreates historical consciousness in the mind of readers. She is presented as a valorous lady obsessed with the spirit to enhance the honour of her forefathers by redeeming the region Thoda from slavery. To redeem Thoda she declared the war. The head note of the poem runs as: "Sootan being deprived of Thoda by Lilla the Afghan, occupied Bednore. His daughter Tarra Baee or the star of Bednore, stimulated the reverses of her family and by the incentive of its ancient glory, scorned the habiliments and occupations of her sex and devoted herself to many sports and exercises. When princes made proposals for her hand, her answer was, 'Redeem Thoda and my hand is thine.'"

According to some historians, the heroic figure Tara Bai appears in the medieval period of India. In seventeenth century, queen Channamma was ruling in Bednore and she enjoyed the status as a star due to her valour and heroism. And so her name is coined as a 'Tara Bai.' This Tara Bai and the Tara Bai from Maratha empire have no similarity in any respect but only in name.

The purpose of this poem is to glorify the past history and thus to promote the feelings of patriotism and freedom in the decadent life of Bengalis. The poem enriches national feelings.

1.2.2 Indian Poetry from 1857 to 1920

The first phase of Indian English poetry ends with 1850 and second phase seriously begins from 1857. The first or early phase of Indian English poetry was imbued with the western scholarship and the result of it, the new zeal and enthusiasm led the Indian poets to depict Indian personality and ethos and thus Indian renaissance commenced. Naturally, the spirit of nationalism asserted in the form of social and reformative zeal. The poets had no concept of nationalism as such; but this zeal itself was nationalistic in spirit.

In the second phase of Indian English poetry (1857-1920), the spirit of nationalism is more distinct and strongly Indian in colour. The glorious aspect of Indian nationalism emanates through the texts of poetry and the spirit of it is more radiant and purely Indian one. Here we find the shift in sensibility—from rationalism to nationalism. Rationalism was the watchword of the first generation of English educated Bengalis. M.K. Naik rightly observes: "The Indian English literature really came of age after 1857, when India's rediscovery of her identity became vigorous all absorbing quest and when she had learnt enough from the West to progress from imitation to creation" (1989: 35).

In the second phase, the rediscovery of Indian identity is purely Hindu in spirit. The spirit of Hindu nationalism locates its roots in religious scriptures and rich cultural life of India. Here Indian nationalism takes the form of Hindu nationalism. Naturally the spirit is fully engaged in casting out religious and cultural identity of India in Hindu garb.

Indian English poetry from 1857 to 1920 is wholly devoted to the revival of Hinduism which is religious nationalism in general. Naturally the contemporary poetry has great obsession with ancient and religious past of India. The poetry of Toru Dutt, Sarojini Naidu, Sri Aurobindo and Rabindranath Tagore is, more or less, manifestation of Hindu nationalism.

V. Toru Dutt

After 1857, Toru Dutt (1856-77) is the first Indian poet who reacted with the Hindu ethos with great fervour and thereby contributed to the regeneration of nationalism. In her poetry, there is a fine assertion of self-identification with rich mythological past of India. The self-identification with the cultural heritage is in a way a search for identity in the historical and cultural continuity of the nation. This is also an attempt to assert that the people of this country are the inheritors of the rich cultural past and, thus, to ensure the national identity.

Next, this search for identity in rich cultural past is strongly influenced by the impact of Renaissance and the derogatory attitude towards Hinduism propagated by Christian missionaries. Besides this, the intellectual reforms and the establishment of religious organizations in the nineteenth century incited the creative minds to assert themselves in their search for Hindu identity.

Toru Dutt expresses her great reverence for ancient Hindu past in her work *Ancient Ballads and Legends of Hindustan* (1882). The shaping influence on Toru's personality was her mother—a religious lady well-versed in Hindu scriptures, myths and legends. Toru Dutt had inherited her strong intellectual and mental qualities from her father and the moral beauty and humanness from her mother.

In *Ancient Ballads* she converted popular stories from the *Ramayana,* the *Mahabharatha,* and the *Puranas* into English verse. Dutt was trying to win a place of dignity for the Indian classics through her renderings. This glorification of the past was with the purpose to strengthen the Indian identity and to reaffirm the roots in racial past.

Toru Dutt's ballads about ancient legends of Hindustan symbolize the Indian poet's return to her Indian identity in spite of her crucial fascination for France and England. In *Ancient Ballads*, there are nine ballads and legends and a single non-mythological poem "Our Casuarina Tree." The ballads served the young poet to reassert her own Indian identity through the legendary figures—Savitri, Dhruva, Prahlad, Buttoo, Lakshman, and Sita (each a household name in Hindu India).

Toru's love of Hinduism may be clearly sensed in the stories collected in *Ancient Ballads*. Her self-identification with legendary past of India is to generate pride among Indians about Hindu ideals, philosophy and thereby to reaffirm the national identity. In the narration of these legends, we rediscover Hindu identity and Hindu nationalism.

All these legends and ballads of Hindustan do one thing—they reveal search for Indian national identity. Hindu philosophy is the source of these ballads. The interest in ancient Indian tradition and culture serves the purpose of developing the spirit of Hindu nationalism and the accompanying sense of self-identification. The ballads together aspire to promote the sense of continuity, unity and integration in the Indian life. John B. Alphanso Karkala emphasises the significance of these stories: "These are not mere fancy tales. Though they were inventions of the poets of the past, they had come down the ages as models of virtue meant to teach and delight the collective conscience of Indian people" (122).

Her greatness as a poet was that she touched the chord of our racial and religious ethos by her rendering of those deathless stories from the Indian classics. Her efforts in poetry were complementary to the efforts of social and religious reformation initiated by the early stalwarts of the Indian renaissance.

VI. Sri Aurobindo

After Toru Dutt, the spirit of Hindu nationalism further enhanced and strengthened in the hands of the great poet-seer and yogi Sri Aurobindo (1872-1950). He realised his roots in Indian culture and thought immediately on his return to India from Cambridge in 1893. 'There is a divinity that shapes our ends,' wrote Shakespeare in *Hamlet* and it seems that Aurobindo's return to India in 1893—the year in which Swami Vivekananda set out to illumine the West with the light of the East—marked the beginning of Aurobindo's journey planned out for him by the divine Mother.

It was during the period of his Baroda State service (1893-1906), Aurobindo experienced a reawakening of his Indian consciousness which had remained dormant in him. It was during this period that the poet in him blossomed, when his mind was drawn not only to the Indian classics and legends but also to the nationalistic upsurge which was just on in the country. Once in India, he had been led to Indian themes and drawing his consciousness nurtured in the Vedic-Upanishadic tradition.

Aurobindo's interest in spiritual heritage of India is developed through via classical and legendary past of India. He struck with spiritual transformation in Alipur jail. His participation in the revolutionary politics of Bengal culminated in his arrest and imprisonment. It was here that Aurobindo had his initiation into the world of spirituality through the mystic experience of *Narayan Darshan* which came to him.

The socio-religious climate at the time of Aurobindo's arrival in India was charged with Hinduism and demand of freedom. The revival spirit was at its apex. Many socio-religious organisations were engaged in rediscovering the cultural and religious past of India. The spirit of Hinduism and patriotism was in air. It was a period of Indianization. The elites in Bengal considered the freedom of India as a spiritual mission and realised that it was impossible to get freedom without religious and spiritual language. For them, India's dominant spirituality was the only factor that was responsible for the survival of India's Indianness before gigantic influence of the West.

This background influenced Aurobindo to nourish his spiritual nationalism. The regeneration of mankind through evolution into higher states of being is the aim of spirituality. In *The Ideal of Karmyogin* Aurobindo stated in clear terms: "The task we set before ourselves is not mechanical but moral and spiritual. We aim not at the alteration of a form of government but at the building up of a nation. Of that politics is not a part, but only a part [...]. It is spiritual revolution that we foresee and the material is only its shadow and reflex" (1950: 2-3).

In Baroda, Aurobindo had a first decisive experience that of *Nirvana.* The *Nirvana* experience developed spirituality in him. He warned the people that it would be an error to think that spirituality is a thing divorced from life. He asked the people to self-surrender to that power within us which rules the world. He induced people to recover the Vedanta, the Gita, the Yoga. He appealed: "You must win back the kingdom of yourselves, the inner Swaraj before you can win back your outer empire."

Aurobindo's spirituality has a strong base of Hindu religion. Ancient Hindu culture and religion is the spiritual home of Aurobindo. He locates his roots and roots of Hindu race in age-old Aryan scriptures and thus, he brings the sense of the continuity of the Hindu race. In his famous *Uttarpara* speech, he raises the question 'What is Hindu religion?' and explains: 'It is the one religion which insists every moment on the truth which all religions acknowledge that He is in all men and all things, that in Him we move and have our being' (1997: 49).

Aurobindo's nationalism has a religious concern. It is an offspring of Hindu religion. It has its roots in the spiritual heritage of India. Aurobindo's creed of 'spiritual nationalism' evolved out of his belief in the fact that 'only by becoming great and free in heart, can we become socially and politically great and free' (1950: 5). Nationalism according to him was "a religion that has come from God" (1974: 23). A nation could rise only when nationalism is worshipped in a 'religious spirit.' He dispelled the fears of those who were uncertain of the victory of nationalism by saying: "Nationalism is not going to be crashed. Nationalism survives in the strength of God and it is not possible to crush it, whatever weapons are brought against it. Nationalism is immortal, Nationalism cannot die because God cannot be killed, God cannot be sent to jail" (23-24).

His vision of free India rose majestically above the narrow confines of political self-interest as his religion of nationalism sought to realise the divine unit in the nation, a unity in which all the components—individual, social and political and economic—are fundamentally one and equal.

By propagating the idea of spiritual nationalism, Aurobindo wanted to build up the strength of the country on a mass basis so that it could stand upon its own feet in a posture of self-reliance which would compel the British to recognise India's right to be free. He himself clarified that the religion of nationalism was "religious not in the sense of doctrine and dogmas—but religious in so far as to evoke the highest devotion and the greatest sacrifice from us" (In Mujumdar 1969: 78).

The spiritual experience in the poems many times attains the mystical plane and such experiences are veiled by symbols and myths.

Sri Aurobindo's epic *Savitri* (1954) can be studied as a serious quest for the spiritual identity of India. As the story relates to Hindu legendary figures like Savitri, Narad, Ashwapathy and Satyavan, it immediately brings out the Hindu ethos. Moreover, the symbolic meaning asserted by these characters has enriched the Vedic heritage of India. Though these characters are allied to human experiences, their tendency is to suggest rich spiritual experiences through symbols. In Aurobindo's poetry these myths manifest as symbols which have a direct allegiance with the philosophy of the *Upanishads,* the *Mahabharata* and the *Ramayana.* Thus the characters are steeped in Hindu philosophy. The whole poem develops as one of the aspects of spiritual nationalism.

The whole plot of the epic is based on the belief in the divine life on earth as the inevitable future of mankind, the fruition of its long and tardy evolution. The protagonists, Aswapathy and Savitri are in the forefront of this grand design. In their vast spiritual journeys, Sri Aurobindo maps out his version of the structure of the universe and its meaning. The symbolic treatment is one of the dimension of the poem which contributes to the consolidation of the divine aspect of the poem. M.K. Naik (1989: 55) asserts the spiritual quality of the poem: "Savitri" is an 'inner epic,' an epic of the soul and the Oversoul. Nor is it, like Toru Dutt's ballad, a simple retelling of an ancient Hindu myth. It is distillation of Sri Aurobindo's philosophy of Integral Yoga. The images and the symbols in the poem rightly reintegrate the Indian identity. The symbolic treatment in the poem clearly reveals the search for spiritual identity of the Indians.

VII. Rabindranath Tagore

Tagore (1861-1941) is one of the finest products of Indian renaissance, who comes closest to Sri Aurobindo in the treatment of Indian spirituality and mysticism. However, Tagore differs from Aurobindo. In Aurobindo we find total manifestation of spiritual experience, but Tagore does not sacrifice the poetry at the altar of spirituality. His poetry is fusion of poetry and mystic feelings. Tagore shows his sympathy with the downtrodden and the suffering masses of India, obliquely criticising the oppression of the British. Though Tagore belongs, like Sri Aurobindo, more to the twentieth century than to the nineteenth, he represents the new tradition which emerged on Indian cultural and literary scenes at the turn of the century as a consequence of the impact of the West.

Tagore was a very prolific writer who enriched our literature with numerous poems, plays, short stories, novels and other prose writings. However, his achievement as a poet mainly rests on his English *Gitanjali* (1912). Almost all those who commended his English *Gitanjali* emphasised Rabindranath's mystical appeal. *Gitanjali* is very spiritually charged, almost galvanized by the mystical power.

The central theme of *Gitanjali* is devotional. Naturally, the *Gitanjali* songs may be considered as a twentieth-century manifestation of the great *bhakti* tradition in Indian poetry, a tradition in which the 'Vaishnava' and 'Saiva' poets of old sang, pouring forth their love of God, expressing the joy and ecstasy they experienced in their communion with the Divine. We can see in these songs a revival of the *bhakti* tradition, the kind of revival brought about by Ramananda in the north and Ramanuja in the south and again by Kabir under the influence of the former and in reaction to the dry intellectualism of the Vedanta. Like the Vaishnava lyrics of Jayadev and the devotional songs of Kabir both of whom had influenced Tagore in a very profound way, *Gitanjali* songs are inspired by what may be called the mystical religion of love. It is a poetry inspired by pure devotion and mystical communion with the divine, by a participation in the *lila* or the total joy of the cosmic play of which the phenomenal world is but a manifestation.

There is no doubt that the songs in *Gitanjali* manifest the Indian tradition of devotion; but these devotional songs are veiled by the spiritual and mystical experiences as embodied in the great *Upanishads.*

The deep desire for God-vision as the sweetest thing in life and as the glory of the soul is expressed in a number of songs. In Song No. 5 the poet yearns for union with the divine and so begs for His permission to stop his worldly activities for a moment and pass the time in the contemplation of the divine. He says that he will discharge his worldly duties after such a moment of contemplation. His yearning for the divine is so acute that he is restless and knows not a moment's peace. His works appear to him to be a constant, never-ending drudgery. He will be able to take interest in it only after he has been face to face with his maker at least for some time.

The relationship between the Man and his Maker or the Finite and the Infinite finds its bold assertion in Vedantic philosophy. The dormant urge to meet the Infinite in the Finite is emphasised in the *Upanishad.* Moreover, the conception of

Divine Love is purely the Vaishnava ideal. This philosophy of Vaishnavism emphasizes an organic relationship between God and man. Its first principle is that everything is God and all the actions of man should be dedicated to Him (Srivastava 1976: 136-37).

The poet's yearning for merger with God constitutes mystic sensibility. This deep desire for God-vision as the sweetest thing in life and as the glory of the soul is also expressed in Songs Nos. 18, 38 and 76.

In song No. 18, the poet reveals his desire of God-vision as:

> If thou showest me not thy face, if
> thou leavest me wholly aside, I know
> not how I am to pass these long, rainy
> hours. (15)

If He neglects the poet and does not give him His *darshan,* the poet does not know how he would pass the dark and lonely hours of night when it rains outside. Here, poet describes his intense yearning for complete identification with God and also the pangs of separation in the path of God-realization. The same desire is expressed in Songs Nos. 38 and 76 respectively.

This deep desire for God-vision refers back to the Hindu mysticism expounded in the *Upanishads.* It rightly promotes pride about the Hindu spiritual heritage.

The human soul as 'beloved' yearning for merger or union with God the 'lover' is a major component of the vision of the mystics all over the world. But Tagore comes closer to Sufi mystics in his divine love conceived in human or earthly terms. In Sufi mysticism we find "the identity of the individual and God, or the lover and the beloved; and the world is seen as the manifestation of God." There is evidently a Sufi strain in Tagore's mysticism. In the poems of Kabir, one finds a mystical abstraction of looking at God as Divine Lover and devotee as Bride. In the visionary deliberations of Kabir and Tagore, love transcends all other barriers for the union of man with God. Tagore has the rarest combination of harmonising human love with spiritual elegance. He has been called the 'spiritual descendant of Vaishnavas and Sufi mystics' (Rama Swami 1988: 138). Both Kabir and Tagore regard God in their worship as "Master," "Lover," "Father," "Beloved," "Mother," "Bridegroom," "Boatman," "Musician" and "Seer." On the instance of Vaishnava cult, both the poets accept soul as bride who always longs for union with her eternal lover, God. In *Gitanjali,* God is Lover and also Beloved; God is Father, King, Master-poet and also Friend.

VIII. Sarojini Naidu

The spirit of Indian nationalism is displayed in varied colours and contours in the poetry of Sarojini Naidu. She followed the footsteps of Toru Dutt, Aurobindo and Tagore and explored the rich ancient heritage of India and the folk culture of the rural India prompted her to distinguish Indian mythology, customs, manners, festivals and, thereby, to generate pride among colonised Indians and thus to reassert their national identity. Aurobindo was interested in the spiritual regeneration of India; on the contrary Naidu's attempt was to depict the common scenes and sights in the country which distinguish the cultural identity of the nation. She was very much interested in the different aspects of Indian life which constitute the heritage of India. Especially the folk themes in her poetry reveal the search for national identity of the Indians. And so her folk poetry is a fine assertion of Indian nationalism.

The folk song "Palanquin Bearers" reveals the Indian reality through folk characters. Palanquin Bearers are depicted as a part of feudal system of Indian life and they glorify their tradition without the least reference to their oppression under this system. Sarojini Naidu composes a 'folk' song out of their reality, in terms which would please the gentry.

Naidu depicts this common scene in Hyderabad as representing the traditional Indian life. She has a high idealised sense for this life and is least concerned about the toil, sweat and oppression of the Palanquin Bearers. The poem rightly brings out one of the facets of the Indian life—the feudal system in India and the Palanquin Bearers as the most natural part of this system. The Palanquin Bearers was one of the sanctioned customs of the contemporary Indian life. Naidu glorifies this custom in a view to reassert the sense of Indianness and thereby, to develop pride among Indians about the rich heritage of folk culture which was vanishing due to the colonisation.

The search for Indian identity is continued in further "Indian Weavers." The weavers' tradition was a part of social life of India. But due to industrialisation, it was losing its colour and strength. Naidu through her poetic discourse has recreated this folk tradition with great reverence.

Weavers constitute the part of the economic structure of rural India and after industrialisation was launched by the British, this Indian tradition was on the verge of dying. Naidu rightly captures the spirit of this Indian tradition so it naturally manifests in her poem.

Naidu's lyrics give expression to the distinct Indian folk personality, in order to reintegrate the Indians with their rich cultural heritage. This spirit is reflected in her "Wandering Singers."

With their musical instruments in their hands, they always keep on singing and wandering. 'Walls,' *i.e.* national, provincial, racial, caste, etc., prejudices do not separate them from their fellowmen. They consider all men to be their brothers, and all the world to be their home. They are cosmopolitan in their outlook. They believe in the oneness of all men. They are votaries of world brotherhood.

In the 'face of modernity,' Naidu affirms the Indian identity through wandering singers. Wandering singers belong to the cultural heritage of India and Naidu is not ready to lose this Indian tradition under the threat of modernity.

Naidu's poetry is deeply attuned to the great ideals which inspire and regulate the life of Indians. She induced pride among the Indians about their centuries old folk-life, culture, customs and nature through her poetry. The Indian ethos thus recreated in the poem rightly reveals the search for national identity of Indians.

While Sri Aurobindo, Toru Dutt, Rabindranath Tagore and Sarojini Naidu were the most important among the poets who emerged on the nineteenth century Indian English literary scene and continued (with the exception of Toru Dutt) to write in the earlier decades of the present century, there were a number of other poets who made significant contribution to the Indian English poetry in the earlier phases of its growth. Not all of them deserve serious attention, except for historical reasons. Only Swami Vivekananda is worth to be considered in the context of the spirit of nationalism.

IX. Swami Vivekananda

Swami Vivekananda (1863-1902) is the last poet of the nineteenth century who gave expression to the spiritual quest of ancient India. The gospel that Vivekananda preached was that each man is potentially divine and it is in the realization of the divinity of men and their essential unity that the future of mankind lay. Vivekananda believed that no enduring solution of the problems of men could be achieved without a religious or spiritual transformation of the character of men. His message to Indians was: "Up, India, and conquer the world with your spirituality."

Vivekananda wrote only a few lyrics, but they give an authentic embodiment to his profound spiritual perception and realization. He is not a poet in the conventional sense of the word, but belongs to the category of 'singers'—Kabir, Chaitanya, Tukaram and Nanak. His vision and voice as expressed in his poetry are a trumpet note to awaken the mass-mind, a clarion call to the spiritual essence in man. His quest in poetry may be treated as a legacy of the spiritual past of India. This rediscovery of the spiritual ethos of India is directed to the assertion of the national identity of Indians.

1.2.3 Indian Poetry from 1920 to 1947

The third phase of Indian English poetry starts from 1920 and ends in 1947. With nearly a hundred years of renaissance and social reform behind, Indians had gained the moral and ideological advantage over the British. The struggle for the overthrow of British power gathered momentum as Gandhi appeared on the political scene of India. In general, there was a sense of exuberance and hope; the prevailing atmosphere was almost millennial. India was going through one of its most optimistic and buoyant periods in recent history. The freedom struggle had reached its peak and there was an unprecedented awakening among sections of society. In literature, some of the greatest writers of the century were at their most productive. In the area of Indian English poetry, this period gives no evidence of any new major voices. Again we find the poets like Sri Aurobindo and Rabindranath Tagore who had consolidated their reputation before the advent of the Gandhian age. M.K. Naik proclaims: "The impact of the Gandhian whirlwind produced no outstanding poetry of any kind" (1989: 140). Though poetry failed to record spirit of Gandhian age, fiction gave an authentic expression of Gandhian movement and socio-political realities of the contemporary period. Thus, we realise that what poetry lost, fiction gained. However, the poets like Armando Menzes and Humayun Kabir were influenced by the Gandhian whirlwind and naturally their poetry articulated the fervour of freedom struggle and the spirit of the decade of 1920s. Their poetry was close to the Gandhian time.

The writers of verse may conveniently be considered as belonging to two groups—practitioners of religious, mystical and philosophical reflective verse, including disciples of Sri Aurobindo and poets mainly in the Romantic Victorian tradition, who treat a wider range of themes.

The trend of mystical and religious poetry established by Sri Aurobindo continued in the period 1920 and onwards. Though it was a period of Gandhi, poetry very casually reacted with the spirit of Gandhian politics. It was engaged in giving spiritual and mystical relations. The nationalist urge was sublimated and realised in spiritual poetry. The flowering of mystical and religious poetry was a logical progression in the construction of identity—both personal and national. The poets who contributed in this period are: K.D. Sethna, J. Krishnamurti, Swami Parmanand and Swami Rama Tirtha.

It is true that the Indian English poetry was not close with the spirit of time. The poetry was still in the hands of Aurobindo's disciples and some mystics. Naturally the spirit of the struggle for freedom very rarely voiced in the text of the poet. Only Armando Menezes and Humayun Kabir have reacted with the contemporary political situation. They have given expression to the political aspect of Indian nationalism, especially the political event of 1942.

According to Hans Kohh, the struggle for freedom is the second phase of nationalism. This phase reflects in the poetry of Armando Menezes, Humayun Kabir and V.N. Bhushan.

The dream of freedom ushered in by the Gandhian movement gets quite rightly revealed in the poetry of Menzes, Kabir and Bhushan.

1.3 Conclusion

Thus, the spirit of nationalism expounded by the poets in the pre-Independence period is solely occupied with the search for national identity. As the colonial rule suppressed the Indian identity, the Indian elites in contact with Renaissance turned to the rich heritage of India. This was the initial attempt at self-expression or self-identification, on the part of Indian poets. In the latter phases, this identity is consolidated through social, historical and political spheres.

The Indian English poets from Henry Derozio to V.N. Bhushan were extensively engaged in defining their own identity and along with it the identity of the nation. For this, they handled various themes which strengthened their search for Indian identity. The themes treated by these poets—Indian culture in all its aspects, Indian spirituality and mysticism, the social and reformative concern, the historical past, Indians' love for Mother India and the Indian nature, and patriotism—amply illustrate the spirit of Indian nationalism. The search for identity in the cultural sphere consolidated the nation and in the course of time, it resulted into the political freedom of India.

The sense of nationality or the spirit of nationalism inevitably grows out of the discovery of identity. During the pre-

Independence period, this discovery is engaged in various ways. The poets, while constructing their cultural identity construct the identity of the nation. Thus, the concentrated endeavour of the poets during pre-Independence period is inevitably directed towards the revelation of the spirit of nationalism.

WORKS CITED

Aurobindo, Sri. *Savitri.* Pondicherry: Sri Aurobindo Ashram, 1970.

——. *The Renaissance of India,* Vol. XIV. Pondicherry: Sri Aurobindo Birth Centenary Library, 1972.

——. *The Present Situation.* Pondicherry: Sri Aurobindo Ashram, 1974.

——. *India's Rebirth.* Paris: Institute De Recherce Evoluties, Co-publisher Mera Aditi, Mysore 2nd edition, 1997.

Derozio, Henery. *Poems of HLV Derozio, A Forgotten Anglo-Indian Poet,* ed., R.K. Das Gupta, Calcutta: OUP, 1980.

Dutt, Toru. *Ancient Ballads and Legends of Hindustan.* Allahabad: Kitabistan, 1941.

Gokak, V.K. *The Golden Treasury of Indo-Anglian Poetry.* New Delhi: Sahitya Akademi, 1985.

Karkala, John B. Alphanso. *Indo-English Literature in the Nineteenth Century.* Mysore: University of Mysore, 1970.

Naik, M.K. *Perspectives on Indian Poetry in English.* New Delhi: Abhinav Publications, 1984.

——. *History of Indian English Literature.* New Delhi: Sahitya Akademi, 1989.

Nehru, Pandit Jawaharlal. *The Discovery of India.* Bombay, 1961.

Paranjape, Makarand, ed. *Sarojini Naidu: Selected Poetry and Prose.* New Delhi: Indus, 1993.

Spear, Sir Perceival. *India, A Modern History.* Ann. Arbor, 1961.

Tagore, Rabindranath. *Gitanjali.* London: Macmillan, 1959.

Verghese, C. Paul. *Problems of the Creative Writers in English.* Bombay: Somaiya POublications, 1971.

Williams, H.M. "Indian Literature in English." In *Galaxy of Indian Writing in English.* Delhi: Akshat Publications, 1987.

——. *Indo-Anglian Literature 1800-1970.* New Delhi: Orient Longman, 1976.

18

A.K. Ramanujan's Conception of the Self

SARANGA D. BARAL

Self at the centre of all search manifests itself in Ramanujan's art from the very beginning of his creative life. And the artist has all through assumed an elusive character till his vision clears. It is important to note that his vision of the self permeates most of his elusive poems, the poems which have so far been faulted on one account or another. The first one comes to my mind is "The Striders," which is not by chance, the opening poem of Ramanujan's first volume of poems, and this volume *The Striders* (1966, London: OUP) is also entitled after this poem. Ramanujan's concern with the self and hence his idea of the individuality of beings is very much there, but misted with an uncanny subject like *water-bug* and more, gone veiled under an objectivist style of the moderns. The *strider* to Ramanujan is a uniquely personal experience, such an experience as characterises "$KMNO_4$ in Grandfather's Shaving Glass" (*TS* 28-29). These two poems, among many others, are not as banal as they are made out to be. The style adopted in the poems is peculiarly a Ramanujan-device to serve best his slowly evolving vision of the self. In the first poem, the poet emphatically focuses on the miracle performed by the strider, a tiny creature, which always escapes our grand-seeing eyes. The poet means what he says: "No, not only the prophets walk on water." He recognises the strider, he recognises the self. It is said that John Keats had the capacity to smell the beautiful even in the garbage. Fairly here, it is Ramanujan who senses merit in the smallest. Well, with Ramanujan, it is not so much a case of appreciating the observed, the outward, as it is an act of inwardising what is seen, what is encountered: there is always some symbiosis between outward observation and self-exploration. Such creative correspondence is natural to the poet, to the artist, the sensitive soul; but to us, normal are it only sounds absurd or seems austere.

"The Striders" is a dramatic self-exploration, a quest for "a tiny strip of sky," for a little space of one's own in a vast world, infested with the masters, the "prophets." Thus, underneath an objective mode of seeing minutely a strider's miracle, there is a deliberate, hidden, absorptive dwelling on the self. The strider's "perch" on "the ripple skin" of a stream gives an easy idea of its outward stability, fixity. But a close look would reveal how the water-bug adapts continuously to the rippling stream, in order to keep itself steady on the continuously changing phenomenon. It is imaginable, even scientifically, how beneath a stable picture of cinematography there are a hundred continuous, swift snaps of photographs, juxtaposed mechanically to give an idea of the living. Thus, instability underlies the life's seeming stability; the self cannot endure fixity; change and flux neatly describe the self's stable truth. Therefore, the strider is a symbol of an individual self, while the ripple skin of a stream is a metaphor for the flux of being. "Towards Simplicity" (TS 35) is also another poem of Ramanujan in his search for the self, and which details the particularities of its physical nature, in especial. It is roughly designed in a 'sonnet' form, which I quote in full:

> Corpuscle, skin,
> cell, and membrance,
> each its minute seasons
> clocked within the bones.
> Millions grow lean and fall away
> in the hourly autumn of the body.
> But fertile in fall, ending as others begin,
> to the native of death they run.
> From the complexity
> of reasons gyring within reasons,

> of co-extensive spring and autumn,
> into the soil as soil we come,
> to find for a while a simplicity
> in larger, external seasons. (*The Strider* 1966: 35)

The image of gyre here reminds us of W.B. Yeats and his idea of the underlying change of history and the recreation of the world through self-conflicting forces.[1] Ramanujan's quest here is limited in scope, limited to the level of body which is such a mysterious house as embodying "to-extensive spring and autumn" and inside which millions of cells, tissues, and corpuscles die their "hourly" death: they are "fertile in fall, ending as others begin." An unending process of change is relevant also to a larger, external world. This poem is an attempt on the part of the poet to understand the "co-extensive" changes, the continuously changing phenomena within this human body, within the self on its physical level. The complexity of birth and growth simplified by death, as the poet sees, characterises the nature of our physical existence. But this is too simplistic to understand the "hourly" deaths and births that go ceaselessly within us; too deductive to comprehend "the complexity of reasons gyring within reasons." Again, the growth of this self and the process of this growth are to be envisioned in "$KMNO_4$ in Grandfather's Shaving Glass" (*TS*). We have to mark very closely how "a tall water column of clarity" which receives "a drop of potassium permanganate" turns into "pallor" till "pallor pales into transparency." but the water column gets "blued by a past sensation." And finally, with the addition of another drop of $KMNO_4$ the water goes "brewed to winedark." The poet is not merely re-enacting a child's wonder, here. But, then, a child's wonder is not for nothing being elucidated in a language of a mature man. A water column of "clarity" to its "winedark" marks the process of change onto its growth, the process of which would also depict the change and growth of a human being, of the self from a childhood to a stage of manhood. We can also notice and feel how sensitively the poet describes the unravelling of $KMNO_4$ in the living terms of human and plant proximity: vein, tress, and filament; past sensation, capillary roots; loosening skein and winedark. Thus, Ramanujan's interest is evidently not of a chemist's in this poem, as his interest is not of a biologist's in "Towards Simplicity." These poems are his inner concerns to understand the vital process or processes that are integral to the moulding or making of the self. Therefore, to dismiss "$KMNO_4$ in Grandfather's [...]" as not worth a poetic experience is an error on the part of the critics.[2] Moreover, every experience leaves its scratch on the self, which our common intelligence or scientific rationalism hardly understands, the least notice. The poet in the above poem could sensitively mark how a drop of $KMNO_4$ plummets into the water column "lensing a scratch on the wall." And not only that, this self also gets somewhat affected by each and every encounter, every experience, each past action, as the water column slowly achieves a clarity but remains "slightly blued by a past sensation." Therefore, every event, each experience shapes our consciousness, shapes our vision; by this I pertinently mean that a new experience does not simply displace our past experiences, nor dismiss our past consciousness. All kinds of consciousness result from their self-absorption, and consequent inner changes, all changes shape the consciousness and the self. More often, a change is not visible because it happens with "the faintest current of stillness" as a drop of colour in the water unravels but "slow-motioned by the element."

"Elements of Composition," the opening poem of *Second Sight* (Delhi: OUP, 1986) introduces the reader to Ramanujan's idea of the self, its composition out of many elements, its process of change through a reciprocal giving and taking, and its sudden transformation to a completely new, unforeseen life-form, such as a "caterpillar." This poem, to my mind, is a culmination of Ramanujan's long search for the identity of the self, its nature and its reality. The poet's idea gets clear expression thus:

> Composed as I am, like others,
> of elements [...]
> father's seed and mother's egg

gathering earth, air, fire mostly
water, [...]
into a chattering self tangled
in love and work,
scary dreams [...]. (*Second Sight,* 1986: 11)

But into the making of one's personality, many incidents, many experiences go like scary dreams; uncle's eleven fingers playing childhood games; the riots of Nairobi; the lepers as well as the goddesses of Madurai; the Muharram tigers and the epileptic saints and all. The self is affected by them, as they are affected by the self. This self evolves, develops and grows through many divisions, decompositions ("Towards Simplicity": *TS*) and not only through additions of experiences or elements. It will not be wrong, therefore, to suggest that Ramanujan's vision of the self comes close to Henri Bergson's *elan vital* as illustrated in his *Creative Evolution* (1911). Life for both the creative artists, is to certain extent a mechanism, moulded out of "father's seed and mother's egg" and other elements added to them. But beyond this psycho-chemical phenomenon, the self remains a mystery which the mechanical theories fail to explain, as it embraces "the complexity of reasons gyring within reasons." Bergson explains lucidly:[3]

> [...] our personality shoots, grows and ripens without ceasing. Each of its moments is something new added to what was before. We may go further: it is not only something new, but something unforeseeable. Doubtless, my present state is explained by what was in me and by what was acting on me a moment ago.

That the life is a creative evolution, and that every moment for this evolution is vital, are also fundamental to Ramanujan's thought. The importance of a moment in Ramanujan's art is also already sensitively reflected by King as he observes the artist's sense of "living from moment to moment."[4] The critic comes almost near the point but misses it as Ramanujan's vision eludes him. The vitality, the creativity of every moment as enshrined in Ramanujan's art can also be explained in Bergsonian terms:[5]

> Each of them (moments of life) is a kind of creation. And just as the talent of the painter, is formed or deformed—in any case, is modified under the very influence of the works he produces, so each of our states, at the moment of its issue, modifies our personality, being indeed the new form that we are just assuming. It is then right to say that what we do depends on what we are; but it is necessary to add also that we are to a certain extent, what we do, and that we are creating ourselves continually.

Ramanujan explains the phenomenon of mutual exchanges between the self and other forces in the similar vein: "I pass through them/ as they pass through me/ taking and leaving/ affections, seeds, skeletons" ("Elements of Composition," *Second Sight).* Bergson also reflects on "these mutual exchanges, like those between two vessels separated by porous partition," while on the biological inner process, he has to observe:[6] "Life does not proceed by the association and addition of elements, but by dissociation and division." With this, Ramanujan's awareness has a striking correspondence, and he has to say:

> [...] even as I add,
> I lose, I decompose
> into my elements,
> into other names and forms,
> past and passing, tenses
> without time [...]. (*Second Sight,* 1986: 11)

Thus, like Bergson, Ramanujan views the life's continuity and discontinuity as fundamental and like the former, he also admits that the change beyond all mechanistic logics or Darwinian adaptation to the circumstances is sudden; it brings a new, unforeseeable form of the life, "a caterpillar on the leaf, eating,/ being eaten." This change is not a complete dislocation but the continuation of the same impetus, that suggests that "change" might be sudden, but the "tendencies" in life towards this change are always up on toes. Bergson emphatically states: "We said of life, that from its origin, it is the continuation of one and the same impetus, divided into divergent lines of evolution."[7] And human life is one divergent force, the most valuable one on this planet.

As evolution moves into no fixed ends, and as it is the expression of a creative urgency to be fulfilled in some novel ends, inventively generated in the process of time itself, Ramanujan's metaphor of "a caterpillar on a leaf" is very apt. This metaphor is a primitive, elemental life-form whose origin is a mystery and whose transformation into another form is more mysterious as butterfly. The idea of the self's sudden disconnection brought about by its own chemistry gets a clear expression in Ramanujan's "Looking for the Centre." He thus says:

> Suddenly, connections severed
>   as in a lobotomy, unburdened
> of history, I lose
> my bearings, a circus zilla spun
>   at the end of her rope, dizzy
> terrified,
> and happy. (*Second Sight* 82)

Therefore, terror in a sudden decomposition and happiness in a new form are simultaneous processes in the life's inner circle. Change is a necessity for the self to endure. And Bergson says that "a psychic state which remains the same so long as it is not replaced by the following state does not endure either."[8] As the critics fail to see Ramanujan's meanings as embodied in his poetry, he satirises them in "Connect" (*Second Sight* 73): "But my watchers are silent as if/ They knew my truth is in fragments."

This process of the self growing, changing and evolving, also informs Ramanujan's idea of memory. Without a little reflection on this aspect, the artist's vision, I think, may remain either incomplete in our understanding or fragmented for his 'watchers,' me included.

Memory occupies a seminal place in the art of Ramanujan. His family poems almost invariably give the impression that memory is their indispensable part, which makes them livelier or more disturbing. That apart, it is also closely associated with Ramanujan's vision of the self. Here, many questions raise their heads. Is memory in Ramanujan a dead deposit, wherein all the present like the past would rush and get dumped? Is it like a memory bank in a computer? Or, is it a graveyard from which time's ghosts are conjured up to be exorcised by the psychoanalysts? In order to answer these questions, one needs to consider Ramanujan's concept of Time which again is intimately linked with memory. 'On a Delhi Sundials' (*The Striders*) helps us understand that Ramanujan grieves for a "sundial time" as opposed to the modern idea of it: 'four and twenty ghostly circles.' The poet says:

> But who, among tourists
> on a five-day tour, can put the clock back
> and run into sundial time?

The sundial time is for the poet, a real and living concept, and it does not "slice the country silence" because time is lived in the living of life; it does not hurry us, as "four-faced clocks on market-towers" do, to feel only the transience of our existence. Ramanujan's sly and ironic comment on our accepted concept of time, which "the clock towers" give us, is noted in his "Time and Time Again" (*Relations*. London: OUP, 1971). What is highlighted in this poem is how by 'a precise act of nature, *i.e.* by real and natural time, a clock tower, symbol of mechanical time, is knocked out. The implication is surely one that distinguishes between *real time,* which is a fact lived and unreal time which is a mechanical *figure,* only *thought.* From our discussion, it is evident that Ramanujan's concept of time is, to a large extent, akin to Bergson's. Bergson has explained at length in his book *Creative Evolution* this difference between real time and "time as an independent variable" which can be shortened or lengthened by modern science. The modern sciences divide a day into hours and minutes, consider a time-period as a mathematical sum of "moments always a virtual stopping-places, always, in short, immobilities."[9] So also for a modern man, time consists of inert *units.* But for the artists, the creative souls, time is "the real duration" (Bergson's term again) which Ramanujan endorses in his work, but which generally escapes the hold of scientific knowledge. Time as *real duration* might assume an infinite stretch of time as in the case of creative pursuits or love: "coupling hands take time to kill the frost" ('Two styles in Love,' *The Striders),* or it might take infinitesimally small click of a second:

History
which usually
changes slowly,
changes sometimes
during a single conversation ("History," *Relations* 51)

Or, as in "Looking for the Centre" (*Second Sight*) this real time is realised "suddenly", on a point of time, when all the "connections" are "severed" from "history" to bring about a completely new and strange beginning. The importance of a moment for Ramanujan's creative consciousness is already dealt with. With Ramanujan as with Bergson, real time is a flux, a continuously flowing phenomenon; it is a living as well as lived fact of life and not a dead concept. Therefore, time past is not a time *passed* for all time to come, as it reveals to the sharpened consciousness of all sensitive artists. It is possible that Ramanujan's other source of influence is Eliot's idea of presence of the past in 'time present.'[10]

Memory, such as commonly accepted as a storehouse for the times past, for the experiences done away with, is not the concept to which Ramanujan subscribes. To Ramanujan, memory like time is, for ever, "real." "On Memory" (*The Striders* 19) would soon reveal this point on a little reflection:

Memory,
in a crowd of memories, seems
    to have no place
at all for unforgettable things.

"Memory" to have "no place" for "unforgettable things" is something that sounds very self-contradictory. How are things "unforgettable" if they are not called up by memory? One meaning is that the unforgettable memory is not the unmixed, pure kind of its first occurrence. Secondly, Ramanujan does not intend to emphasize a self-contradiction. On the contrary, he brings to light a living paradox, which is immanent to the true nature of a living memory. This can, of course, be substantiated only in the light of the entire poem. Here Ramanujan suggests of two kinds of memory: the one is of facts, of history, of data, of informative knowledge gained through reading and recalling, the other is of intimacy, of experience, perhaps mingled in the "blood beat." While the first kind gives away its "tangent" answers, the other kind of memory, very distinct in scope and nature from the first, can not bring up sudden, ready-made "images" or exact answers. This is because the living memory has undergone some imperceptible change in the process of being mixed with the other felt experiences. Memory hardly keeps on original reality. Thus, its successful evocation is truly creational with much of its original simplicity or complexity as being shred, but its original impetus not completely obliterated. Ramanujan reflects in the poem "On Memory":

> [...] But not
> for all my blood-beat
> nor the drill of that woodpecker beak
>   my will,
> can I hold or keep
>   one face
> and those words random-thrown
> in a tumble of your multiple faces
> as they turn in this day's dazzle [...]. (*The Striders* 19)

However, Ramanujan's "The Past" anthologised in a P. Lal's *Modern Indian Poetry in English* (1969)[11] is more revealing on this aspect of memory. I quote the full poem:

> The cavern's sculpture quickens
> an actinic process
> in the eye.
> But it's frozen again
> into the stone's oblivion
> as the moment's retina roves
> and moves
> in the white suspense
> of all the stalactites of remembrance.

A sight turning inward into experience and finally moving into the domain of a living memory is an entire process of the life's growing vision itself. The concept of real memory and the vision of the self informing it are also embodied in "Carpe Diem," another poem of Ramanujan which features in P. Lal's anthology. In the poem, the poet by means of the metaphor like 'tree' and 'fruit' explores the living continuity of real memory as well as of the self. He says that a fruit when plucked does not forget the tree's inverted image. This also affirms the fact that no single moment can be separable from real time, the flux. Memory is all the time alive there as the time past is always present. Ramanujan's "A Lapse of Memory" (*Relations* 20) also illustrates this truth about real memory and suggests that the lost memory of an amnesiac is not lost really, perhaps gone asleep or gone suppressed "somewhere."

Many of the myths and legends, that some of Ramanujan's poems enshrine, unravel another significant facet of living memory, which pertains to the "collective unconscious" in Jung's phrase. For the memory of the family relations is not the only type, individually lived or consciously presented in Ramanujan. No less important is the memory which comes from a distant past, perhaps even from time immemorial. "Prayers to Lord Murugan" (*Relations* 57-61) and "The Difference" (*Second Sight*) among others disclose such a memory. In "The Difference" (67) the poet says: "But today, out of the blue,/ when Vishnu/ came to mind, the Dark One you know/ who began as a dwarf [...]."

Therefore, real memory can also synchronise the time span of a thousand ages (Dwarf: the *Vaman avatar* of Vishnu may be traced back to a pre-Ramayan era) to a point of the present. Thereby, memory is a way to realise how the past persists in life, in the present. Ramanujan comes near Bergson again in his concept, of memory. Bergson says, "Memory is there, which conveys something of the past into the present." He further elucidates that man's "mental state, as it advances on the road of time, is continually swelling with the duration [...]."[12] An uninterrupted change really inheres in each of

Ramanujan's concepts like memory, time or self. Our scientific intelligence, our rational mind could see only an interruption here or a dislocation there. But the truth remains, as the poet means, that we change without ceasing. The fact that our life is not a reality divided between times is substantiated by Ramanujan himself in his interview to Rama Jha. There he answers[13]:

> Because you cannot entirely live in the past, neither can you entirely live in the present; *we are both these things.* The past never passes [...]. It is with us, it is what gives us the richness [...] understanding, the richness of expression. [italics mine]

Ramanujan's statement can be supplemented by some textual evidences also. This persisting of the past into the present is present in "One Reads" (*The Striders*):

> Our night's pomegranate mines
>   that cast
> their ember seeds
> into the future and the changing past
> of files, charts and last year's twins.

And, in "A Poem on Particulars" (*The Striders*), the poet, aware of the continuity of time as well as of an imperceptible presence of the future in time present itself, writes:

> [...] every one of these (oranges)
> had an absurd, almost human
>   umbilicus
> at the top
> where once the Tree
>   had poured its
>   future
>   from forgotten roots.

From our discussion so far, it is now increasingly obvious that memory and time in Ramanujan are a twin concept rather than two separate ideas. Memory which conveys to us the idea of real time as flux and that of the self as a ceaselessly changing reality is, to Ramanujan, not a dead deposit, nor a graveyard, not even a mechanical unit. It is however not a means of "protecting his Indian psyche," as Devendra Kohli[14] would like to find it. Memory constitutes Ramanujan's interior landscape and is "a means of self-exploration" as G.N. Devi[15] rightly points out. Bruce King also aptly considers that 'memories' in Ramanujan are "at the foundations of the self" and they "form his inner self."[16]

From the above discussion, it is manifest that Ramanujan's concept of the self is not analogous to the Upanisadic *Brahman,* which is considered as the source of origin for the phenomenal world and into which it dissolves. *Mundak Upanisad* in this regard says[17]:

> That is the truth (the unoriginated one). The embodied selves in millions are born of Brahman the way thousand sparks spurt out from a radiant flame. Likewise, the created selves (*bhavah*) get dissolved into the very source.

In order to reach or realize Brahman, it is said, one has to abandon all dualism, and go beyond time, memory, and all mental conceptions. So Ramanujan's changing, evolving self cannot really correspond to Brahman, which according to Samskar, is alone the truth and the world is a myth. Ramanujan like Bergson is more empirical and scientific in spirit. This may be observed that his creative mind *vis-á-vis* the essential Indian ethos but remains ambivalent, and not alienated.

NOTES AND REFERENCES

1. Ward, David. "Yeats' Conflicts with His Audience," *ELH,* Vol. 49, No. 1, 1982, 143-44.
2. Raffel, Burton. Review of *The Striders. Mahfil,* 2-3 (1966), 86. The critic criticises the image of the "Striders" as not rising from "authentic poetic experience," and "$KMNO_4$ [...]" as "a catalogue" and "superfine objectivity" gets some consideration. The critic is noted by E.N. Lall (*The Poetry of Encounter,* 1983, 52) who supports the reviewer.
3. Bergson, Henri. *Creative Evolution* (trans.) Arthur Mitchell. New York: Modern Library, 1911, 8.
4. King, Bruce. *Modern Indian Poetry in English.* Delhi: OUP, 1987, 115.
5. Bergson, Henri. *Creative Evolution* 10.
6. Bergson 99.
7. Bergson 60.

8. Bergson 6.
9. Bergson 336.
10. See Eliot, T.S. *Four Quartets.* 1962; rpt. Delhi: OUP, 1977 (2nd Impression).
11. P. Lal. *Modern Indian Poetry in English.* Calcutta: Writers Workshop, 1969, 448.
12. Bergson 4.
13. Jha, Rama. "A Conversation with A.K. Ramanujan," *The Humanities Review,* 3(1), Jan.-June 1981, 5-13. Noted by Bruce King, *Modern Indian Poetry in English,* 1987, 214-95.
14. Kohli, Devendra, "Landscape and Poetry," *Journal of Commonwealth Literature,* XII (3), April 1979.
15. Devi, G.N. "Alienation as a Means of Self-Exploration: A Study of A.K. Ramanujan's Poetry," *Chandrabhaga,* (ed.) Jayanta Mahapatra (1981) 6.
16. King Bruce 212.
17. *Mundak Up.* II.1.1 (translation mine).

19

The Contours of Individualism in the Poetry of Kamala Das

BHABANI S. BARAL

Individualism as a term is closely related to haecceity, originally employed by Duns Scotus, the thirteenth century scholastic philosopher of Scotland to denote the formal property of a person by virtue of which one individual is to be identified in relation to others.

E.M. Forster, the doyen among the believers in individualism in the essay "What I believe" writes:

> [...] as for individualism—there seems no way of getting off this, even if one wanted to. The dictator-hero can grind down his citizens till they are alike, but he cannot melt them into a single man. This is beyond his power. He can order them to merge, he can incite them to mass-antics, but they are obliged to be born separately, and to die separately and, owing to these unavoidable termini, will always be running off the totalitarian rails. The memory of birth and the expectation of death always lurk within the human being, making him separate from his fellows and consequently capable of intercourse with them. (Two cheers for democracy)

Not only Forster but a large number of writers who believe in individualism are "iconoclasts" of their own times and sometimes take recourse to what is called confessional literature. The issue becomes all the more pinpointed because Kamala Das, though not directly influenced by the feminists of sixties and seventies, takes up the causes of women with all the zeal and vigour at her command. In this respect she is essentially different from individualists of male species who deal with the same or similar themes of love and sex in their poetry. A comparison with Andrew Marvell's "To his Coy Mistress" clarifies the issue much better.

In "To his Coy Mistress" the reader discovers that the poem is a proposition or in other words, an offer of sexual intercourse. The male speaker seeks to frighten her into sexual compliance. In the opinion of *A Handbook of Critical Approaches to Literature* written in the context of Renaissance poetic tradition of equating the female body with a fortress that must be assaulted, and phrased in terms of the seventeenth century's fondness for morbid and grotesque metaphysical imagery, the poem powerfully depicts the secondary status of the female body [...]. "The feminine is thus portrayed as a negative state: that is, she does not assent; she is not in the poem; her final decision is not stated."[1] The feminist critic further continues: "No mention is made of procreation in the poem, nor of marriage, nor really of love. It is about sex."[2]

In much of Kamala Das's poetry the stuff is no different. It is the attitude of the speaker, she being mostly a female one, to subjects such as marriage, love and sex that is different. What the British author and critic Rebecca West says about the Feminist movement seems to have a ring of truth in it: "I myself have never been able to find out precisely what feminism is, I only know that other people call me a feminist whenever I express sentiment that differentiates me from a doormat or prostitute."[3] The title feminist attributed to Rebecca West here can also be unequivocally extended to Kamala Das (even though her first few volumes of poetry were published during the movement's infancy and depict her personal views on women's condition in the contemporary society). In her poems the first person account of women's sexual encounters, description of the plight of the socially oppressed women and description of the private lives of women have thoroughly made the picture of suffering women complete. Hence, the protests of the feminist ciritic in case of Marvell's poem become the staple content of female speaker's narration in Kamala Das's poetry.

The crux of the matter is that from the very beginning, human society has been dominated by the male, otherwise literature of the world would have been very different. However, it is perhaps worthwhile to mention here that the attitude of literature to love and sex is opposed to that of religion and ethics. And in this context, a female poet like Kamala Das takes advantage of her poetry to undo this historical imbalance in the society. Here is poetry which like the seventh-century anthology of erotic verse "Amarusataka" or medieval Sahaja poetry espouses free love as a means of self-realization. Verse 40 of "Amarusataka" runs as follows:

> her breasts
> were dwarfed
> in a tight embrace
> the hair of her body
> bristled with desire
> that cloth
> on her glorious hips
> melted away
> in the heat
> of the moment
>
> and with weak words
> she urged me
> Don't, Don't
>
> Thief of my pride
> Don't
> For me
> it's more than enough
>
> then I don't know
> was she asleep
> or dead
> did she merge
> with my heart
> did she dissolve
> into nothing.[4]

If "Amarusataka" glorifies love and sex and portrays "Shringara Rasa" of Indian literary criticism, deviations from this traditional Hindu approach (possibly due to seclusion of women under Muslim influence and Christian sense of guilt) comes under attack by a poet like Kamala Das. Commenting on the issue Adya Rangacharya in his essay "Sex and Indian Literature" writes:

> It is enough to note that an early and well-known proponent and commentator of the theory describes the distinctive feature of 'Rasa' as the quality of "losing oneself" in the enjoyment. It is not pleasure or joy or even ecstasy as such but the state where one loses one's identity. This is exactly a feeling that distinguishes sexual experience. This particular feeling in literary appreciation is called "Rasa" a word which has no equivalent in English. It is no surprise, in view of the origin of the conception, to find that Rasa of Love (Shringara) is called the king of all the Rasa. Sex experience is at the root of the conception.[5]

What Kamala Das laments in her poetry is the absence of this "losing oneself," *i.e.*, the *Shringara Rasa* in the lives of Indian women. It is not strictly the ideology of feminism rather her individualism as a female writer that comes to the fore when she advocates a concept of love that does not impede her impulse to freedom:

> The long waiting
> Had made their bond so chaste, and all the doubting
> And the reasoning
> So that in his first true embrace, she was girl
> And virgin crying
> Everything in me
> Is melting, even the hardness at the core
> O Krishna, I am melting, melting, melting
> Nothing remains but
> You [...]. (Radha)

In spite of the portrayal of the relationship that exists between the legendary Radha and Krishna, the poet's concern here is not religious. Like Vidyapati who exemplifies the sexual relationship of Radha and Krishna, Kamala Das through her poem "Radha" tries to express the intensity of human sexual relationship. This totality of human relationship or fusion "offers contrast to the *ardhanareeswara* concept where woman is fused to man but (sic) yet remains distinguishable."[6]

How different is this from the experience of the poet's usual protagonist who finds herself as a victim of oppression and is tempted to disobey the conventional life of the male-dominated society.

N.V. Raveendran seems to be right when he says, "[...] in her poems one can see the male characters only in relation to her and not as separate individuals."[7] In an early poem "An Introduction" which is considered as her 'manifesto' she makes her individualistic spirit soar to new heights by "asserting her right to speak, write and select a male companion. The so-called categorizers are there to offer a contrast to the speaker's assertions as a free individual. The contrast therefore yields what seems to be the preference of the speaker."[8]

The speaker of the poem "The Looking Glass" giving instructions to her fellow women shows her strength as an individual. The much used imperatives in the poem are indicative of that:

> Only be honest about your wants as
> Women. Stand nude before the glass with him
> So that he sees himself the stronger one
> And believes it so, and you so much more
> Softer, younger, lovelier [...] Admit your
> Admiration. Notice perfection
> Of his limbs, his eyes reddening under
> Shower, the shy walk across the bathroom floor,
> Dropping towels, and the jerky way he
> Urinates. All the fond details that make
> Him male and your only man. Gift him all,
> Gift him what makes you woman, the scent of
> Long hair, the musk of sweat between the breasts,
> The warm shock of menstrual blood, and all your
> Endless female hungers. (The Looking Glass)

The lines present a comparative statement of attributes of males and females before the readers. In comparison to the only male attribute of physical strength, the female possesses three—softness, youth and loveliness. In the opinion of the poet, by challenging traditional social norms, women should derive satisfaction out of their sexuality. This could be by standing "nude before the glass with him" or by watching "the jerky way he urinates." The individualistic tendency of her poetry shocks the readers particularly when she talks of gifting the male partner "The warm shock of menstrual blood."

The individualistic self of the poet which always believes love to be some sort of a reciprocation gets a severe jolt when it discovers that "Life is quite simple now-/ Love, blackmail and sorrow" (Substitute). A few lines later she finds that lovers have become a nameless, faceless crowd and the speaker a whore:

> After that love became a swivel door,
> When one went out another came in
> Then I lost count, for always in my arms
> Was a substitute for a substitute
> Oh, what is the use explaining—
> It was a nameless faceless crowd.

(Substitute, II.43-48)

This resentful attitude of the speaker becomes all the more pronounced in the poem 'Herons' when objecting to the act of coitus under sedatives she brands her husband a pervert and says "my ragdoll limbs adjust better/ To his versatile lust" (II.8-9). True to the critic's words, this gives the reader a "vision" of an "illegitimate" sex experience with a legitimate partner.[9] However, to observe this kind of an attitude on the part of a female poet is something unheard of before. Even her male counterparts in spite of the inherent freedom of their gender, writing poetry, sometimes feel hesitant to make such allegations against their female partners. What Kamala Das complains in her poetry is the exploitation of women by the male of the species and in this she has few parallels in the realm of Indo-Anglican poetry. One brilliant example of such iconoclasm in Indian literature is in the realm of drama and that too, by a male dramatist, Vijay Tendulkar. His play "Kamala" which provides an evaluation of the role of an Indian woman within the institution called marriage shows that women are still slaves to their male partners in the Indian society even in recent times. It may be worthwhile to mention here that all the three female characters, Sarita, Kamalabai and Kamala are in some way or other subjected by the dominant male character Jaisingh Jadav.

The traditional Indian concept of love is that it is a feeling where man and woman both forget their individualities. It is an eternal moment and once they come out of it they feel as if they are reborn. This is the only experience where, despite physical fatigue like perspiration or straining of nerves, fresh vigour and strength are felt by the partners. However, Kamala Das's speaker in the poem "The Old Playhouse" is far away from this kind of reciprocated love. In spite of the speaker's cooperation in the act of love-making, the male partner's egoistic invasion of her body violating all norms of individual decency is what the poet protests here:

> You were pleased
> With my body's response, its weather, its usual shallow
> Convulsions. You dribbled spittle into my month, you
> poured
> Yourself into every nook and cranny, you embalmed
> My poor lust with your bitter—sweet juices. You called
> me wife,
> I was taught to break saccharine into your tea and
> To offer at the right moment the vitamins.
> Cowering beneath your monstrous ego I ate the magic
> loaf and
> Became dwarf. (The Old Playhouse)

Here despite the voice of protest, sometimes the readers do suspect the very motive of the speaker. Is it the female partner which becomes dwarf because of the monstrous ego of the male or *vice versa*? Isn't it a fact that sometimes the individualistic traits of the female speaker resents the intrusions into the female ego which is often considered necessary in a traditional Indian man-woman relationship? The answer to this and some such allied questions is really vital in consideration of Kamala Das as an individualistic writer with her inherent concern for women's issues.

If the Sahaja tradition of Indian love poetry is inversely instrumental for making the poetry of Kamala Das a poetry of rebellion, the confessional tradition which is western made her poetry more endearing to the readers. In the opinion of P. Mallikarjuna Rao, "This mode of expression suits her as she ventilates her personal experiences and humiliations and also the intensity of her experience. In conformity with the confessional tradition, she talks in poetic terms about her unpleasant sexual experiences. Invariably her poems are autobiographical. This lends a kind of authenticity to her poetry which is found lacking in much of love poetry written today."[10]

However, writers belonging to a school like that of the confessional are believed to be lacking in individual uniqueness. But a critic like Mukarovsky feels that the writings of these authors is an expression and consequence of their individual uniqueness.[11] Raveendran writes: "A writer of spontaneous emotional expression with a capacity to dominate over others in that mode becomes a significant personality influencing the rest. Personalities converge in some aspects and diverge in others. Hence, individual writers have definite places in the suprapersonal development, that is, the school."[12]

Confessional poetry is often considered as the product of romantic emphasis on the individuality of the poet. Looking from this standpoint Kamala Das is not alone to write confessional poetry in the twentieth century. D.H. Lawrence in Britain and poets like Sylvia Plath and Anne Sexton on the other side of the Atlantic made earlier forays into the domain of this school of literature. However, direct influence of these practitioners on a poet like Kamala Das is not discernible. In other words, Kamala Das continues to remain overwhelmingly an individualistic poet in spite of her periodic forays into literature branded as confessional.

REFERENCES

1. Guerin, Labor, Morgan, Reesman and Willingham. *A Handbook of Critical Approaches to Literature* (New York: OUP, 1999) 216.
2. Guerin *et al.* 217.
3. West, Rebecca. *The Young Rebecca* (Ed.) Jane Marcus. London: Virago, 1982, 219.
4. *Amaru, Amarusatakam* (Eng. translation by Chintaman Ramachandra Devadhar) New Delhi: Motilal Banarsidass, 1984, 30.
5. Rangacharya, Adya. *Sex and Indian Literature in Indian Literature* (New Delhi: Sahitya Akademi, Sept.-Oct. 1991) 144.
6. Raveendran, N.V. *The Aesthetics of Sensuality: A Stylistic Study of the Poetry of Kamala Das* (New Delhi: Atlantic Publishers, 2000) 87.
7. Raveendran 33.
8. Raveendran 43.
9. Raveendran 84.
10. Rao, P. Mallikarjuna. "Love Poetry of Kamala Das," in *Triveni* (April-June 1989, Vol. 58, No. II) 52.
11. Mukarovsky, Jan. *The Word and the Verbal Art* (Trans. John Burbank and Peter Steiner. New Haven and London: Yale UP. 1977) 155.
12. Raveendran 119.